T0329405

CAMBRIDGE LIBRARY COLLECTION

Books of enduring scholarly value

Technology

The focus of this series is engineering, broadly construed. It covers technological innovation from a range of periods and cultures, but centres on the technological achievements of the industrial era in the West, particularly in the nineteenth century, as understood by their contemporaries. Infrastructure is one major focus, covering the building of railways and canals, bridges and tunnels, land drainage, the laying of submarine cables, and the construction of docks and lighthouses. Other key topics include developments in industrial and manufacturing fields such as mining technology, the production of iron and steel, the use of steam power, and chemical processes such as photography and textile dyes.

Correspondence of Josiah Wedgwood

Josiah Wedgwood (1730–95) was a master potter who pioneered the industrialisation of pottery manufacture during the early years of the Industrial Revolution. His experimental work on ceramics resulted in many innovations in the production and decoration of pottery. This three-volume work, edited by his great-granddaughter Katherine Eufemia Farrer, and first published between 1903 and 1906, contains Wedgwood's letters to his business partner, the Liverpool merchant Thomas Bentley (1730–80), and others. The highly successful partnership with Bentley is credited with the expansion and development of Wedgwood's reputation across Europe. The letters cover the years 1762 to 1794 and provide a lively account both of the growth of the business partnership and of Wedgwood's domestic life. Wedgwood and Bentley also maintained a keen interest in current affairs, and these volumes provide a fascinating insight into the life of the emerging middle class of the late eighteenth century. Volume 1 covers the period 1762–72.

Cambridge University Press has long been a pioneer in the reissuing of out-of-print titles from its own backlist, producing digital reprints of books that are still sought after by scholars and students but could not be reprinted economically using traditional technology. The Cambridge Library Collection extends this activity to a wider range of books which are still of importance to researchers and professionals, either for the source material they contain, or as landmarks in the history of their academic discipline.

Drawing from the world-renowned collections in the Cambridge University Library, and guided by the advice of experts in each subject area, Cambridge University Press is using state-of-the-art scanning machines in its own Printing House to capture the content of each book selected for inclusion. The files are processed to give a consistently clear, crisp image, and the books finished to the high quality standard for which the Press is recognised around the world. The latest print-on-demand technology ensures that the books will remain available indefinitely, and that orders for single or multiple copies can quickly be supplied.

The Cambridge Library Collection will bring back to life books of enduring scholarly value (including out-of-copyright works originally issued by other publishers) across a wide range of disciplines in the humanities and social sciences and in science and technology.

Correspondence of Josiah Wedgwood

VOLUME 1:
1762 TO 1772

JOSIAH WEDGWOOD
EDITED BY
KATHERINE EUFEMIA FARRER

CAMBRIDGE
UNIVERSITY PRESS

CAMBRIDGE UNIVERSITY PRESS

Cambridge, New York, Melbourne, Madrid, Cape Town, Singapore,
São Paolo, Delhi, Dubai, Tokyo, Mexico City

Published in the United States of America by Cambridge University Press, New York

www.cambridge.org
Information on this title: www.cambridge.org/9781108026468

© in this compilation Cambridge University Press 2010

This edition first published 1903
This digitally printed version 2010

ISBN 978-1-108-02646-8 Paperback

truly, & affectionately yours

J Wedgwood

Etruria 14th Feb: 1772

LONDON HURST & BLACKETT

LETTERS

OF

JOSIAH WEDGWOOD

1762

TO

1772.

London :
Printed by the Women's Printing Society, Limited,
66 and 68, Whitcomb Street, W.C.

1903.

I am Sr your obt Servt

Thomas Bentley

Burslem May 18 176

LONDON: HURST & BLACKETT

This volume contains the greater part of a series of letters written by my great-grandfather, Josiah Wedgwood, to his friend and partner, Thomas Bentley; and though extracts from them have been published in the "Life of Josiah Wedgwood," the letters seem to me to gain so much in interest by being read consecutively, that I have reproduced them with a view to the enjoyment of many who might naturally care for them and who have not had an opportunity of reading the originals.

Bentley's letters, deeply prized as they were by Wedgwood, and bound up in volumes known in the family as "Josiah's Bible," on account of his having them so constantly by him, are unfortunately not extant, and we know nothing of the means by which the family became possessed of his own letters to Bentley.

These letters begin in May, 1762, when Wedgwood was thirty-two. His great-grandfather, Thomas Wedgwood, had begun business as a potter in Burslem, about 1680, on a piece of land adjoining the church and known as the Churchyard Works. The business was con-

tinued by his son, Thomas Wedgwood. The
third Thomas Wedgwood, father of Josiah,
married, at an early age, Mary Stringer,
daughter of a dissenting minister, and had a
family of thirteen children. This Thomas
Wedgwood, on the death of his father in 1714,
removed from his own small pot-work to the
Churchyard Works, and here Josiah, the
youngest child, was born in 1730. He was
sent at first to the dame school in Burslem,
and later to a Mr. Blunt at Newcastle, but
remained there only till the death of his
father in 1739. He seems to have begun at
once to work at the Churchyard Works, which
were now carried on by his eldest brother
Thomas, but was not apprenticed till 1744.
In the meantime, a severe attack of smallpox
had left the boy with an affection in his right
knee, which was the cause of much subsequent
suffering. At the end of his term of apprenticeship he joined Alders and Harrison in a
small pot-work near Stoke, and afterwards
entered into partnership with Thomas Wheil-
don at Fenton. During the latter partnership
he was laid up for some months in consequence
of an injury to his diseased knee. This gave
him an opportunity to supplement the meagre
education he had received at school ; he studied
arithmetic and chemistry, and read history

and general literature, In these studies he was helped by his brother-in-law, the Rev. William Willet.

The date of Josiah Wedgwood's beginning business on his own account cannot be determined, but by the year 1759 he was established at Burslem in premises known as the Ivy House, rented from John and Thomas Wedgwood, of the Big House, with a distant cousin, another Thomas Wedgwood, as his journeyman. The business increased steadily, and Wedgwood, being now his own master, was able to devote much time to making experiments towards the improvement of his manufacture, especially in the matters of form and glaze. He was keenly interested in public affairs; we find him giving a handsome subscription towards a free school at Burslem, throwing himself heartily into the question of turnpike roads, and working enthusiastically in the cause of inland navigation by means of canals. His business necessitated journeys to various parts of the country, and in 1762, while riding to Liverpool, an accident to his diseased knee laid him up in that city for many weeks. It was this circumstance which led to his making the acquaintance of Thomas Bentley, to whom he was introduced by his surgeon, Mr. Turne

Probably in this year, too, Wedgwood removed from the Ivy House to larger premises known as the Brick House and Works, where he lived till 1769. In 1766 he bought some land known as the Ridgehouse Estate, lying between Burslem and Newcastle. To this he gave the characteristic name of Etruria, and at once began to build on it works for the manufacture of ornamental ware, dwellings for the workmen, and a large house for himself. A smaller house was also built for Mr. Bentley, in the expectation of his coming to settle there, but this plan not being carried out, and the smaller house being first finished, the Wedgwood family occupied it from November, 1769, to September, 1770, when the final move to Etruria Hall was made.

Thomas Bentley was a Liverpool merchant. He was born in 1730—the same year as Wedgwood—and was educated at a large Presbyterian school at Findern, near Derby. At the age of fifteen he was apprenticed to a Manchester warehouseman, and at the end of his apprenticeship he spent some time on the continent. On his return he settled in Liverpool as a Manchester warehouseman, taking as a partner a Mr. James Boardman.

He married Miss Hannah Oates in 1754, but became a widower two years later.

Bentley's death took place in November, 1780. In the following year Wedgwood's nephew, Thomas Byerley, undertook the warehouse in Greek Street, and by securing the services of Alexander Chisholm as his secretary and chemical assistant at Etruria, Wedgwood obtained a comparative degree of leisure, which enabled him to pursue his scientific enquiries and to enjoy the society of many of the distinguished men of the day. Dr. Erasmus Darwin was his intimate friend during the remainder of his life.

Wedgwood died at Etruria, January 3rd, 1795. My brother-in-law, Godfrey Wedgwood, remembers the old carpenter, Greaves, telling him how he had had to climb into the bed-room window—the door being locked—and found Josiah Wedgwood dead in his bed.

Unless otherwise specified, all the letters in this volume are addressed to Mr. Bentley. I have omitted much business and technical detail.

KATHERINE EUFEMIA FARRER.

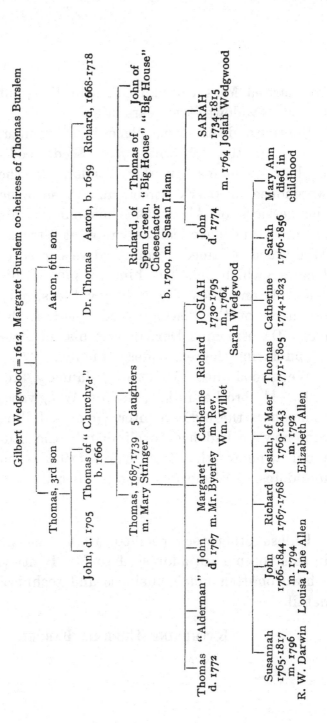

To Mr. Thomas Bentley.

My much esteemed Friend

If you will give me leave to call you so & will not think the address too free, I shall not care how Quakerish or otherwise antique it may sound, as it perfectly corresponds with the sentiments I have & wish to continue towards you; nor is there a day passes but I reflect with a pleasing gratitude upon the many kind offices I reciev'd in my confinement at your hospitable town. My good Doctor & you in particular have my warmest gratitude for the share you *both* had in promoteing my recovery & I know he is too well acquainted with the influence of a good flow of spirits (whatever they are) upon the whole animal Œconomy, to refuse you your share of merit in this instance. Believe me I could with pleasure dwell much longer upon this subject & say a great deal more without offending against that excellent rule in your MS. upon the article of letter writing which teacheth not to belye our own faillings in *writeing better things of any person than we think is strictly true,* but I know your delicacy in this point & have done. I find by the papers that the subscription for

1

Thompsons works is open'd again & intend
to add my name to the list, or at least become
a purchaser, which may do as well. I wish I
could do the same by an excellent piece upon
female education, which I once had the pleasure
of reading in MS. Why will not the benevolent author be prevail'd upon to publish a thing
which would benefit thousands without hurting
one! "It is not perfect."—Why should *you* or
the Publick expect it should be so? do you know
any publication, *on this side Rome,* that is so in
every respect? I can honestly tell you & from
some experience that it is perfect enough to
do a great deal of good, & for my own part I
did not, nor do I imagine those it is wrote for,
will see the faults you father upon it; therefore in behalf of myself & many others, his
Majesty's good improveable subjects, as well
male as female, who are daily lamenting the
want of a proper education, & would gladly
make use of such an help as you have prepared,
I say in behalf of myself and 10,000 fellow suf-
ferers, I do now call upon you to publish the
above mention'd book, but if after this admoni-
tion you still persist to keep such a *talent buried*
in your study, at your own peril be it, I have
discharged my conscience & for this time at
least shall say no more, but appeal to your good
sister Miss Oats, whether a few hypercriticks

(for such only, I think, you have to fear) should be put into competition with the best if not the greatest part of the lady's of Great Britain & I may add many of the Gent[n]. too.

Since my return home I have been very busy but have found time to make an experm[t]. or two upon Æther, the result of which I have ventured to trouble my good Doct[r]. with & I can tell you that you as well as myself may be thankfull if he permits me to write to him on these subjects. You have perhaps escaped this time reading a tedious acc[t]. of acids, alcalies, precipitation, saturation, etc. But not to make this equally tedious it will be necessary to conclude and am very respectfully

  Dear Sir

Your gratefull friend, & most obed[t]. servant

    Josiah Wedgwood.

Brother & Sister Willett do not know of my writing to you, but I have by me a general commission to send their compliments whenever I write to any of our friends and I am sure they would be very angry if I neglected to make use of it when I write to you.

*My respectfull compliments wait upon Miss Oats.

---

* This formula or something like it appears in almost every letter.

My dear Friend

It is now so long since I was favoured with your kind letter, & have not yet thanked you for the very great pleasure it gave me, that I feel a secret reproach every time I think of it, which mixes itself with & allayeth that pleasure which ever accompanies the idea of my worthy friend. I am indeed too sensible of your candour to imagine you will impute my silence to anything that borders upon disrespect. No : to be ranked amongst the number of your friends is a priveledge I too highly esteem & am too proud of to treat it with anything like indifference : but when I reflect on the polite & numerous correspondents who are capable of returning the pleasure they receive which you must already be engaged with—the time your business, now you have lost your partner, will necessarily require at your hands ;—with the many other objects of attention which will ever present themselves to a person of your disposition, I confess I am allmost discouraged from writeing to you at all and taking up that time, which you would otherwise employ to better purpose. And per-

4

haps when I have told you what a troublesome correspondent you may have of me, you may think it more for your ease to drop than continue the correspondence.—However I will be quite honest & tell you what you have to expect from me—that I may as the necessitudes of life may furnish occasion, sometimes call upon you for advice—at other times I may call upon you for assistance to settle an opinion —or to help me form a probable conjecture of things beyond our ken and sometimes I may want that valuable and most difficult office of friendship, reproof. If you will promise me to be faithful in the discharge of this last office, I will not doubt the rest, but trust to that instinctive goodness, if you will call it so, I am already so much indebted to ; though I am not fond of the term *instinct* as you apply it, and if it does not include *all the charities* & the finest feelings of the improved human mind I renounce it & must make so free as to tell you that in this instance you have made use of an improper term.

Your favourite author,* and particularly his fine poem on Liberty, has more than answered my expectation, though not a little by your just enconiums. His descriptions of ancient

* James Thomson (1700-1748), author of " The Seasons."

Greece & Rome are truly grand, & place those theatres of liberty and publick virtue in the strongest light of anything I ever met with. And his resurrection of the masterpieces of antiquity is highly entertaining & instructive, & is as strong a proof of his fine taste in the works of art, as the whole of his works are of his extensive benevolence & goodness of heart. His zeal seldom or never omiteth a fair opportunity of introducing his favourite subject. Happy would it be for this island, were his three virtues the foundation of British liberty—independent life—integrity in office & a passion for the common weal more strictly adhered to amongst us.

When you favour me with a line, I shall be glad to hear if you have fixed upon another minister for your Octogon, as I hear Mr. Sedan has not accepted your invitation & when your prayers are published, I should be glad to buy two or three copys of them. I wish they had been published two or three months ago, we should have stood a chance of having them made use of in our neighbourhood. A gentleman at Newcastle has built a chapel in one of our villages which lay at an inconvenient distance from the mother church. When the building was finished he applyed to the Bishop & prayed his Lordship to give it his blessing,

which was refused from motives that do no
honor to the cloth & are not worth troub-
leing you with. The old gentⁿ. who was late an
attorney, now one of his Majesty's Justices of
the Peace, being unwilling that his pious
endeavours to instruct the ignorant should be
so lost to the poor inhabitants, went to work
himself with his prayer book; altered it to his
own liking & sent the MS. to have two or
three hundred copys printed for the use of his
chapel, for which he has now took out a license
& agreed with a good orderly schoolmaster
his neighbour, for the valuable consideration
of £15 p. ann^m. to officiate as priest and he is to
enter upon his new employment on next L^{do}.
day. You naturally conclude that the hearts
of these vilagers must overflow with gratitude
to their benefactor, who has made his way
through so many difficulties to serve them.—
Nothing like it S^r. indeed.—*The Church is in
danger* with them even before it is well built
& many of his intended flock are afraid of
being cheated out of their religion before they
have any to lose. His prayers are found great
fault with before they are seen & they cry
mainly out, *we will have them like other folks'
prayers*, or have none. The ferment is so strong
amongst them at present that 'tis thought the
poor Chaplain may sell his sacred vestments

again, for in all probability they will not let him enter upon his function. If you have any curiosity to see the prayers I will endeavour to send you a copy.

Pray how could you think of my knowing the author of that little piece on prayers for publick worship in the last number of "the Library"? 'Tis true I have the advantage of a particular acquaintance with the author, but I did not imagine you were well enough acquainted with Mr. Willett's manner of writing to find him out there. I remember some time reading a sermon, with some such title as, *a full answer to all the sermons that have, or ever shall be* preached on the 30th Jan*ry*. which tittle I think might with a very little alteration suit that excellent little essay. I was glad to find it had not escaped your notice & have thanked the worthy Author in your name. Oh! for a more ample effusion of such a truly Christian spirit amongst all professed teachers of the religion of the benevolent Jesus.

I hope my good friend is puting the finishing hand to his valuable MS. which it seems is not yet deemed fit to appear in publick. Indeed I am afraid that you are too severe in your criticisms upon it & may keep it private much longer than is necessary for its doing the good you intend in the world. And though it is with the greatest sincerity I assure you that you have not a friend in the world who wou'd be more anxious for your litterary credit in this article than myself, yet as your benevolent intentions in writing it were directed chiefly to the younger part of our species, when one reflects how soon our young folks nowadays grow up to be men & women & enter into the busy world I cannot help regreting that unless you get the better of your scruples soon, one generation at least must lose the benefit they might otherwise receive from your generous labours.—Consider d^r. S^r. so many young persons everyday geting out of the way of instructions by the various connections of riper years, is an object worthy of attention.　I shall leave it with you & know it will not be disregarded.

If you have seen Rousseau's Emillia I should be glad to know your thoughts of that piece & now it is translated I should be glad *by your recommendation*, to purchase it, notwithstanding his Holiness has forbid its entrance into his domains; & as I am about to furnish a shelf or two of a book-case, if you would assist me with your advice in the furniture, I should esteem it a particular favour. Mr. Willett & I are perswaded that you could inform us more concerning the intended institution in favour of liberty, than has yet appeared in the Gent^{ns}. Mag.* but if it is not proper any more should be known at present we are far from desiring it, but will wait with patience till towards Xmass when we hope M^r. J. S. agreeable to his promise will be more explicit. You will now perceive one reason I have for concluding; another is I am afraid I have already encroached too much on your time & patience by this unconscionable epistle, but I hope you will pardon it & let me have the pleasure of hearing from you soon.

Adieu d^r. S^r. believe me with all the cordiallity of friendship

Y^r. much obliged fr^d. & humble Servt.

---

* In the *Gentleman's Magazine* for September, 1762, is a letter signed "J. S.," apologising for delay in developing a scheme to institute a society in defence of liberty, first mentioned in the February number, and promising a public meeting before Christmas. The writer asserts that the scheme is intended for the general good, and begs all friends of liberty to give their attention to the matter. Nothing seems to have come of it.

LONDON, SWAN Wᵀᴴ TWO NECKS, LAD LANE,

31st March, 1763.

Dear Sir

This day I had the mortification to hear the royal assent given to the odious Cyder etc. etc. Bill.*—You have no doubt heard that the City of London petitioned the House of Lords against it, but to no purpose. Lᵈ. Bute harangued a long time in favour of the Bill & his own administration—

"He was well acquainted" he told their Lᵈships "with the clamour which was raised without doors against him and his administration & despised it all; nor would he ever stoop to such mean methods of gaining popularity as some others had done before him"— "A popular minister he knew he never should be, nor did he ever intend or desire to become so, but shoᵈ. continue to advise his Majesty to such measures as woᵈ. bear the strictest scrutiny." The city of London, he own'd, was a respectable body, but they were very apt to be clamorous etc. etc. In this lofty strain the Minister & his friends went on a long time, but not without some rubs from the other party. Upon a division of the House (wᶜʰ. sat

---

* Bute proposed to pay for the war by a tax on cider.

11

till near nine at night) there was 81 (Proxies included) for the Bill & 13 ag^t. it—out of which numb^r. there was 15 L^{ds}. only who spoke. When the Citizens found their petition had not the desired effect in the House of L^{ds}., they had recourse to the throne and last night presented a petition to his Majesty, by whom they were very graciously rec^d. and all that, but the success of this last effort, I have already inform'd you of. I had a great deal more to say to you, but have my Bro^r. & three or four more Gent^n. wait^g. of me very impatiently whilst I scrawl this line or two, wch. I must beg you will not show to anybody unless their candour is equal to your own.

Mr. Wilks ye author of ye N. Briton is gone to France, but I cannot learn on w^t. acc^t.— I sh^d. be glad to know amongst other things how you digest this extension of the Excise laws : it gives universal disgust here & is the general topic of every political club in town —Adieu my good friend—ever your oblig'd & very respectfull Hb^{le}. Sev^t.

Dear Sir

I am favour'd with your very agreeable letter, but have it not now before me, however I remember so much of it—relative to L^d. Bute (his dying speech)* that I shall certainly believe you possess'd of the gift of *second sight*. My principal motive for writing to you tonight is just to inform you that the Irish Butt^r., or rather Grease Bill is this day after some warm debates pass'd the H^o. of Com^{ns}. but it extended to all the ports of England & is upon any dispute arising, betwixt the importer & Custom H^o. officers, to be decided by a Justice of the Peace & two dealers in Butter, whether it shall be deem'd Grease or Butter. L^d. Strange exerted his talents greatly, or I believe it had been thrown out for some irregularitys in form caused by the alterations & which there wo^d. not be time this Session to go through the due forms of to make it regular.

I spent Sunday evening wth. some gent^n. who support poor Annett in his confinement and by voluntary contribution wch. I find runs rather short & they will be very thankfull to any friends of liberty who are dispos'd to

---

* Bute resigned 8th April, 1763, in consequence of the unpopularity caused by the Cider Bill.

contribute their mite for that purpose. I do believe you w^d. be against the extension of the excise laws, as they are most certainly calculated in their very nature to abridge the liberty of the subject & I do my dear friend for the first time differ somewhat from you in my sentim^{ts}. on that subject.

Yours in all the cordiality of friendship.

———————

BURSLEM, *16 June, 1763.*

My dear Friend

Your acc^t. of the opening of your Octogon gives me great pleasure both as a friend to your society & a lover of rational devotion & I most sincerely sympathise with you in the exalted pleasure you must feel in this leading the way to a reformation so long talked of & so much wanted in our Church Millitent here below. I long to join with you, but am alass tyed-down to this rugged Pott-making spot of earth & cannot leave it at present without suffering from it.

My nephew* arrived at N:castle on Sunday

———
* Tom Byerley, son of Wedgwood's eldest sister.

night on his way to visit friends of his late
father at Durham. Whilst he was with me at
Burslem, his trunk came down with all his
papers etc.; these unraveld a part of his history
which we before were strangers to. Poor Tom
could not stand the shock, wch. was the cause
of his elopem^t. & what we shall do now with
a lad of his turn of mind I cannot tell; what
that turn of mind is I cannot so well explain
to you as a few of the said papers I have
enclosed will do. What can be done with so
young a subject of authorism so terribly
infected with the cacoethes scribendi as to take
possession of a garrett at fifteen!

N.CASTLE. (Xmasing & wanted at play)
Jany. 9th, 1764.

Dear Friend

I had acknowledg'd your very kind letter
before now, but hoped by waiting a post or two
to be able either to tell you of my happiness or
at least the time I expected to be made so: but
" O grief of griefs " that pleasure is still denyed

me & I cannot bear to keep my friend in
suspense any longer, though I own myself
somewhat asham'd & greatly mortify'd to be
still kept at bay from those exalted pleasures
you have often told me attend the marriage
state. If you know my temper & sentiments
on these affairs you will be sensible how I am
mortify'd when I tell you I have gone through
a long series of bargain making of settlem^{ts}.,
reversions, provisions, etc. etc. Gone through,
did I say! Wo^d. to Hymen I had—No, I am
still in the Attorney's hands, from which I
hope it is no harm to pray "good L^d. deliver
me." Miss W. & I are perfectly agreed &
could settle the whole affair in three lines
& so many minutes—but our Pappa, over
carefull of his daughter's interest wo^d. by some
demands which I cannot comply with, go near
to seperate us, if we were not better determin'd.
On Friday next Mr. W. & I are to meet in
great form, with each of us our Attorney, which
I hope will be conclusive. You shall then hear
farther from your obliged & very affec^{te}. friend.

BURSLEM, *23rd of Jan^{ry}., 1764.*

Dear Sir

All things being amicably settled betwixt my Pappa elect & myself, I yesterday prevail'd upon my dear girl to name the day, the blisfull day! when she will reward all my faithfull services & take me to her arms! In three words we are to be married on Wednesday next. On that auspicious day, think it no sin, to wash your philosophic evening pipe with a glass or two extraordinary, to hail your friend & wish him good speed into the realms of matrimony.

Adieu my good friend, I am very busy today, that no business may intrude on my pleasures for the rest of the week.

———————

BURSLEM, *28th May, 1764.*

My dear Friend

I am very glad to hear of your & Miss Oats' health by your very agreeable neighbour Mrs. Forbes. I sho^d. have wrote to you again though you were in my debt but have been extreme busy on may acc^{ts}.: have sent you a sam-

17

ple of one hobby horse (engine turning) wch. if Miss Oats will make use of she will do me honour. This branch hath cost me a great deal of time & thought & must cost me more & am afraid some of my best friends will hardly escape. I have got an excellent book on the subject in french & latin. Have enclosed one chapter wch. if you can get translated for me it will oblige me much & will thankfully pay any expense attend^g. it. Tom Byerley is learning that language but I cannot wait his time; he is a very good boy & I hope will make a usefull member of society.

Accept the best respects of two married lovers happy as this world can make them—believe me ever

Your very affec^{te}. fr^d.

My worthy friend

The moment I returned from Liverpool I had one of the printed papers you refer to put into my hands which astonish'd, Confounded & vexed me not a little. I was told the writer was Mr. Gilbert, M.P.,* & that he had given it out as a scheme to obviate every objection. His Broth^r. Mr. John Gilbert call'd upon me the same evening to whom I gave my sentiments of the four last paragraphs, that they were dark, mysterious, & ungenerous & much better calculated to overturn than support our design. That his printing & circulating such a paper without once consulting the Persons who had hitherto lent their heads, hands & purses too in planing & forwarding our scheme of Navigation† was as indelicate, as the insinuations were gross & illfounded.

Mr. Gilbert replyd that he wished his Bro^r. had not taken so unadvised a step & desired I wo^d. meet L^d. Gower, Mr. Garbett‡ & his

---

* Thomas Gilbert was member for Newcastle; his brother John was agent to the Duke of Bridgwater, the inaugurator of the scheme of inland navigation furthered by Wedgwood.

† The Trent and Mersey Canal, called the Grand Junction Canal, from Wilden Ferry to Preston Brook.

‡ A manufacturing chemist in Birmingham.

Bro^r. at Lichf^d. on sunday evening, for these Gent^n. with Mr. Councelor Beard of Newcastle were it seems to settle preliminaries for monday, & fatal wo^d. have been the consequences thereof.

Mr. Beard was sent for, Mr. Sparrow nor anybody else ever mention'd, I plainly saw the necessity of our going, but had a very great sacrifice to make, such as no one can feel stronger than yourself in consenting to intrude myself unasked upon a junto which I then thought did not want my company.

Mr. Sparrow, Mr. Brindley (Engineer) & my Bro^r. saw our critical situation in the same light with myself and stifling every other sensation in that of promoting our *General Cause*, we altogether posted away to Lichfield, where we arrived about 10 minutes after his L^d.ship. Mr. Garbitt was there in conference with Mr. Gilbert, & we soon found that they were both very sanguine in supporting their chimerical plan of a medium betwixt Proprietors & Comm^{rs}. As I had thought more on this subject than most of our people had, they served me as poor Uriah of old was served & placed me in the forefront of the battle. After a slight skirmish with Mr. Gilbert, in which he did not choose to answer *point blank* to some questions which I had prepared for him,

he desired I would go & speak to Mr. Garbitt
& his friends who were in another room. I
obeyed, & soon perceived by what each of
them s^d. compared wth. what they had wrote
to myself & others that the *medium scheme*
was the joint production of those two Gentle-
mens brains, or at least that they had concerted
or adopted it together. Mr. Garbitt at my
request explained to me the whole plan, &
answered my questions rather more explicitly
than Mr. Gilbert had done, the consequence of
which was that in 10 minutes time he found his
baseless Fabrick tumbling down to the ground
& deserted it immediately without one attempt to rear it up again. I am afraid you
will think me rather too figurative, but remember I am not reasoning now I am only
huzzaing and singing Io' after a conquest.

To return—Mr. Gilbert w^d. neither speak
quite out nor give up the point, but we were
call'd to sup with L^d. Gower in the midst of our
debates. After supper the subject was introduced before his L^d.ship which I was very glad
of as I knew him to be *sensible* & *Humane* &
the scheme proposed to be either *weak* or
Tyranical.

His L^d.ship desired that both the plans might
be explained to him. Mr. Gilbert opened his
own & made his remarks upon it at large.

Think my friend how I was delighted to find
that he had not one argument, inference, or
flourish to make in the whole harangue but what
I *felt* myself able with the greatest clearness to
confute. In this situation I was call'd upon
to make my reply & most joyfully enter'd
upon the task, my *heart* was ingaged in the
cause, & that I believe made my thoughts
& expression obedient to my wish.—You will
know what could be said on the subject, which
may save you the trouble of reading, & me
of writeing half a doz. sheets at least—if I
had time for it—but I am now interupted
by a Gent^n. who wants to subscribe £1000 &
tell me some interesting facts. In short then
I concluded in *very honestly* endeavouring
to interest his L^d.ship's candour and humanity in favour of the Proprietors, by appeal-
ing to him—if it would not be very cruel,
when a set of men had employed their time,
their talents & their purses for ten years
together—the best part of their lives—in the
execution of a design by which the Public
wo^d. gain 300 ⅌ C^t., & when they have executed
this Laborious task—what is their reward?
why a new sett of Masters are raised up to
controul both them & their works, they have
hitherto had but bare interest for their money
& now perhaps they will be permitted to have

1 or 2 $\tilde{p}$ C^t. extra out of 300 they have saved
to the Public, which poor pittance wo^d. not at
the highest calculation pay them 4^d. $\tilde{p}$ diem
for their past Labour. L^d. Gower turned to
Mr. Gilbert. " It wo^d. be hard," he s^d., " Gilbert,
it would be very hard, & if the Proprietors can
save so much to the Public as Mr. W. hath
proposed I do not think their plan can be re-
jected by Parliam^t."

Our Plan was accordingly fixed, and L^d.
Gower declared & everyone join'd in the
opinion that if we had not met that evening
at Lichfield, nothing could have been done at
Wolsley Bridge, & as that was the last meeting we could have, we should scarcely have got
over these difficulties.

Your favour of 31 gives me great pleasure
& I do most sincerely congratulate you on
the advantages you must recieve from your
infant institution, your being of the committee
gives me a very favourable Idea of the good
sense of the members. What a pity it is that
a man so capable of serving the interests of
millions should be at all confined to the circle
of his own affairs. I know your expanded
bosom, & I have some knowledge of your
talents. O my friend ! that I had but power
equal to my wishes, your station sho^d. then be
more adapted to your abilitys.

You want a good plan for raising the money That I hope is now fixed, & am in no fear of the subscription being filled, & as to a general letter on the advantages of Inland Navigation, I have no time to think or write about anything, but the *immediate business of the day*, Public business I mean, for as to my private concerns I have almost forgot them, I scarcely know without a good deal of recollection whether I am a Landed Gentleman, an Engineer or a Potter, for indeed I am all three & many other characters by turns, pray heaven I may settle to something in earnest at last.

Adieu, God bless you and continue your health and usefullness to mankind.

Y^{rs}. with the truest affection.

To Bro^r. J. WEDGWOOD.*

BURSLEM, 1st Feb^{ry}., 1765.

Dear Bro^r.

It gave me great pleasure to have it under your own hand that your health & spirits are so good & your affairs in so promising a way of being settled agreeably & with dispatch—this gives us some hopes of haveing the pleasure of your company this spring which I doubt not you will find very salutary, especially as we now have got such pretty employment for you. Sukey† is a fine sprightly lass, & will bear a good deal of dandleing & you can sing—lulaby Baby—whilst I rock the Cradle but I shall hardly find time for nursing as we have another Turnpike broke out amongst us here betwixt Leek & Newcastle & they have *vi et Armis*—mounted me upon my hobby-horse again, & a prancing rouge he is at present, but hope he will not take the route of London again. He carried me yesterday to Leek from whence I am just return'd much satisfied with our reception

---

* Nine years Wedgwood's senior, and in rather better circumstances than the rest of the family.

† Susanna, afterwards wife of Robert Waring Darwin, and mother of Charles Darwin.

there. Tomorrow I wait upon D^r. Nigil to beg
his concurrence & on Monday must attend
a meeting to settle the petition, etc., at Mony
Ash at y^r. fr^d. Isaac Whieldons—We pray to
have the Utoxeter & Burslem Turnpikes join'd
& to have the Road made Turnpike from Buxton & Bakewell to Leek & from Leek to
N:castle. Whether or not our good fr^{ds}. at
Newcastle will give us battle on this occasion
we do not know, if they do, there will be
some probability of my haveing a comm^n. &
seeing the great City again.—£2000 is wanting
for this road. My Uncles* Thos. & Jno. have
—I am quite serious—at the first asking subscribed—I know you will not believe me, but
it is a certain fact—*five hundred pounds ! ! !*—I
have done the like intending 2 or 300 of it for
you, and if you choose any more you must let
me know in time—it will not be wanted till
summer though it must be subscribed now,
turn over if you have not had enough. Mr.
Willet† hath took the Bank and desires you'l
come a fishing as soon as your affairs will
permit.

We have now added another Christian‡ to

---

* His wife's uncles.

† Unitarian minister at Newcastle, married to his sister
Katherine. The Bank was his house at Newcastle.

‡ Susanna, baptised January 17th, 1765.

our family, & her Mamma, who is very well
—please now to observe that I do let you know
by this present writeing that she is *Bona fide*
in good health, & as I was saying before is—
privately—Churched, but the weather is too
bad to carry her to our Abbey at present.
Your Lobsters made an elegant dish, were
extreme good, pleased my Daddy* vastly who
stay'd with me three days upon the occasion,
& was as usual very merry & very good
company.—" Tell Jn°. Wedgwood," says the
old Gent^n., " that I drink his health & thank
him for his Lobsters, they are very fine,
& a creature that I like." Now whether there
was any design in this I cannot pretend to say,
far be it from me to judge betwixt you on so
nice & knotty a subject.

Will you have Taffy again this summer, or
some better beast? if you do not choose to
ride him ag^n. I intend parting with him as two
horses (now I have got an increase of my
Family another way) are rather a needless
expence to me.—Sally sends her love to you
& Tom with

D^r. Bro^r.

Your very affect^e. Bro^r.

All well.

* His wife's father.

To Mr. John Wedgwood,
    Cateaton Street, London.

Burslem, *Feb. 16ᵗʰ, 1765.*

Dear Broʳ.

In all your letters you do not say a word about coming into Staffordshire again this spring. I hope you will now soon have settled your affairs so as to leave Town, for I do not think that close, smoaky place will ever agree with your constitution, & I do very earnestly intreat you to come & take the benefit of your native, salutary, country Air this Spring, even though it shoᵈ. be something inconvenient to your affairs in other respects.

Mr. Bentley will be in Town on Wednesday Evenᵍ. next. I am just to kiss his hand as he passeth thro' Newcastle in the Coach on Monday next & shall direct him where to find you. Lʳˢ. to him will be directed—at Mr. Wards Haberdasher in Holbourn.

I hope Mrs. Blake is *coming on in the world* as the phrase is, my best respects ever wait on that most Agreeable Lady. I hope you will carry Mr. Bentley to Turnham Green* & am

* The residence of Mr. Griffiths, editor and publisher of the *Monthly Review.*

well assur'd those two Geniuses will be highly delighted with the interview. I insist when that happens that I am consider'd as *present in spirit* though alass *absent in body.* I can hardly concieve a Scene I sho^d. be better pleased in partaking of, but I am going to be very busy, haveing come to a full resolution of attempting in earnest the French ware, & am every night forming schemes for that purpose.

I mention nights for whilst Tom is from home I am too closely confined to the Counting house to do anything of that sort in the day. Your next will I hope tell me he is coming home to me.

Adieu.

Yours affectionately.

Sally sends her love to you & best wishes for the continuance of your health & joins me in love to Tom & Comp^{ts}. to all. I need not say how agreeable the first part of y^r. l^r. was to us all. Sist^r. Byerley's eyes sparkled like——at it the similie is not at hand & I can't wait for it.

To Sir Wm. Meredith.*

March 2ⁿᵈ, 1765.

Sir

You have heaped your favours on me so abundantly that though my heart is overflowing with sentiments of gratitude & thankfullness I am at a loss where to begin my acknowledgem^{ts}. Your goodness in lead^{g}. me into improvm^{ts}. of the manufacture I am engaged in, & patronizing those improvem^{ts}. you have encouraged me to attempt, demand my utmost attention. With such inducem^{ts}. to industry in my calling, if I do not outstrip my fellows, it must be oweing either to great want of Genius, or application; the first your candour would lead you to excuse, as it might be less my fault than misfortune; the latter is in my own power, & I sho^{d}. be utterly unworthy of your farther notice if I did not double my dilligence in prosecuting any plan you are so kind as to lay out for me.

Your very acceptable pacquets I rec^{d}. by the last post. The true taste & Elegance of the

* Of Henbury, near Macclesfield, member for Liverpool.

Contents charm me greatly, & I shall immediately make that use of them your generosity intends by so kind a present.

I am afraid of encroaching too much upon your time & patience with my trifling concerns & shall therefore conclude them here. But permit me S^r. just to ment^n. a Circumstance of a more Public nature which greatly alarms us in this neighbourhood. The bulk of our particular manufacture you know is exported to foreign markets, for our home consumption is very trifleing in comparison to what is sent abroad, & the principal of these markets are the Continent & islands of N. America. To the Continent we send an amazing qu^{ty}. of white stone ware & some of the finer kinds, but for the Islands we cannot make anything too rich & costly. This trade to our Colonies we are apprehensive of loseing in a few years as they have set on foot some Potwork there already, & have at this time an agent amongst us hireing a number of our hands for establishing new Pottworks in South Carolina, haveing got one of our insolvent Master Potters there to conduct them. Haveing material there equal if not superior to our own for carrying on that manufactorie, & as the necessaries of life & consequently the price of labour amongst us are daily upon the ad-

vance, I make no question but more will follow
them & join their Brother Artists & Manufacturers of every Class who are from all quarters
takeing a rapid flight indeed the same way!
Whether this evil can be remedyed is out of
our sphere to know but we cannot help appre-
hending such consequences from these emigra-
tions as make us very uneasy for our trade, &
our Posterity.

Your well known attention to the arts &
Commerce of y^r. Country encourages me to
give you this trouble,—pardon my freedom
& believe me with the greatest respect
S^r.

Your very gratefull & most Obed^t. humble serv^t.

To Mr. John Wedgwood.

Dear Bro^r.

Your last very kind Letter of 12 days long gave us the greatest pleasure as it assur'd us you were recover'd to your former state of health & spirits again, & we pray God to continue you those invaluable Blessings.

Though I have time now only to write a few lines it being near post time, I shall be so unreasonable as to expect a very long one in return. You will I doubt not have a Copious subject—*the Confabulations of the Triumvirate.*—My good fr^d. Mr. Bentley I know hath given up our liberty as a Chimera—have you convinced him of his error ? or hath he bro^t. you to be of his opinion ?

Tom arriv'd here last night & is set in earnest to his business, & I hope will settle again, he was grown really fond of his business, before your giddy Town set his spirits afloat again, but I have great hopes a little encouragem^t.—a set of *new* books, & one months serene air will bring them to subside again.

One piece of news Tom brings which I hope is premature, that is your staying in London all summer. I cannot give my consent to this

33

C

step believing it will indanger your health, which certainly sho^d. be your first care.

I have just begun a Course of experiments for a white body & glaze which promiseth well hitherto. Sally is my chief helpmate in this as well as other things, & that she may not be hurried by having too many *Irons in the fire* as the phrase is I have ord^d. the spining wheel into the Lumber room. She hath learnt my characters, at least to write them, but can scarcely read them at present.—This business I often think if you could but once enter into the *spirit* of it, wo^d. be the prettiest employment for you imaginable.

I do not intend to make this ware at Burslem & am therefore laying out for an agreeable & convenient situation elsewhere.

Three pacquets by one post from S^r. W^m.! two of them enclosing birds, insects & flowers. I have since wrote two l^{rs}. to him directed to S^r. W^m. Meredith in London—that direction I suppose will find a Gentⁿ. of his eminence, if you think otherwise as he is removed to Chelsea pray do the needfull for me.

Accept our best wishes for your health & happiness, present our respects where due & believe us ever

Your very affect^e. Bro^r. & Sist^r.

J. & S. WEDGWOOD.

To Mr. Jno. Wedgwood.

Burslem, *11 March, 1765.*

Thanks to my dear Bro^r. for his last very
agreeable & entertaining epistle, & the kind
offers of transacting any business in London I
may want to employ such an hand in.

I have had too much experience of your
affection & partiality towards me to doubt of
your regard for my interest & readiness to pro-
mote it, & you are too well acquainted with
my business & connections in Town to believe
I shall let such offers pass with me as mere
compliments only, no, I have already some
tolerably solid business cut out for you, if I
pursue my scheme of white glazed ware, some
materials for which must be bo^t. & disguised
in London before they are sent to me—but
more of this hereafter.

I congratulate you on the offer of so liberal &
honourable an appointm^t. made you by the
Society of Gent^n. Merch^{ts}. &c. but you are not
explicit enough for me to have a tolerable Idea
of the plan, or business of this Society, who
can afford their Chairman so handsome an
appointm^t., or what service they expect in return for it.—I can readily concieve this employment would be an honourable one & that the

Gent^n. concern'd must have a great opinion of the abilities, & integrity of any Gent^n. they employ'd in it, but as to the lucrative part that must depend on circumstances I am entirely a stranger to. I hope in your next you will favour me with a farther explanation on this head.

Your feast at Turnham Green (mental feast I mean) was just what I expected, from the meeting & collision of such Geniuses as were there assembled, & from your description with a little of the art of designing I could spread a yard of Canvas over with an excellent group of figures.—How happy sho^d. I have been in partaking of so instructive, & elegant an Entertainm^t.!—but alass I must be content with *fashioning my clay* at an humble distance from such comp^y. & live, breathe, & dye, amongst animals but one remove above the Earth they are teazeing.

I do not envy my friends their more refined enjoyments of life, but I do sometimes wish for a pair of wings, & a learners seat amongst them, & had the good Bishop Wilkins* scheme for flying been bro^t. to any tolerable perfection, you had most certainly seen me fluttering at

* John Wilkins, Bishop of Chester 1668-1672, wrote a treatise entitled " Discovery of a New World," in which he gravely discusses the possibility of communication by means of a flying-machine with the moon & its supposed inhabitants.

your Dineing room Window at Turnham Green.

I sho^d. be glad to know how my good friend Mr. Bentley's scheme proceeds, & sho^d. have wrote to him to-day but have half a do^z. other l^{rs}. which must be wrote & will prevent me. That accomplished man is sure to make a figure on allmost any subject, & in any company capable of doing justice to his eminent talents.

Pray what were the Chief subjects of your conversation with S^r. W^m.? I suppose you attended that worthy Gent^{ns}. summons along with Mr. Bentley & others—perhaps, & have no doubt of your being elegantly and agreeably entertain'd.

On Friday last I dined with Mr. Brindley the Duke of Bridgwaters engineer, after which we had a meeting at the Leopard on the subject of a Navigation from Hull, or Wilden Ferry to Burslem agreeable to a survey & plan before taken. Our Gent^n. seem very warm in setting this matter on foot again, & I could scarcely withstand the pressing solicitations I had from all present, to undertake a journey or two for that purpose. We are to have another meeting at Hanley to-morrow & per Wednesdays post you shall know the result.

Mother, Bro^r. & Sist^r. Wedgwood are poorly of colds, mine hath quite left me. Sally &

Sukey are well & send love & duty.   The finest
Girl!—So like her father!

Y^{rs}. in the truest affect^{n}.

My best respects allways wait on Mr. Bentley
& the triumvirate.

––––––––––

To Mr. John Wedgwood.

Dear Brother

I'll teach you to find fault, & scold, &
grumble at my not writeing, I warrant you, &
as to your going to France, I do not believe I
can spare you out of London this summer, if
business comes in for you at this rate, for
instance

—An ord^{r}. from St. James's for a service of
Staffordshire ware, about which I want to ask
a hundred questions, & have never a mouth
but yours in Town worth opening upon the
subject.

The ord^{r}. came from Miss Deborah alias
De^{b}. Chetwynd, sempstress, & Laundress to
the Queen, to Mr. Smallw^{d}. of Newcastle, who

bro‘. it to me (I believe because nobody else
w⁴. undertake it) & is as follows.

A complete sett of tea things, with a gold
ground & raised flowers upon it in green, in
the same manner of the green flowers that are
raised upon the *mehons,* so it is wrote but I
suppose it sho⁴. be *melons*—The articles are 12
Cups for Tea, & 12 Saucers, a slop bason, sugar
dish wᵗʰ. cover & stand, Teapot & stand,
spoon trea, Coffeepot, 12 Coffee cups, 6 pʳ. of
hand candlesticks & 6 Mellons with leaves.

6 green fruit baskets & stands edged with
gold.

I have just begun an Enamel work & am in
great want of some gold powder such as is
burnt in upon China. It is made by one Mr.
Shenton (only) & sold by him at 7 guineas per
oz. Mr. Giles Enameler in Berwick S‘. Old
Soho, can tell you where Mr. Shenton lives,
which is the best direction I can get. I sho⁴.
be glad to have a few pennywᵗˢ. by way of
tryal, Mr. Shenton may perhaps give you instructions about the best manner of useing it
& when I have his address will write farther
to him & settle him a Cr‘. in Lond". for wᵗ.
Gold I order in future. May send this small
parcˡ. along with some leaf gold I have ord⁴.
from Mr. Gifford in Maiden Lane Wood S‘. unless you find a quicker conveyance. You may

conceal a little of it in a frank. Miss Chetwynds ord^r. must be done with this gold if
burnt in.

My post boy waits—adieu.
Yours most cordially.

Do not waste a frank on a single l^r.
All well.

Pray put on *the best suit of Cloaths you ever
had in your life,* & take the first opportunity
of going to Court.

Miss Chetwynd is Daughter to the Master
of the Mint.*

———————

To JOHN WEDGWOOD.

BURSLEM, *3rd Apr^l., before breakfast.*

Dear Brother

I find Tom hath made you acquainted
with my late Tour, & in part with our success
in it.—Mr. Taylor is just enter'd into partnership with one Mr. Loyd in the Banking business, & Mr. Loyd it seems is one of the Proprie-

* 3rd Viscount Chetwynd, & a great friend of Bolingbroke.

tors in the Burton Navigation which will be injured by our intended Canal, as it is proposed to carry it beyond Burton to Wilden in order to keep clear of their Locks and shallows.

We made it appear pretty evident to the Gent[n]. of Birmingham that £10,000 per ann[m]. would be immediately sav'd to them in the Article of Land Carr[ge]. to and from the River Trent, so soon as the Canal was bro[t]. to their Town which wo[d]. it is apprehended be in less than three years after it is begun upon. We are inform'd by a very intelligent Gent[n]. (Mr. Garbitt) of Birm[m]. that this Navigation would be a great advantage to the Russia Merchants as they wo[d]. then be able to send their Iron & Flax with much greater certainty & at 15s. per Ton less expence to Birm[m]. Wolverhampton Walsal &c. & between 30 & 40s. per Ton less into these parts. We have not yet been with the Gent[n]. of Liverpool, but have rec[d]. instructions per last post from Mr. Bentley in w[t]. manner to make our address the most acceptable there. This scheme of a Navigation is undoubtedly the best thing that could possibly be plan'd for this country & I hope there is a great degree of probability of its being carried into execution.

I met our fr[d]. Mr. Bentley at Trentham & spent the evening with him (till 3 o'Clock

morn^g. when he took Coach again) at Talk, &
I need not tell you was greatly entertain'd
with his acc^t. of Men and things in London.

The last post bro^t. me five pacquets from S^r.
W^m. inclosing prints of different sorts which
he is so obliging to employ his good taste in
picking up for me at the Printshops, he hath
likewise sent me some orders from S^r. Geo.
Savil & Gent^n. of his acquaintance & hath
many more he says for me & in order that I
may work after the best models he hath sent
me a Dessert service of Dresden China to pattern from. How shall I make any return at
all adequate to this Generosity? When you
see S^r. W^m. you will let him know I am at
least sensible of his distinguishing favours.

A VOICE this moment breaks in upon me
with—NEWS, NEWS, NEWS, & what do you
think it is? why truly, the Marriage writeings
are making between my Unckle Thomas, &
my Cousin Molly, both of venerable memory*.
This may serve as *a Choice drop of Comfort to
Old Maids, & Batchelors*, & I hope it will have
its proper effect. It is farther whisper'd in my
ear by a Voice which allways gives me pleasure
that the chief stumbling-block to this marriage
was removed when she secured a third Person

* The bridegroom (Mrs. W.'s uncle) was 55 & the bride much
younger.

for her own. We have no other very particular news with us that I know of.

Sukey smiles this morning & sends Duty to
her Unckle, & wo^d. be very glad to see this
Unckle John she hears so much of, in Staffordshire, Sally is very well & joins in best wishes
for your health & pleasure with

D^r. Bro^r.

Your obliged, & very affectionate Bro^r.

———————

To John Wedgwood.

Burslem, *May 29 , 1765.*

Dear Bro^r.

You do not say one word about our worthy
friend S^r. W^ms. illness. I was told last week
at Liverpool that he had been siezed with an
Apoplectick fit & lay a dying but did not give
any credit to the report, as I had rec^d. a letter
from you the even^g. before I left home, which
was the same post they must have their intelligence by, & you did not mention anything of

it, but a report is now current here of his being carried from the House of Comm^{ns}. in some sort of a fitt, & that he now is extremely ill of a fever. Do let me know by return of post how it is with him, whether he is sick or well, & if I may yet expect the honour of waiting upon him at Burslem, & if you wait upon him, pay my humble respects in what manner you shall think proper, but pray let me know how his health is affected, for since the last report I have been much concern'd about it.

If I had time and room for it you should have a good scolding for beginning your last letter in such a manner. Am not I teazeing you with my scrawls every week? & sometimes every post? & sho^d. have no sort of objection to writeing oftener still if Journeys, Navigations, & other things did not prevent me. You know I do not want inclination,—you know that ever since I have been capable of distinguishing, I have had the truest & most affect^e. regards for you, & I am sure you have allways given me sufficient reason to believe that our affection was mutual; therefore do not talk of my forgetting such a Brother & friend as you have ever been to me, nor of my being forgotton by you. I cannot bear to think or say any more about it.

The latter part of your letter delights me

greatly as your poetical description of Groves
& springs, the feather'd Choir &c. &c. indicates
the flow of spirits you enjoyed at the time of
writeing it, & let me tell you that a pint of
new milk & a Role & half a Role by way of
finishing a breakfast shews a tolerable good
natured stomach, at least we should think so
in the country. But I am afraid by your acc^t.
of this new chalybeat Inn & the Comp^y. who
resort to it we are not to have the pleasure of
your company in Staffordshire this summer,
this I can by no means consent to—we have
chalybeats with us, & new milk too, for the
very day I knew your quantity, we sold our
barren Cow in order to buy a new milch one,
& now come as soon as you will there will be
enough for us all. Sally says your niece Sukey
is worth your coming 150 miles to see, but
she may see & talk like a mother, however we
do expect to see you some part of the summer
amongst us, & the sooner the pleasanter.

  Believe us ever
   Your truly affect^e. Bro^r. & S^r.
    J. & S. WEDGWOOD.

Success to the minority.

To Mr. John Wedgwood.

My dear Brothers letter of 28 June rejoiced us all very greatly as it left us no room to doubt of the return of his health & spirits again, pray God preserve to you those invaluable blessings.

Your mother sends her love to you, with her blessing provided you do not take her son John into France, she is not willing to trust him with that *false-hearted* People, & hopes he will not be so hardy to venture himself amongst them, but rather come & visit his friends in Staffordshire.—I cannot help thinking the advice is good & hope it will meet with due attention.

I should have wrote to you sooner but have been waiting upon his G— the D— of Bridgwater with plans &c. respecting Inland Navigation. Mr. Sparrow went along with me, we were most graciously recᵈ. spent about 8 hours in his G—'s compʸ., & had all the assurances of his concurrence with our designs that we could wish. His G— gave me an ordʳ. for the completest Table service of Cream colour that I could make, shewed us a Roman Urn 1500

46

years old at least, made of red china, & found
by his workmen in Castlefield near Manchester. After his G— had dismiss'd us we had
the honour, & pleasure too of sailing in his
Gondola nine miles along his Canal, thro' a
most delightfull vale to Manchester, the next
day we waited upon the Cheshire Gent^n. at a
meeting of the Comm^{rs}. for the Weaver Navigation at Northwich, who promised likewise
to use their interest in favour of our design,
provided we fall into their Navigation. But
no more of this 'till you are better acquainted
with the subject.

I am greatly delighted with the picture you
give of yourself, & the short journal of your
exercise & diet—pray let us as soon as possible
be favour'd with a sight of the Original, &
edify by your example in early rising, & eating
of buttermilk.

I shall be very proud of the honour of sending a box of patterns to the Queen, amongst
which I intend sending two setts of Vases,
Creamcolour engine turn'd, & printed, for
which purpose nothing could be more suitable
than some copper plates I have by me. I can
adapt the Vases so that the designs & they
will appear to be made for each other, & intended for Royalty, nor must you hint to the contrary—but I am one group or design short

which I have sketched out & inclos'd & desire you'l get it done by Wale unless you know a better hand. It must be engrav'd, any of the print shops, (Mr. Bowles in Cornhill in particular) will direct you to Wale or some other: the sooner I have it done & sent me, the sooner I shall be able to send the patterns.

TO MR. BENTLEY.

BURSLEM, *Augt. 1st, 1765.*

Dear Sir

I am favoured with your very agreeable L^r. dated Sunday Evening & intirely approve of your judicious remarks, & desire you will finish the Pamphlet* upon the Plan you mention—I shoud. like that part abo^t. the Pottery pared down a great deal, I am afraid of mentioning too much abo^t. our manufacture, least our Governors shoud. think it worth taxing.—

* A pamphlet entitled "A View of the Advantages of Inland Navigation," drawn up by Mr. Bentley.

We were at Trentham yesterday waiting
upon L^d. Gower & the Duke of Bridgwater, Mr.
Gilbert Member for Newcastle was there &
made us promise to send our Pamphlet to his
House the beginning of next week in such a
state as we coud make it by that time—his
Reasons were, that he sh^d. then have a Gent^n.
with him who is exceedingly clever in these
matters.

The article of Fuller's Earth may be left out
till we are better assured about it, or anything
else that you think is doubtful, there will be
enough besides & I do not think it will be
worse for being reduced in it's Bulk.—I
entirely agree with you that the second part
will be more properly the first, & that Compliments Piety &c. &c. are very improper for
this Work.—But why then did I put them in?
you ask! That, my Friend, is a kind of mystery
wch. I shall take some opportunity of revealing
to you, but not till you have done your business.—

So much for Authorship!—

Pray let me know by Post, or Coach if that
will arrive sooner, when our good friend Sir
Willm. arrives at your Town. It does me good
every time I think of his new station,* which

---

* Sir W^m. Meredith had been made a Lord of the Admiralty.

there is no doubt of his filling with honour to himself & advantage to his Country & Constituents. Pray make my Congratulations on this happy Event, to the worthy Society at the Dog & Partridge.

———————————

To Mr. John Wedgwood, Junʳ.

BURSLEM, *2nd Augᵗ., 1765.*

Dear Brother

Broʳ. John* is here in his way to London so could not miss the opportunity of sending a line by him.

On second thoughts it may not be amiss to know all one can about this burning on gold polishing, & burnishing the same—burnishing is a different operation to polishing, & I shᵈ. be glad to know wᵗ. instrument they make use of & be furnished with one of them.

I wish you woᵈ. buy & send me per Coach Vol. 1st of the Handmaid to the Arts published in 1758 for Nourse in the Strand.

* His wife's brother, a cheese-factor at Smallwood, Cheshire.

And now as to the price of this ware. I
foresee that if the gold must be laid on to have
a full metalic appearance the price will be very
high, whether they may be deemed dear or not
I cannot say, but sure the great Personage
they are for wo^d. have them perfect, & can
afford to pay for them, but I wo^d. rather not
fix any price at all upon them if that wo^d. be
approv'd of, but farther on this subject another
time. . . . .

Pray how are you for business, or schemes
of pleasure? for I wo^d. by no means break into
the latter, but if it wo^d. be consistent with
both & you sho^d. choose it I wo^d. send you a
pattern or two & a list of my Chaps,* & more
bills if you choose such employm^t. 'till a *better
place* offers. I have this year sent goods to
amo^t. of abo^t. £1000 to London all of which is
owing for & I sho^d. not care how soon I was
counting some of the money.

You know I have often mention'd having a
man in London the greatest part of the year
shewing patterns, taking orders, settling acc^{ts}.
&c. &c. & as I increase my work, & throw it
still more into the ornamental way I shall have
the greater need of such assistance & sho^d. be
glad to have your advice upon it. Wo'd £50

---

* Customers,

a year keep such a Person in London & pay rent for 2 Rooms (both back rooms & St. Giles's wo^d. be as good as St. James's) about so much I think it might answer for me to give.

If your Clark hath not full employm^t. a thing of this sort might make a little appendage to his salary.

My father sends his respects service &c. to you by his son, but he is a Leaky vessell to freight wth. Comp^{ts}. I shall expect answers to all my l^{rs}. very soon from your experienc'd punctuality & am with the truest Affection

D^r. Bro^r.

Your greatly obliged Bro^r.

To Mr. JOHN WEDGWOOD.

BURSLEM, 7 Aug^t., 1765.

Dear Bro^r.

I have just had the honour of the D. of Marlb^o., L^d. Gower, L^d. Spencer & others at my works.—They have bo^t. some things & seem'd much entertain'd & pleas'd.

Sally & I are taking a ride to look at poor
S^r. Nigil's* goods &c. which are to be sold in a
fortnight, he hath left Knipersley with his
family, & it is much feared his affairs will
never suffer his return.

Our best affection waits on you.

Adieu.

I have succeeded the first tryal in making
powder gold which I have allways been told
one man only in England could make, & desire
you'l send me an oz. of *pure* gold either in
Ducats or grain or some form, send the powder
too.

I am just teazed of my life with dilatory,
drunken, Idle, worthless workmen which prevents my proceeding in the tea service, to w^{ch}.
more sorts of workmen are necessary than one
wo^d. imagine.

The Gent^n. above ment^d. (not the workmen
though) wonder I have not a Wareh^o. in Lond^n.
where patt^{ns}. of all the sorts I make may be
seen.

Our love to another J. W.

---

* Sir Nigel Gresley, one of the lords of the manor of Burslem.

To Mr. Thos. Bentley.

My dear Friend

To-morrow I shall set out for London & therefore need not tell you that to-day I am very busy, but cannot help sending you a correction or two for our Navigation Pamphlet wch. I have just rec^d. from a friend*.

In general he thinks the style rather too flat or tame, but be it remember'd that he is himself a Poetical Genius.

That it is not wrote enough to the Landowners, & they, if any body of men does, will ruin our scheme.

Secⁿ. 1. Sentence 1st. "Whose int^s. are more immediately concern'd in its success" not approv'd as it reminds the Landowner that the contributor is interested more than he is in it.

This objection does not appear to me to be well founded, as the "immediately concern'd" may relate to the Landowners as well as any other Persons, for who are more than they concern'd or interested in its success ? . . .

In the Article of *pleasures.*

* Dr. Erasmus Darwin.

54

"Gentlemen in other situations &c." is offensive, is nobody to wish for such things but *Gentlemen*? A Correction attempted— " wch. your honour, in another situation, if it please your honour, would wish for in vain ! "—

This appears to me more witty than just— who are not *Gent^n*. when addressed in print? besides the Articles of luxury refer'd to belong more properly to Gent^n. than either Farmers or Mechanics.

"To have a Lawn terminated by a Canal &c." Why change a more elegant & equally simple word for a worse? Why a Canal is as straight as *Fleet Ditch*.—A Canal at the bottom of your meadow ! Foh ! it can't be born by the Goddess of modern taste, but " *Water* " ay *Water* give me *Water* to terminate or divide my Lawn.

This seems a real emendation, if you think so pray alter it accordingly, for I have the fear of the Goddess before my eyes.

"Is the circumstance of our trade being safer in war time omitted least the Gent^n. concern'd in the Coasting trade sho^d. be alarmed ? "

"The acc^t. of China is Curious if one could believe it."

"Several other malchanges will be pointed out if leisure permits."

To Mr. Thos. Bentley.

UTOXETER, *27th Sept^r., 1765.*

My worthy Friend

Your agreeable favour of 23 inst. was wrong sent to Stone which kept it a day longer out of my hands & prevented my answering it by yesterdays post, however it now lies before me & I find to my great mortification that according to the old adage "when luck is in the lane, I am in the field," had I been fortunate enough to have kept at your hospitable mansion 'till S^r. Ellis's arrival, I should have expected no less than to be presented with the freedom of your Opulant Corporation, & unless you can procure me the same honour from S^r. W^m's. party I will not now, after the notice S^r. Ellis hath favoured me with, promise you my weight & interest in Liverpool, for as you say of money, so I may say of honour, 'tis hard to say w^t. enough of it may do.—Seriously, the meaning of this compliment, any further than as p^d. to you, thro' your friend, is to me incomprehensible, but I have no more time to bestow upon *trifles light as air.*—To the business of your l^r.

The Booksellers at Newcastle are partners, you may put in Messrs. Gore, Johnson & who

56

N 6

To

Mr Thos Bentsley March 4

in

Liverpool

My worthy friend

Worcester 27th Septr. 1765

Your agreeable favour of 23 Inst was wrong sent to Stone which kept it a day longer out of my hands & prevented my answering it by yesterdays post, however it now lies before me, & I find to my great mortification that according to the old adage "when luck is in the lane, I am in the field," had I been fortunate enough to have kept at your hospitable mansion till Sr. Ellis's arrival, I should have expected no less than to be presented with the freedom of your Opulent Corporation, & unless you can procure me the same honour from Sr. Wm's party I will not now, after the notice Sr. Ellis hath favour'd me with, promise you my weight & interest in Liverpool, for as you say of money, so I may say of honour, 'tis hard to say wt. enough of it may do, — Seriously, the meaning of this compliment, any farther than as pd to you, thro' your friend, is to me incomprehensible, but I have no more time to bestow upon trifles light as air to the business of your Cr.

The Book sellers at Newcastle are partners. you may put in Messrs. Gore, Johnson & who you please as Booksellers ———— Dr. Darwin at our Inn, & just made his appearance! was ever anything so apropos', adieu till we get to Derby Derby past eight — Well as I was saying — Booksellers

Book sellers — you'l write to Johnson perhaps, & by the
time he can rec͟v͟e a line from you I will give him
a call.

D͟r͟ Darwin says nobody writes Grace, &
R͟t͟ honourable, but Taylors & such like folks, so do
as seemeth good in your own eyes. nor wo͟d͟ the D͟r͟
have anything farther than ingenious or so, so M͟r͟
Brindleys name, but that matter is left entirely
to your own discretion, feeling, &c.

A few copys on a finer paper may not be amiss.

M͟r͟ Gilbert & L͟d͟ Gower (I ask his L͟d͟sh͟ps͟
pardon) have seen your Dedication this morning
& approve of it, but D͟r͟ Darwin does not like
Legislature & some other things in it, & thinks
Inhabitants in the article of pleasures. more
unexceptionable, than Gent͟n͟ — but he hath
promis'd me to write you his sentiments himself
on these & some other things in the Pamphlet in
a day or two at farthest.

I am very sorry our good friend S͟r͟ W͟m͟ is
likely to have the trouble of a contested Election
amongst you & wo͟d͟ gladly throw in a mite if I
had it for his service, — If a hint I have picked
up in my way hither will be of any use to his fr͟ds͟
in securing his Election pray take it, & may it
prove as successfull as it hath lately been at a

a Burrough in our County

No. 5, Bullocks roasted whole — Quantum sufficit

6. small Cannon to be fired at every vote gained from the Enemy

a Fighting Captain to be made use of occasionally with the wavering, & timerous.

Get Mr. Scaigs (a Person well known in Tamworth) to make queer faces

a Poet is absolutely necessary & he be heard of at Birm^m.

Adieu

y^rs affect^ly
J Wedgwood

Pray charge postage to — Navigation

you please as Booksellers.—D^r. Darwin at our
Inn, & just made his appearance! was ever
anything so apropos? adieu 'till we get to
Derby. . . . .

D^r. Darwin says *nobody* writes *Grace*, & R^t.
honourable, but Taylors & such like folks, so
do as seemeth good in your own eyes. Nor
wo^d. the D^r. have anything farther than ingenious or so, to Mr. Brindley's name, but that
matter is left intirely to your own discretion,
feeling, &c.

A few copys on a finer paper may not be amiss.

Mr. Gilbert & L^d. Gower (I ask his L^d.ships
pardon) have seen your Dedication this morning & approve of it, but D^r. Darwin does not
like *Legislature* & some other things in it, &
thinks *Inhabitants* in the article of pleasures,
more unexceptionable than *Gent"*.—but he hath
promis'd me to write you his sentiments himself on these & some other things in the Pamphlet in a day or two at farthest.

I am very sorry our good friend S^r. W^m. is
likely to have the trouble of a contested Election amongst you & wo^d. gladly throw in a mite
if I had it for his service. If a rec^t. I have
picked up in my way hither will be of any use
to his fr^{ds}. in securing his Election pray take it,
& may it prove as successfull as it hath lately
been at a Burrough in our County.

RECEIPT. Bullocks roasted whole—Quantum sufficit.

6 small Cannon to be fired at every vote gained from the Enemy.

A Fighting Captain to be made use of occasionally with the wavering & timerous.

Get Mr. Scaigs (a person well known in Tamworth) to make *quere faces.*

A Poet is absolutely necessary & may be heard of at Birm[m].

————————

To Mr. Thos. Bentley.

London, *7 Oct[r]. 1765.*

Dear Sir

I doubt not but you have rec[d]. my letter from Utoxeter & Derby, & a long, Critical epistle from our ingenious & poetical friend Doct[r]. Darwin, which I doubt not, if it be such as he generally favours his friends with, hath afforded you entertainment, & shook your diaphragm for you, whatever it may have done respecting your Pamphlet on Navigation.

I am greatly pleased with your judicious remarks, on composition, Truth, Simplicity, Pathos & Eloquence. Am intirely of your sentiments respecting those subjects, & that is all I can now awhile to say about them.

The Plan will be engrav'd in 10 days, when will the Pamphlet be ready?

Yesterday I spent at Turnham Green & did your message to our friend Ralphs.

If you mean the letter respecting Mr. Priestley's* Publication, Mr. Griffith sent it to the manager of the St. James's Chronicle with a letter acquainting him it came from Mr. Bentley, a sensible & ingenious correspond^t. of theirs, & desir'd it might be published, & he hath sought it sorrowing in every paper since, 'till a few days agoe he was in comp^y. with Mr. Baldwin & desir'd to know the reason why it was not inserted, & rec^d. for answer that they did not choose to meddle in disputes betwixt Reviewers & Authors or their friends for if they did that their papers wo^d. be filled with little else. But there is it seems a more potent reason for their refusing your paper, for the manager of the London Chronicle hath

---

* Joseph Priestley, at this time Tutor of Languages & Polite Literature at the Warrington Academy. The publication referred to was " An Essay on a Course of Liberal Education for Civil & Active Life," which was reviewed in the *Monthly Review* for September, 1765.

particular connections with the Critical Reviewers.—But be comforted, we will rescue the paper out of their hands, & try it in another quarter, unless you forbid it by return.

I must leave you to do *the needfull* with Mr. Tarlton, if he was from home when you call'd upon him with the MS., does not that sufficiently excuse us of our promise?

I have been three Days hard & close at work takeing patt^{ns}. from a set of French China at the Duke of Bedford's, worth at least £1500, the most elegant things I ever saw, & am this evening to wait & be waited upon by designers, modelers &c. Adieu.

Qu. Does *Legislature* signify the Legislators or the act of Legislation, vid. Dedication.

To Mr. Thos. Bentley.

London Lawrence Lane. Messrs. Berrys & Co^y. Manchester Warehouse.

15 Oct^r., 1765.

D^r. Sir

Before you recieve this you will see your spirited & manly paper in the St. James's Chronicle, & I wish it may have the desired effect upon the Public. S^r. W^m. read it there last night, at his own house, & I took the liberty of telling him to whom the Public was indebted for it, he said it was very clever &c. & I hope it falls in with his own sentiments.

I have not read the Monthly Review for Augt. or Sept^r. & therefore have not seen the Review of Mr. Priestley's work, indeed the truth is I have scarcely read anything at all, or thought of anything at all but Pottmaking & Navigating, & when it will be otherwise with me I cannot tell.

The Booksellers you know how to deal with & deal by, much better than myself & shall leave that business entirely to you.

I have mention'd the affair of Dedication to Mr. Griffiths before I was favour'd with yours, we had no very deliberate discussion of the matter, but *offhand* he thought the *Legislature* if it meant the *Power* rather than the *Persons* could not with propriety be Dedicated to, but if as you say it means King, L^{ds}., & Comm^{ns}. I sho^d. think that objection entirely took away.

I am my good friend very sorry that this Pamphlet turns out so troublesome an affair to you who I am sure have full employm^t. for every moment of your time. As to our friend of Lichfields* remarks if you can avail yourself of them in the part not yet print^d. I know you will, but the condemnation or postponing of the whole I can by no means agree to nor perswade myself that there is any necessity for it. Must the Uniting of Seas & distant countrys depend upon the choice of a phrase, or monosyllable? Away with such hypercriticisms, & let the press go on, a Pamphlet we must have, or our design will be defeated, so make the best of the present, & correct, refine, & sublimate, if you please, in the next edition.

P.S.—My Bro^r. is now with me, & is very certain that if you wo^d. come & fix in London, & enter a second time into the holy estate of Matrimony that you might choose your Lady, have your Chariot, lead the World in a string, and do what seemeth good in your own eyes.

* D^r. Darwin.

By the same authority that I mention this,—
every Wife, maid and Widow that hath seen
Mr. Bentley in London join in this opinion.
This deponent farther sayeth not. I am only
his emanuensis, if you require an explanation
write to him.

To Mr. Thos. Bentley.

London, 2$^{nd.}$ Nov^r, 1765.

To the right Honrable. & Honrable. both
Houses of Parliament this design to enhance
the value of land & to extend the manufactures & Commerce of Great Britain is most
humbly Dedicated.

S^r. W^m. Meredith says this is enough & he
thinks better than more; *Legislature* is not he
thinks proper to dedicate to, both houses of
Parliament he likes much better & does not
apprehend any impropriety in leaving out the
King, perhaps this may come too late but you
must depend upon your own taste, feeling, &
judgement whether to let it go as it is or print

that part over again. I shou'd have wrote to
my worthy Friend sooner & thank'd him for
his very acceptable letters but my late illness
wou'd not suffer me to do anything & I had
not before to-day a convenient opportunity of
consulting our good Friend, this Afternoon I
had the honor of Dining with him alone he
tells me there is the greatest probability of Mr.
Pitt joining the present administration.* He
greatly laments the death of the good Duke of
Cumberland† & is sorry that Prince Henry
Frederick has so soon followed his unckle, he
died this morning.

I hope you rec^d. the plate which I sent you
by Sundays Coach so you will get what quantity are necessary struck off suppose you send
a hundred Pamphlets to each of the two Booksellers in town and six to S^r. W^m. Meredith &
six to my Brother which may be made up in
the parcel to Mr. Becket & my Brother will
deliver them.

[The letter so far is in the handwriting of Mrs. Josiah Wedgwood.]

So ends the Female Scribe.

Now sir I do warmly thank you for your
kind Letter & advice, the Reason for my stay

---

* The Rockingham Ministry.
† "The Butcher," died Oct. 31st, 1765.

in London was the very same that has prevented you from doing many things—my Concerns
& Business here Prevented me, & I had no
hand I cou'd well leave it in.

I will take Care of the Review. The Language I am not afraid of, & the Plan will have
Justice. I have consulted with Griffiths who
begs his respects.

In my Opinion D^r. Darwin's Criticism is below a Man of Letters. I fancy the Author
was sore—you know the old Proverb.

I am sir with the Greatest sincerity
Y^r. real Friend, well-wisher & Humble Servt.
JOHN WEDGWOOD.*

LOND^N., *2nd Nov^r., 1765.*

Though these good Folks have concluded
the letter without me I dare not omit puting
my name to it least you should think me dead,
lame, or very lazy. I believe they have told
you everything I have to say respecting the
Pamphlet you have been so teized about. I
shall for the future be very cautious how I

* Josiah's brother.

E

hook my friends into such thankless, profitless business again, & how I engage in them myself too, but there is no retreating now without both loss & shame therefore must make the best of a bad matter.

Mr. Gilbert tells me that the D. of Bridgwater wants to know how we proceed in our design as he hath not heard anything of it lately. I am glad to find he has not forgot the subject & hope he will be our steady & potent friend.

I cannot find any French book on Chymical affinitys, without the title or authors name.

We hope to leave this dismal, smoaky place on Monday next.

To Mr. John Wedgwood.

Burslem, *11ᵗʰ Novʳ., 1765.*

Dear Brother

Nothing prevented us having a pleasant journey home but the badness of the roads which were very bad indeed.

We spent half a day very agreeably at Blen-

heim House and in the evening went with the
Steward, his Daughter & four sons to see a
play at Woodstock, but alass, we had seen the
London Theatre too lately to have much en-
joym^t. from poverty, rags & blunders on the
Woodstock stage.

As you talk of sending down a box I must
just hint to you that Sister Willets little
Lasses will go to bed without their nightcaps
soon if they do not rec^{ve}. an old shirt from
their unckle. They send love & duty to you
from the Bank, your cousin Sally bids me
send her best love (next to her husband or so)
to you & tell you she was providing some pork
pyes & will now send the puddings along with
them for y^r. Xmas fare before the holydays.

To Mr. Thos. Bentley.

NEWCASTLE, *18th Nov^r., 1765.*

Dear Sir
Accept my thanks for your kind letter
& good wishes for my health. I am got pretty

well but not perfectly recover'd. Dr. Darwin who stop'd all night with me at Burslem last week, hath prescribed something for me which he says will strengthen the machinery & set it all to rights again.

The Dr. acknowledg'd he had wrote you two or three very rude letters, & said you had drub'd him genteely in return, which he seem'd to take very cordially, & to be very well pleas'd with his treatment.

The Pamphlets came to hand on friday or saturday last. I saw them yesterday only but have been so much employ'd in dispersing them that I have not yet had time to read one but have dipped upon some alterations which please me much.

The word, *revive*, in the dedication may possibly give offence to the late administration* & their friends, on some of whom we chiefly depend for success in this undertaking. The papers have been so full of complaints that our trade & manufactures are ruin'd by the blunders of the late administration that when we pray them (as a part of both houses of Parliamᵗ.) to favour our design for *reviving* our (decayed) manufactures & commerce, they must be affected either with shame for their

* The Grenville ministry, which succeeded Bute.

own maladministration, or with anger for the reproof, which last I think is most probable, & though they may deserve it ever so much, we should not make our Dedication a channel for anything of that sort. I know you would have me write my sentiments without any reserve, on this, or any other subjeçt, & so you see I do. I am quite open to conviction, & shall be glad to know my fears have no foundation.

Excuse the trouble which I am truly sorry to give you & believe me yours affectionately in haste.

BURSLEM, *Dec. 12ᵗʰ, 1765.*

Dear Sir

. . . .

I have now learn'd all I can from the D. both Mr. Gilbert & Mr. Brindley, & the whole amounts to this, that his Grace intended to bring you a Canal to Liverpool *some way* & *sometime*, neither of which Circumstances were determin'd, & whether the Duke will like to join any other Navigation, or have the time, manner, or road of bringing this Canal to you

chalk'd out to him is much doubted by Messrs.
G. & B. & I most sincerely wish our great
Patron may prove in every respect the Patriot
we both would be glad to find in him. He
has done great things for his Country & for us,
& seems to be intending farther good for both,
it grieves one to suspect such a Character
sho^d. mean to serve himself only at the expence
of what is most dear to a people by whom he
is so much beloved. I hope his views are more
liberal, more extended & more worthy a Character so greatly respected, but it will be our
truest policy as you advise, that, whatever be
his *motives*, we endeavour to make his *actions*
contribute to the execution of our plan which
is certainly calculated to serve the Public more
effectually than any other that hath yet been
chalked out.

Saturday noon.

I am just return'd from waiting upon S^r.
Walter Bagot, & his son who is Member for
our County, they were on a visit at Mr. Sneyds
of Keel S^r. Walter's son in Law, & sent for me
to come & explain the plan of our intended
navigation to them. I spent the evening &
morning 'till noon with this good company,
chalked out all the plans in agitation, &
answer'd all their objections in the best man-

ner I was able, & had the satisfaction to find my labour was not bestowed in vain, for they acknowledg'd themselves convinced of some errors they had imbibed, & said they now understood our plan &c. much better than they had ever done before, & when they knew the sense of the County in general & had considered a little upon the subject they would be glad to see some of us at Bliffield. S^r. Walter & his son have hitherto been avowed Enemies to canal navigations, but I hope their eyes are opening & we are takeing proper measures to let them know the sense of the County.

Mr. W^m. Bagot has been much abroad in France, Italy &c. he hath seen the famous Canal of Languedoc & says that though it is navigated upon only about three months in the year it is of so much consequence to the Inhabitants in exporting their wine & oyl & importing corn for their subsistance that the country bordering upon it would scarcely be habitable without the conveniences it furnishes. Its importance he says may be known by the great annual expence they are at in keeping it Navigable, he has seen vast numbers employ'd in clear^g. it of the weeds which choak it up in the nine months it lies idle. This Canal is vacant so long every year for want of Tonnage to be conveyed, & not through any defect in the

Canal & this vacancy creates the expence of Clearing &c. I was glad to learn these facts from so good Authority, as the expence attending the Languedoc Canal & its insufficiency to answer the purpose it was intended for hath often been mention'd as an objection to ours, where hills are to be level'd, cut through, &c., but no weeds grow in the Dukes Canal, & I hope we shall have motion enough in ours to prevent any great degree of vegitation in its waters. Mr. Bagot says the Languedoc Canal is too small to be ever intended for shiping, that it now keeps a communication open between the Mediterranean & the Ocean & would if there was tonnage enough to keep it clear of weeds answer the purposes it was made for.

Sunday morning.

I am favour'd with your letter of 13 & could forgive this navigation all the trouble it gives me for the pleasure I recieve in reading your repeated & very valuable letters. You want an answer to your doubts, first whether we are not all intended to be humbug'd. I cannot answer for another mans intentions, but I believe we are in very little danger, we have fixed upon an expedient to avoid it, & that is to insist as much as decency & propriety will

permit us of L^d. Gower's coming down into
Staffordshire & *PUBLICLY* at a meeting of
the Gentlemen in this County to be appointed
for that purpose to put himself at the head of
our design & take it under his patronage. This
I told Mr. Thomas G. on Tuesday last was the
only measure that could give us any of that
importance with the Landowners & Country
Gentlemen which was necessary for carrying
our great design into Parliam^t. this Sessions,
& without it, we despair'd of succeeding in
any other way than complying with proposals
from another quarter where the Gent^n. would
appear openly in our support. This had the
desir'd effect : my L^d. Gower had been wrote to
& Mr. G. rec^d. a letter from his L^d.sh^p. the
day after we were with him promising his
assistance in Parliam^t., &c., but Mr. Gilbert
immediately despatch'd an express to London
& told his L^d.sh^p. that a letter would not do
for us. That we desired nothing more than to
put our intended Navigation under the protection of his L^d.ship & the D. but then we
were so circumstanc'd that it was necessary
his L^d.ship sho^d. come into the country to recieve it, that the Potters were determin'd to
accept the best Navigation they could get if
they could not get the best they wished for.
I have wrote to the same purpose by last post

to his G. of Bridgewater at Mr. G.'s request.
Now if L^d. G. sho^d. publicly espouse our cause
& take the lead in it, & afterwards desert us
when the D.'s purposes were served, the County wo^d. never forgive him & I do not believe
any private connect^n. wo^d. induce him to do it.

Anybody may build their own boats & do
what business they please upon the D.'s Canal
paying the Tonnage fixed by act of Parliam^t.
which I think is a very moderate one, the
Landowners may likewise build wharfs &
warehouses along his Canal so that I do not
think it can be made a monopoly. I have seen
Mr. Brindley again & told him that our present
situation oblig'd me to put a few serious &
very important questions to him, that I consider'd his connections with the D. & did not
desire him to do anything inconsistant with
them, but that a whole Country depended
upon his well known abilities & integrity to
prevent their being decieved in such important
points, from any quarter.

The first was if there really was a practicable
path for our Canal to join the D.'s without too
great an expence to answer to the Public or
the Proprietors. He says there really is. The
next was whether when other Peoples business is done, it is meant that we should
be permitted to do our own. Answer—we may

depend on it that it is so meant. Thirdly whether the D. wo^d. cause an estimate to be made of Crossing the Dane* (the great difficulty) & enable any engineer to give security to complete the Aqueduct in a given time & for a certain sum, or whether he chose to do it himself. He could not answer for the D. but wo^d. consider of the subject himself.

Monday morning.—I have just rec^d. a letter by a special messenger from S^r. W^m. at Henbury desireing me to come there on Tuesday evening next. I hope you have rec^d. the same invitation.

Oh! that we may meet there, to lend our assistance together in reconcileing these Jarring interests & conducting this Grand Design in the best manner possible for the Public. We must meet somewhere to settle matters for a 2nd Edition of our Pamphlet. The plate of the plan must be alter'd greatly, or a new one made. Mr. Brindley recommends Mr. Oldham of Manchester as a proper Person to lay it down anew. If you do not choose to come to Henbury, suppose we meet at Macclesfield or Knutsford & in your way thither you send a messenger for Mr. Oldham to meet us

---

* The Dane is a small river forming part of the boundary between Staffordshire and Cheshire : it flows into the Weaver at Northwich.

there. I am enabled to bear your & all expences attending our journeys on the subject
of our Navigation. We shall want to spend a
full day or two together & I shall bring all my
papers &c. with me to Henbury in hopes of
seeing you there or reciev^g. a message where to
attend you.

I need not tell you this L^r. is for your own
perusal only, I have this moment an express
from Mr. Gilb^t. to answer, this is the sixth l^r.
on Navigation I have dispatch'd to-day. Adieu,
I wish this bustle was over & I was quietly
settled a Potter *only* again.

Dec. 16, 1765.

NEWCASTLE. *Monday morning before
sun rising.* [*Dec. 1765*]

I have stole a few moments from my
wife this morning to converse a little with my
friend 'till the world is wide awake, for then I
must of necessity mix with the bustling crowd.
Everything is in the most violent agitation
here, by *everything* you know I mean *Navigation*—but I will confine myself at present to

the subject of your last two letters which I
rec^d. by Saturdays post, & first I am sure I
ought to thank you for them, which I do very
sincerely, & esteem them as the most valuable
part of my Literary treasure, & the kindest
testimonies of your friendship.

My health is now perfectly restored, I could
not say so much a few days agoe, & when I did
write to you I really forgot to say anything
about it, which I blame myself for, as I know
assuredly from my own feelings that the health
of a friend cannot be a subject of indifference
to you. But to business of greater importance. I intend to advertise the pamphlet
again at Birm^m. & think it would not be amiss
to do so in the London papers, if you think
so, pray send a proper advertisem^t. to my
Bro^r. or Mr. Johnson in Town, & I should be
glad to have a coppy of yours by Tuesdays
post. His Grace the D. of Bridgwater told
me of some deficiencies in our advertisem^t.
in the Lond^n. papers but I have forgot what
they were, & have not seen the advertise-
m^t. myself. The pamphlet his Grace approves of much & thinks it can recieve very
little improvem^t. in any respect. It is universally admir'd & will be more so the more it is
read. A few phrases may perhaps be alter'd
for the better, but they are too trifleing to

merit a serious thought. The whole is sterling, & you will have the honour you justly merit.

The D. of Bridgwater lay at Trentham on Wednesday evening in his way to London & sent for Mr. John Brindley & me to attend him there. We had the honour to sup, breakfast, & spend about eight hours with his Grace. The subject you may be sure was *inland Navigation*, & I had the best opportunity to mention my friend & his improvem'. that I could wish & in such a manner as I thought they deserv'd. Mr. John Gilbert (his steward of the works) was present, they looked at each other as though some secret design of their own had been discover'd by another before the time they thought proper to avow it, & therefore were very shy in saying anything about it. On saturday Mr. John Gilbert was sent to Burslem to us to give us some farther hints, instructions & encouragm'. in our design, & amongst other things desir'd your scheme might not be mention'd at present, & with a significant nod told me *great things might be done at a proper time* but we had enough under our hands at present.

You will now have an opportunity of conversing with Mr. Brindley as I sent a line by him to you & will make the most of it I doubt not.

Our good & worthy friend S^r. W^m. is at present I fear with the Cheshire Gent^n.—in their designs I mean.

The Comm^{re}. of the Weaver Navigation have made us an offer of reducing their tonnage if we terminate there to 6d. per Ton, for all Canal Tonnage. Mr. Brayne & Mr. Pownal were sent to make this & some other proposals to us last night. Another material one is that they will in effect remove Liverpool so much nearer to us as Northwich by making the River navigable for Vessels of 120 Tons burthen, this if we agree with them they will do by cutting past the bridges, & our Clay ships & other coasting vessells will not discharge or take in their Loading at your Port, but Northwich will in most respects be to Liverpool what Gainsb^{ro}. is to Hull.

This needs no comment of mine.

I hope you will be able to engage S^r. W^m. in our favour, our interests are certainly mutual, for I think all the advantages the Cheshire Gent^n. have or can offer us are not equal to the prospect there is of carrying the general plan of Canal Navigation you have pointed out into execution in *due season*, but if the two schemes now in agitation do both terminate in the weaver there is not a grain of probability that that *Grand scheme* sho^d. ever take place &

Liverpool must feel it the first & severest too.

I am ord^d. when our battle waxeth hot, which it soon will do, to keep 4 or 5 runing footmen at my elbow & trust nothing of consequence to the post. To send any important intelligence to the Duke himself unless I know Mr. Gilbert to be in Town, & I beg that you will write anything you think may be of service to the *general cause* & convey it by what Channel & to whom you think most proper. No necessary expence is to be spared, & we have reason to expect L^d. Gower publicly to espouse our cause in a few days.

The D. we know will exert all his talents, & interest all his fr^{ds}. in the support of our design.

BURSLEM, *Jany. 14, 1766.*

The above* is copy of a letter my Bro^r. takes with him to Warrington, to-day I believe, in order to set on foot a subscription there. You have strange heterodox notions amongst you at Liverpool about your Port being ruin'd, your not being principals, & I don't know what stuff. Pray who are *principals by the rules of common sense,* in a design of this sort, but those who will recieve the *principal* advantages from it. I do not mention this for your edification, I know you are thoro'ly converted from such heathenish doctrines yourself & will use your best endeavours to convert your Bretheren. However we have thought it needfull to send a Missionary amongst you, Mr. John Brindley who is coming near your Town on another errand, by whom I sent a line to you, & hope he will bring a better report from your Town than the following extract seems to promise.

" The subscription or sum voted by this Corporation you may have at comm^d.—when you wo^d. have the first £100 remitted please to send a rec^t. to be a Voucher for the

* A letter urging further subscriptions towards the £3000 needed to get their bill through Parliament. Liverpool has only subscribed £200, while a few villages in Wedgwood's neighbourhood have taken all the trouble and subscribed £700.

F

Treasurer. We are making a survey for the Lancashire part of this great design, which undertaking we apprehend will be solely subscribed by this Town. We may justly therefore say our hands are full & be excused aiding you any otherwise. I am, &c."

FROM MR. J. TARLETON. 12 Jan^{ry}.

Pray now seriously what will your Lancashire Canal be without the Derbyshire, Staffordshire, & Cheshire additions—it dwindles so that I can scarcely see its *importance* without the assistance of a *mental microscope.* Whilst I am writing Mr. Brindley is returned without going to your Town which I am sorry for. . . . .

I am greatly pleas'd with Mr. Hodson's Letter—which fully convinces me that if any of us Navigators are slip'd besides ourselves, it is our quondam Friend of Macclesfield.* Poor Man! how he raves! I hope one Month's Confinement to the Debates in Westminster Hall will perfectly cure him.

Time obliges me to conclude myself
Your affectionate Friend
J. W. for y^r. perusal only.

---

* Sir William Meredith.

My dear friend

So poor Scarrat is Married! & in the next line allmost you tell me—*his head is turned*, which I suppose are synonims with you wicked Batchelors & Widowers—Well I could in mere spite wish to see you fairly noosed again, & bro^t. down into the Country, there to be immured in a little Rustick Cott, such as I could fashion for you—you know where, for the Diversion & emolument of the whole Country. Are your *last & first* thoughts ever employ'd on these subjects? Have you thought upon either of them more frequently since the Congress? Pray let me know how your head, & heart are affected of late when these subjects come across you, that I may know what to think of you & form my schemes accordingly.

P.S.—The case you suppose of your head being Corrupted is a very possible one, it is a kind of Original sin of which you are not thoro'ly cleared—so pray take care.

My dear Friend

I am a little sorry for your being oblig'd to take the field again before the scars of the last Campaign are closed up, but take courage my friend, fatigues & hardships are very necessary in forming great Characters, & you will by these frequent attendings on Parliam'. be the better prepar'd for filling a seat in that August assembly your self when the time comes, & who knows how near that may be ? but let this happen when it will I percieve very plainly by the good sense your Corporation hath now shewn, that whenever anything of moment to the Port of Liverpool is to be transacted in Parliam'. you must be their Agent with the Senate, & as you desire my advice & as I think myself very capable (for who does not ?) of giveing it take what I have to give in two words.

Do not give up your opinion too easily to Men who know not the matter so well as yourself.

Do not let your modesty prevent your making a proper advantage of your abilitys.

If I may add a third, take care of your health, & so God bless & prosper you & all your laudable undertak^{gs}.

To Mr. John Wedgwood.

Burslem, *4th June, 1766.*

Dear Brother

Perhaps you will not be angry at paying for the intelligence that we had yesterday a very Noble, Numerous & amicable General assembly of the Comm^{rs}. & Proprietors of the *Navigation from the Trent to the Mersey.* L^{d}. Gower, L^{d}. Grey, Mr. Bagot, Mr. Anson, Mr. Gilbert & the Gent^{n}. of the County did us the honour of attending this Assembly which was conducted through the whole of it with the utmost order, Harmony & as far as appear'd, to the entire satisfaction of all parties. I have inclos'd you an abstract of the business done, by which you will see the honour done me, which was quite unexpected & voluntary, with-

out the least previous sollicitation on my part,
& without one dissenting voice. The reason
I accepted it was that some of our friends suspected a Candidate wo^d. offer who liv'd at too
great a distance from the Centre of the business, & of the bolk of the subscribers, to be
convenient, on which I was urged to accept it
& comply'd. Mr. Smith of Fenton then propos'd me to the Assembly, & I was asked if I
wo^d. accept it, & what security I was willing to
give. To the former I answer'd in the affir-
mative, & referr'd myself to their pleasure for
the latter. The sum fix'd upon was £10,000.
All this was begun & ended in about quarter
of an hour. Immediately after it was over Mr.
Sam Robison took me aside and very genteely
offer'd to join in my security for so much as
his bond wo^d. be took for, which unexpected
favour I shall ever remember with gratitude
whether I accept it or not. I own I sho^d.
rather have no other name but Wedgwood in
the security, & sho^d. be glad of your advice on
this head. The utmost I ever expect to have
in my hands at once is 5 or £6000.

P.S.—Mr. Steveson of Stafford was the
Person expected to be a Candidate for Treasurer, so you will know where not to mention
that Circumstance.

AT A GENERAL ASSEMBLY OF THE PROPRIETORS
OF THE NAVIGATION FROM THE TRENT TO
THE MERSEY. *3 June, 1766.*

Commitee appointed. 1st Meeting ordered
to be held 10th June 1766 at the Crown at
Stone at 11 o'Clock.

Officers appointed :

James Brindley Surveyor   £200 per ann.
  General
Hugh Henshall* Clerk of   £150 per ann. for
  the Works   self & clerk
T. Sparrow Clerk to the   £100 per ann.
  Proprietors
Jos. Wedgwood Treasurer at £000 per ann.
out of which he bears his own expences.
Ord^d. That the work be begun on immedi-
ately both sides of Harecastle & at Wilden.

BURSLEM, *12 June, 1766.*

I most sincerely congratulate you on the
success your labours have again been crown'd
with, & on the new worlds which are opening

* Brindley's brother-in-law.

to our view. *Giants & Pigmies* you say! discover'd by one Captⁿ. Byron*, & you do not
think him a Descendant of Gullivers! Well I
suppose we are to have a trade opened with
these two extremitys of the Human species &
amongst other [things they] will no doubt
want some of [our commoditys so that it will
be as well] to be prepareing for them, though
[I do not know what size they will want their]
services. Terrines for instance (as [such
things are sure to be used] amongst them) of
two Gallons, one Gallon [is the largest we
make & I sho^d.] be sadly at a loss to know
whether a dish that [wo^d. be used] amongst
the what d'ye call 'ems, the 9 feet Giants [for
a lark would do] for a rump of Beef with the
Lillipution tribe. [Amongst other] things I
shall be much oblig'd to you for the [descrip-
tion of] the rest of the animals in those Regions, [in what proportion they are] to their
Lords & Masters, & whether a Lettuce [& a
Cabbage are as] different in each Country, . . .
[in size] & Capacity I mean, that I may be
ordering my [materials] accordingly. You see
I am for makeing an immediate [proffit] of
these new worlds, & I hope to reap some *spirit-*

---

* The account of Commodore Byron's Voyage Round the
World in the *Dolphin* (1764-1766) contains a description of the
Patagonians, whose average height is stated to be eight feet and
upwards.

ual benefit too, for if it is once confirm'd to me that there are *really & truly Nations* of *Giants & Nations* of *Lilliputions* existing upon this Globe of ours, my faith in other matters & things will certainly grow again, & I may become a sound *Believer* yet.

BURSLEM, *26 June, 1766.*

My worthy friend

I am extremely happy in the thoughts of haveing our connections increased in any way & the pleasure will grow in proportion as those connections can be made more agreeable or advantageous to you, & as you are to be a Pot merch^t. you may rest assured that in everything I can make or purchace you shall be enabled to serve your friends to the utmost of their wishes, so take in orders for anything this country produces, & in what way you think fit, but whole crates will certainly be attended with the least trouble.

With respect to commission or proffitt upon

the goods you sell I shall very readily conform to any plan you may have determin'd upon, or if you have not settled that matter, I wo^d. make a proposal a very simple one to you respecting this new branch of Trade betwixt us, which is that whatever goods I purchace to send you we divide the proffit laid upon them equally betwixt us which is to pay you for the trouble of selling & me for that of buying in the goods, & for the goods of my own manufacture I allow you 10 ℔ C^t. Comm^n. as before & I hope by this plan a trade may be struck out worth our attending to.

On this plan if approv'd of I must know whether the goods you order at any time are for wholesale or retail customers, as the prices must be made accordingly. For this reason I sho^d. know if the Waggon Crate now ord^d. is for Exportation, a shop, or a private family. If for the former the profits must be more moderate & a disc^t. of 5 ℔ C^t. allow'd for ready money, but we never allow any disc^t. to the latter, as that is properly selling them retail.

I shall from time to time as you send me Commissions buy the goods on the best terms that ready money can purchace them for, & charge them in the inv^e. sent to you with the proffits laid upon them & at the same time inclose you an Acc^t. what that is upon each parc^l. I sho^d. be glad to have your thoughts on this business when convenient.

On Thursday next you may expect another Cargoe of Creamcolour & perhaps a little green and Gold for hot Climates, with some pretty things for the Ladys who honour you with their company.

I expect a small ship L^d. of Clay at your Port in 3 weeks at farthest, pray what are the Port dues I am to pay. If you could get one the honour of being made free of your Corporation now it might be of some use to me & I wo^d. be exceedingly good & vote just as I was bid, you cannot think how passive I feel myself to be, & that is surely qualification sufficient for an honorary Burgess.

July 4, 1766.

Yesterday our Committee sat at Sandon to examine the bills of the several claimants for expences in obtaining our Navigation Act, they did not quite finish this business but

have allowed our bills of expences, & ord^d. you
ninety pounds besides the ball^e. in your hands,
for your extensive services. I do not think it
an adequate compensation nor was it possible
to *insense* them in this instance unless they
had gone along with you from the beginning
as I have done. They have ord^d. me 150
Guineas for my trouble, for which I made them
a very low bow, & told them I was perfectly
satisfied. I cannot pay any of these matters at
present (as Treasurer) but as plain Jos you
may command it at any time. I am call'd
away.

July, 1766.

I rec^d. my dear friends most acceptable letter
of the 13th inst. & am much pleased with the
farther hints you have given me concerning
these late discoveries. If they despise our
baubles I hope it proceeds from their superior
wisdom, & if we cannot add anything to their
present stock of felicity, may they ever remain
free from our impertinant visits, & not fall a
sacrifice to the ambition or avarice of Uropeans.

I am glad to find you have some doubts about their bodily stature, but should be glad to know in what sense men of five feet high can be called Giants, & whether the Captain & his Crew assert them to be 8 or 9 feet in Mr. Vane's conference with them. You will no doubt think me very inquisitive about these newly discover'd mortals, but as you have raised my curiosity to such a pitch I shall expect it from your humanity either to satisfy it as soon as possible, or to bring it down a step or two lower.

I wish you could make one of our Committee sometimes if it was only to hear & edify by some of Mr. W——hs wise speeches, but as I am not one of that respectable body (for such I really esteem them in general) & am present at their debates by indulgence & not by right I must not make any remarks upon them, but from the good sense, spirit & unanimity of their councils & resolutions, I have the most sanguine hopes of this great work being carried into execution with the utmost dispatch & to the general satisfaction of all concern'd in it as proprietors, & so as to be of the greatest possible advantage to the Public.

I hope the Runkhorn bridge scheme is not forgot amongst you as that shoᵈ. be the grand finishing point to this design in your parts.

The Clay I wrote to you about is to be sent from John Calcroft Esqre. M.P. for Poole in Dorsetshire, from whose Agent I suppose you will recieve a bill of Loading.

Messrs. Marshals of Northwich are the Gent^{n}. my former Cargoes of Clay were consign'd to there, & to them I have promis'd my future business of that sort.   I believe they perform'd their parts very regularly & well, & when that is the case I never like to alter my connections, but am nevertheless equally oblig'd to our good friend Mr. Green for his recommending Mr. Rogerson, which wo^{d}. be a sufficient motive for my employing him if I was not preingaged.

Please to give my compliments to Mr. Vigor & desire he will send the few pounds of earth he has by him that I may give it a fair tryal but I find others have been dabling with it before us, for a Bro^{r}. of the Crockery branch call'd upon me on Saturday last & amongst other clays he had been trying experiments upon shew'd me a lump of the very same earth which surpris'd me a good deal & I sho^{d}. allmost have thought myself robb'd if it had not been much larger than my pattern.   He told me it came from South Carolina, that he had a large boxfull of it sent to him by a Gent^{n}. of his Acquaintance, but he could make nothing at all of it & had return'd the remainder to his friend again. I was not sorry to hear the latter part of his story which I could the more easily credit as I find by the tryals I have made that it will require some peculiar management to avoid the difficulties attending the use of it.

———————————

BURSLEM, *18 July., 1766.*

Dr. Sr.

I am very sorry to know by yours of 18th that the white ware is not come to hand, I rather think they wait for this spring tide to float them. You know we prov'd they could not allways sail without that convenience, & now we feel the effects of it, my only motive for not sending it by land was the expence, which I thought was more than such low pris'd goods wod. bear.

What do you think of sending Mr. Pitt upon Crockery ware to America.* A Quantity might

* Pitt's popularity in America was owing to his vigorous denunciations of the Stamp Act.

certainly be sold there now & some advantage
made of the American prejudice in favour of
that great man. L⁴. Gower broᵗ. his family to
see my works the other day & asked me if I
had not sent Mr. Pitt over in shoals to America.
If you happen to do anything in that way we
can divide a tolerable proffit & sell at the same
price with Sadler.

I have not heard anything of the intended
Navigable Canal you mention, but imagine if
carried into execution it must robb us of a
good deal of Tonnage & as to its joining us
betwixt Wiggan & Runkhorn, by an inspection
of my map of Rivers it seems quite out of
compass, but I am very easy about those matters, pray will you get the canal from Liverpool to Runkhorn made, & then we may (you
& I) along with our fellow-subjects reap the
advantage of our labours more completely than
we ever can by being drowned in the Tideway
at Runkhorn. When I can send you in two or
three days any goods you ordʳ. from my Wareho. at Burslem to yours in Liverpool we
shall stand some chance of making our new
connection worth our attention. It greatly
behoves the shops and warehouses in yʳ. Town
to oppose this scheme.

Pray sell all the green and gold for Pensacola,
the new discover'd Islands, or where you can,

for I never will take it again, so make your best of it. I am quite clearing my Wareho. of Colour'd ware, am heartily sick of the commodity & have been so long but durst not venture to quit it 'till I had got something better in hand, which, thanks to my fair Customers, I now have & intend to make the most of it.

Green desert ware is often wanted, *in reality* for the West India Islands. I have a few crates on hand, some gilt, some plain, Ergo— sho^d. be glad to part with them on very moderate terms, for the reasons assign'd above I wo^d. sell them 20 ℔ C^t. less than I ever sold any before.

I have now bo^t. the Estate* I mention'd to you, for which I am to pay £3,000 at Michaelmass next.

Burslem, *15th Sept^r., 1766.*

I thank you most cordially for your two last very kind & entertaining letters, & for a great share of the pleasure & benefit I rec^d. from my late excursion.

* The Ridgehouse Estate.

G

I am sorry your shoulders sho^d. take upon them so much & grumble so long for a little shakeing, the Alderman* I think contributed not a little to their motion, but I hope he did not leave any *soreness* behind him, as you are perfectly acquainted with his *manner*. My Sally says your *fat sides* require a good deal of shakeing & wo^d. recommend a journey on *horseback*, not in the Coach, to Burslem, & is half angry with me for comeing home without you, but your last letter hath brought her into a little better temper, as she expects not only the pleasure of seeing you here in a little time, but likewise a jant to Liverpool in consequence of your Visit, besides she will not fix upon a spot for either house or Gardens no nor even the Stables 'till you have viewed & given your opinion of the premises, so now my dear Sir you are invited to the Ridgehouse Estate in the quality of a *Brown*,† & this may remove my only objection to seeing you here, I mean, your takeing so long a journey to so little purpose. Ten Guineas if I remember right is the price of a single call, with or without the advantage of his direction, to make a Lawn & piece of Water here—Cut down that

* One of Wedgwood's brothers.
† An imaginative landscape gardener to whom the nickname of " Capability " was given.

wood & plant it there, level that rising ground,
& raise yonder valley &c. &c. But for ten
times the business, fifty miles rideing, & a
hundred times the genius, why we must expect
to be sure to pay accordingly. One thing farther permit me to mention, that we shall be
affronted with a short visit, but very thankfull
for a long one, so pray settle your business
accordingly before you mount your Rosinante,
& as a Salvo, or Quietus, to your Conscience
for the loss of so much time, which I know to
be very squeamish, & am glad it is so, on these
occasions, tell the troublesome sprite, that as
our connections are to become extensive in the
Potting business, it is absolutely necessary
you sho^d. visit the Manufacture, see what is
going forw^d. there, make your bargains accordingly, & lend your assistance towards its farther improvement. Tell him y^r. fr^d. Wedgwood
hath some pretty things laid up for you which
he cannot send without your first seeing them,
& I hope he may be prevail'd upon to let you
spend a fortn^t. or so in this neighbourhood.

We are sending by Morriss to-day the B^p. of
Mans service & several others for you, the T.
ware, Vases & all other pretty things I shall
let alone 'till I have the pleasure of seeing you
here. . . . . .

Our dear friend Griffiths hath left this dirty spot of Earth (as it appeared to his elevated mind) & this morning took his flight to the realms above.

The rainy weather we have had for some days past affected him greatly, & increased the malady which we expected woᵈ. seize him about this time, & by his frequent desire of being shifted from place to place, attended with sudden starts, & other bad symptoms, plainly indicated that he could not continue long with us.

We spent the evening with him at Newcastle last night when he appeared to be much better, but this alass! was only the last blaze of an expireing Taper, for this morning his disorder return'd upon him more violently than ever, & a violent fit he was seized with held him, as we say, from seven O'Clock in the morning 'till near two in the afternoon, when he departed suddenly, & left us to lament the loss of our much lov'd friend.

The plain matter of fact is, he waited, *impatiently enough,* so long for your Machine, which not appearing at seven hours after its usual time, he got into a Chaise, determining to be

at any expence rather than be kept another
day from his beloved Turnham Green.

If you wo^d. wipe the tears from our eyes &
gladden the hearts of your afflicted friends,
surprise them with the *unexpected visit*. The
Alderman & Sally both earnestly wish that
such an event may take place, & you have my
free consent to fall in love as soon & as often
as you please, provided allways, that you pay
your devotions in propria Persona.

Mr. & Mrs. Blake made Burslem in their
way to Town, but we were most unfortunately,
all of us, that evening at Newcastle, we just
saw them the next morning at Burslem, & had
much more chagrin than pleasure from the
visit. Mrs. Blake is a Charming Woman,
there is such a happy mixture of female soft-
ness, Vivacity & good sense in her composition
that she commands both our love & Esteem,
& though it is ten to one, my Sally may see
what I am now writeing I cannot help confess-
ing myself amongst the number of her admirers,
& to be even with you I sho^d. very gladly fall
in love with a Mrs. Bentley if you durst give
us Married men the opportunity. Shake off
your idle fears & once more act the part of a
MAN,—step boldly into that state in which
alone you must expect (& nobody better knows
it) the highest sublunary happiness, you have

little to fear & everything to expect from that holy estate, as I am very certain you may have choice enough, & know well how to make it.

I do not know whether to thank you, or to be affronted at the *first part* of the *first sheet* of your *last letter.*—What! do you think the whole circle of your friends are only a company of Celestial Imps, & not flesh & blood as well as yourself? you have a strange sort of belief indeed, but I remember a saying of yours, that no man will be condemned for want of a *sufficient quantity* of faith, every man having his full portion of some sort or other, but you have certainly been reading Shakespeares Tempest, & have not yet took a due portion of sleep & fresh air to clear the upper . . . . from the vapours which are apt to be raised by such warm applications.

Time,—Traveling,— & a better acquaintance with your friends are specifics in this Case.

I am just sent for by three Gent^n. to the Wareho. & it is high post time, & I have not yet said a word of what I intended to write you.

Thank you for your very acceptable letter by Mr. Swift. I like him well upon sight, we have agreed upon £25 per Ann^m. for the two first years and £30 for the third, but if he is dilligent & deserves it he shall not want encouragem^t.

> With all our respects & loves I am
> > Yours most sincerely.

BURSLEM, *25th Sept^r., 1766.*

Dear Sir

Crests are very bad things for us (Potters) to meddle with & I never take any orders for services so ornamented. Plain ware if it sho^d. not happen to be firsts, you will take off my hands as seconds, which if Crested wo^d. be as useless as most other Crests, & Crest wearers are, for this & other reasons, the additional expence is more than the buyer can be perswaded to believe it ought to be.

Sadler will make no scruple I daresay of doing it in his way for you, or I will get him to do it for me if you had rather, I will write to him by this post to know his price & let you know the result.

I have a sister in Newcastle a Milliner* who wo^d. be glad of three pieces of Manks cloth of three sorts for tryal, we shall send next week to you, but perhaps you may have an opportunity of sending sooner.

The Alderman is not quite clever, but sends his best respects to you, I am going to take him a ride out & shake the dust & rust off his spirits a little, Sally sends her love to you & will be looking out every day for you after the return of this post.

BURSLEM, *9th Oct^r., 1766.*

My dear friend

I have just rec^d. your very acceptable present by Mr. Swift who is arrived safe at Burslem & enter'd upon his employm^t. & Mrs. Wedgwood joins me in thanks to you for these kind instances of your attention to the pleasure & amusement of your absent friends. We are glad to know you arrived safe amongst your friends at Liverpool & by *prudently*

* Mrs. Byerley.

steping into a Chaise I hope you & your
fellow traveler were secur'd from takeing cold
on which acc^t. we were in some pain for you
both.

I am much pleas'd with your disquisition
upon the Capabilitys of Electricity, & sho^d. be
glad to contribute in any way you can point
out to me, towards rendering Doct^r. Priestleys
very ingenious experiments more extensively
usefull, & whatever is the result of your farther thoughts, & the Doct^{rs}. experim^{ts}. on this
subject I am ready, so far as I can be concern'd, to ratify & confirm y^r. resolutions.
But what dareing mortals you are! to rob the
Thunderer of his Bolts,—& for what?—no
doubt to blast the oppressors of the poor &
needy or else to execute some public piece of
justice in the most tremendous & conspicuous
manner, that shall make the great ones of the
Earth tremble!—But peace to ye Mortals, no
harm is intended,—Heavens once dreaded bolt
is now called down to amuse your wives &
daughters,—to decorate their tea boards &
baubles!—well—if you think this business
may be pursued without presumption, & with
safety to ourselves, I sho^d. very gladly meet
you at Warrington, if you let me know when
you can spare a day for that purpose. I beg
my respectfull comp^{ts}. to the Doct^r. & wish

him all possible success in his delightfull &
ingenious researches into the secrets of nature.

———————

Nov. 17, 1766.

I am of opinion with you that the Pensacola
Clay is better worth attention than the Cherokee, for the reasons you mention, & do not
think the price extravagant, or too high to
answer for manufacturing here, if it be *equal*
to the Cherokee, & I sho^d. be glad to have a
Ton by way of sample as soon as may be.

It must be got as clean from soil, or any
heterogenious matter, as if it was to be eat, &
put into good Casks or boxes, & if they were
to get several parcels, at different depths, &
put them in seperate Casks, properly number'd,
I could by that means easily ascertain what
depth of the mine is best for our purpose, as
it is very probable there is a great difference
in that respect if the stratum be a thick one.

I have sent you a few Vases & flowerpots,
which may serve to fill a vacant shelf in your

pattern room, if you sho^d. not sell them. Will you have a few better for the same purpose?

I do not suppose Mrs. Hughs intends to pay me & sho^d. be glad if you wo^d. ask Mr. Clegg sometime when you see him at Change, or perhaps you can tell me yourself, if you had any compendious & easy method of obliging People to pay small debts in y^r. County, or Corporation.

Manks Cloth wo^d. sell much better if it was a little broader, it is too narrow for shirts. My sister Byerley wo^d. be glad to have 2 peices at 12d. & one at 13d. the first opportunity, please to debit my acc^t. with the Cloth.

Am glad to know my Bro^r. is well, happiness in the situation he now is, will follow of course, & I congratulate you on the return of your good sister, well knowing what forlorn Animals the best of us are when destitute of a *Female* head of a Family, my best respects wait upon Miss Oats, & all under *her* roof.

Our Country is the worst in the World to find such a Man in as you want, everybody in a manufacturing country is ready to catch at such animals when they happen to be found loose, which is not often the case here.—I have wanted such a convenience myself for some years past, & am unprovided still.

I have an hundred things to say to you & thank you for, but want *TIME*—I hope your good sister is recover'd, & shall be glad to hear she is so.

I believe we must build our house in the Stone-pit field at last. Adieu my good fr^d. God bless you—write when you can, & I will do so too.

Yours with the truest affectⁿ.

BURSLEM, *14th Feb., 1767.*

How much am I indebted to my dear friend for his affectionate & sympathizeing epistles, & the interest I know he takes in all that con-

cerns me, more—much more than I shall ever
be able to pay, unless he will, as usual accept
of a *gratefull heart* to ballance all deficiencies.

But notwithstanding I owe so much, would
you believe me so void of shame, Grace or discretion that I am every day wishing to owe
more.—I wo^d. scarcely believe it of myself, but
the symptoms are too strong upon me to deny
the charge, for every post day I catch myself
greedily runing over the directions of my letters, & if a well known hand does not appear,
Sally is ready to ask what has so suddenly
alter'd my countenance. I am too pettish (for
you know I am subject to be cholerick on a
disappointment) to give her any answer, but
read my letters, & unless a good order, or some
such circumstance intervenes, few things go
right with me that day.

I rec^d. some consolation on a disappoint-
ment of this sort from a certain article in the
Review for Decr. which as I was going through
in the common ord^r. of reading for the amusement of Deary she observ'd me to read with
more spirit, & emphasis than usual & inter-
upting me cryd out—Why Joss! one wo^d.
think thou wast reading one of B—'s letters—
& so I am I am very certain—but I will give
him a triming for keeping me in the dark, & the
Alderman too, who I afterwards found was in

the secret, as I suspected, but purposely kept me ignorant to try if I could make the discovery myself, which indeed was very easy to do without makeing any great merit of my penetration, & I sho^d. not wonder to hear that G— G—* had sent to inquire of the Publisher, who it was that wrote that article. Oh my friend! that your time, & station would permit you to set our *Great & little* folk right. —Those I mean who have a real intention of serving their Country, if they knew how to set about it. Your province should certainly be to guide, & superintend others, rather then to be busied in any little mercantile affairs of your own.—Pardon the epithet *little* for with the view I have before me, such they must appear be they ever so great.—Nay do not frown, I do not, I will not *flatter*, but *pray* for you—And to *Mammon* shall my prayer be directed, That it may please him to grant, & continue to you, such a portion of his *Divine Essence* as may qualify you to take a seat in a certain assembly, grant this one petition, oh! thou sovereign disposer of the *Honours, & good things* of this World, & I ask no more. Join with me my good friend in this Pious prayer, & at the same time remember that *prayer* as well as *Faith* without works, is dead, endeavour

* George Grenville.

therefore, not after *knowledge, & literary wisdom*, of which you have enough, but after the *wisdom* of the *Children of this world*, in plain English—get money—you want some such matter as 4 or £500 per ann^m. in Terra firma (such is the constitution of things in this sublunary Planet) to make the knowledge & abilitys you have acquir'd of the greatest utility to your Countrymen. If I can at any time be of use to you in this pursuit, you know you will oblige me in leting me know it, my mind is ever willing, & my Body is now better able to serve my friends than it has been for some time past, I have pretty well recover'd my strength, & my spirits flow again in their usual Channel.

Pray what paper is the advertisement in of the Stone Manufactory you mention, I have not seen or heard anything about it, & unless it sho^d. happen to be in the St. James's Chronicle, it will not fall in my way. I suppose sand to be the Basis of the stone, & to make it extensively usefull, a plain & simple method of converting sand into stone should be publish'd. If the secret, & materials for stone-makeing are local it will be rather a matter of curiosity than utility. If the process can be applyd to covering buildings with one complete sheet of stone it will be a valuable acquisition indeed, the roofing may be laid so flatt, & will at the same time be so light that a great saving will be made in the article of Timber, & several other advantages wo^d. arise from such an invention.

Yours at all times.

Feb^{ry}., 1767.

Are not you my good friend a very unreasonable Mortal to desire me to tell you, not only, *all I know, & all I wish to know,* but even, *all I do not know!* However as you desire it, I will attempt somthing in that way. [*Discusses Bentley's suggested improvements on the engine lathe.*]

But this is a sad way of conversing on these subjects—one half days conversation *face to face,* with the book before us, wo^d. be more effectual to the purposes we are aiming at, than an age spent in writing, & I greatly long for such an interview on many accounts. But how can it be accomplished?—You have business of too much consequence to be neglected, to fill up every moment of your time, & I am seldom unemployed. The first week in May I have allmost promised to go to London with my Bro^r. for a fortnight or three weeks. Is it impracticable for us to meet at Knutsford, or some such half way place in the interim?—I propose this as a journey of *business* to myself, from which I have views of *pecuniary* advantage from the art you are to instruct & perfect me in, & therefore I shall expect that you will permit me to act agreeable to my situation & expectations in that respect, therefore the first preliminary article in settling this interview is—That it be no expence to you,—you must be convinced of the reasonableness of the proposal, & I shall allmost think you do not wish to see me if you object to it.

Takeing it for granted that you have agreed to this preliminary article, I will gladly meet you at Knutsford any day next week you shall appoint & will keep clear of engagem^{ts}. for that purpose.

We shall want the book on Engine turning with us, & if you have found anything curious in the Pottery branch in the antiquitys if you bro^t. a volume or two of them along with you, they wo^d. serve as a diversion from the other subjects at proper intervals. But this Luggage requires that you sho^d. bring a serv^t. & Cloak bag with you, or take a Chaise & prevail upon your good sister to fill the other seat.

The last will certainly be most agreeable to us both, if you can prevail upon Miss Oats to take an airing with you, as you will have the benefit of such good Company, & I shall have the pleasure of waiting upon two of my worthy friends instead of one.—Very true—I had forgot the Plans—They must be talked over & settled upon, & that work cannot possibly be done without the assistance of a Lady. But what must become of Miss Oats whilst we are poreing over our turning & trumpery?—I have a Wife & sister at her service, & a good & worthy fr^d. at Knutsford, Doct^r. Colthurst to whom we owe a visit. The Doct^r. has a sister housekeeper who is seldom from home if the Doct^r. sho^d. be out.

I have not consulted my Females upon this plan, indeed it wo^d. be impossible I sho^d. have done it unless they were at my elbow as I am writing it to you, for I put the several parts of it down the moment they occur to me, & do not yet know how they will coincide till I read them over by & by. But as I was saying though I have not consulted the Females, I shall expect *submission* & a *ready acquiessence* from that quarter as they are in duty bound to give it.

I will bring the Alderman with me too if possible, pray write to me in time, & bring the plans along with you to Knutsford.

Pott Business.

I was sorry to refuse Miss Wright but found it necessary when I declin'd dealing with the shops, & continue still in the same way of thinking. Suppose you tell her that your commission extends only to private familys & for exportation.

The proffit upon white stone is small, but your shareing it does not make the ware come a farthing higher. You sho^d. not if you can help allow disc^t. upon lowpriced white ware, few of the Potters will allow it me.

Newcastle, *Saturday morn^g.*
[Feb. 1767.]

My dear friend

It seems allmost an age since I wrote you a line, though I have two or three of your favours to thank you for, but I know *where the heart is right* you will pardon many sins of omission.

I have not your former letter with me, but rememb^r. pretty well the Contents, & agree with you in most of the particulars respecting Mr. P.s plan. We had (Sally & myself I mean) pronounc'd its doom before we rec^d. yours, indeed we did so on the first inspection, but were willing to have your unbias'd opinion, & sent it to you the evening, I think, that it was sketch'd out for that purpose. I propos'd to Mr. Pickford an alteration or two in your plan, which I think very necessary.—To lay a foot at least to your back passage, & add the same to your long room. In the first, two Persons could not meet, especially if one of them had a dish or anything in their hands.—And the latter is, I should think, too much like a Gallery—too narrow to dine, or sup in *comfortably*. The door under the stairs is very convenient on some acc^{ts}., but three outside doors are too many for your small house, & would render it very windy, cold, & uncomfortable. Then the brew house, in its present situation, is abominable, but that may be provided for elsewhere, & with these trifling alterations your plan is infinitely superior, in my opinion, to Mr. Pickford's—within doors, I mean.

I had forgot the last sketches you have sent me, & have not time to examine them, as I am leaving this place in a few minutes, but think they will do very cleverly wth. the alterations you have made.

I have a large packet of letters from America, I wo^d. give a great deal for one days conference with you upon the subject of them, for I do not choose to commit the contents to paper, as our Postmasters open just what letters they please, & seem to have a particular curiosity to be peeping at mine. Last week I had a letter to one of my Foreign Correspond^{ts}. broke open at this office, & how often that practice may have been follow'd before I do not know. Several other matters want you here.

The American business is in a critical condition, & I do not know what to determine upon without you, for you will be concern'd in the event as well as myself.

The conclusion of the whole matter is that I shall expect to see, or hear from you on Monday, that you are on the road, & pray direct, not for me, as that will carry it to Stone, but to the Rev^d. Mr. Willett at Newcastle, & I will send to him on Monday for it.

Adieu my dear fr^d.—put on your boots, mount your Rosinanty, & let me see you at Hetruria in a day or two.

My sister Byerly . . . . desires me to tell
you that the Manks People are *no honester than
they should be,* two or three of the pieces of
Cloth she hath had being of two sorts in each
piece, about a third, or half of the piece being
of the quality it is sold for, & the rest of the
piece 2d. per yᵈ. worse, this inferior part is
sewed to the other where they join, & does not
appear till so much of the cloth is unwrapped.

If you go to Manchester soon I wish you
would see Mr. Vigor, & know if he hath done
anything towards procuring some of the Cherokee Earth, he promis'd me to see or write to
his friend about it, & I think I was to have
had a letter with his frᵈˢ. proposals, but have
heard nothing from either. Have you sent to
Pensacola for a sample of that earth? I have
recᵈ. a box to-day from Mr. Wilkinson with
some sparr which is Calcarious, some white
Earth a kind of bastard (if you'l allow the
epithet) Steatites, & a very peculiar red metalic substance, I cannot class it by its appearance, these I have not yet had time to try,
but am afraid the sparry substance of which
there is a great deal in the Steatites will prove
calcarious & then it will be of no use in our
business.

I shall send you some gold things, & the feather edged Compotiers, dishes I have none of that size. I shall send too a service of feather edge & a service of plain, we shall have feather edged En⁸. soon, as allmost all the best now ordᵈ. are of that pattern.

I can serve you with Creamcolor teapots of 12 : to 24 to the doz. . . . . . I will sell them to you at *Warehouse price* at 3s. 6d. ea. but then you must lay the carrᵍᵉ· & your proffit upon them. There is an inferior sort made here* at 3s. ea., but they are seldom half fired & woᵈ. be cracked all to pieces by the time they got to any foreign market, & are in other respects such goods as I would not put my name to in a bill of parcˡˢ.

I shoᵈ. have made an attempt at the *Boling-broke Jug* but my modeler hath been fully employ'd for two months past, in modeling various articles for his Excellency Mr. Mello the Portugueze Embassador, & Lᵈ. Pembroke wᶜʰ. are not yet finished, & I have been several times afraid the Embassador woᵈ. be sent home without his *Crockeryware*. Several of these articles are very pretty, but am afraid they will most of them be unsuitable for your market, such as Glauciers for Brandy & spirit-

* *i.e.*, by other manufacturers.

uous Liquors, do. for wine, do. for Cream, with a long &c. of such useless Gimcracks.

I have innoculated my Boy & Girl, the latter is at Newcastle & I am just going to see her, she begun to be Ill yesterday being the eighth. I have your pleasing letter before me, but you see I am so absorb'd in business—such a mere Earth worm, that I have not left room to say a word to it, does not the Idea fright you— Durst you attempt such drudgery as the mere *man of business*, alias y^r. h^{ble}. serv^t. is confin'd to.—

Cordially y^{rs}.

J. W.

Burslem, *2nd March, 1767.*

Dear Sir

I thank you for your kind solicitude for our Children, they are now past the worst, & I hope out of danger from that terrible disorder the small pox.

They both had Convulsions at the first appearance of the eruption, & have had a *pretty smart* pox as our Docter terms it. I believe they have had no dangerous symptoms, but have been so very Ill that I confess I repented what we had done, & I much question whether we should have courage to repeat the experiment, if we had any more subjects for it, however I am very thankfull that all is so well with them, & I hope they will not have reason to wish their Parents had acted otherwise than they have done.

I have just now rec^d. a letter from my nephew Tom Byerley acquainting me that he had quitted the Stage from a "*Conviction of his inability to succeed in any tolerable degree.*" He is gone to London & desires we will get him a writers place, or some such birth in the service of the East India Co^y. I do not know what we shall do with him, to keep him out of mischief, & put him into a way of being of some use in the World. . . . . .

We have several Navigation schemes in embryo. One from the *GRAND TRUNK* to Coventry, Banbury & I don't know where. The money was subscrib'd for surveying &c. & Mr. Brindley applied to, but he told them they were too precipitate (for they wo^d. have been in Parliam. this Session) he wo^d. look over the Country in a year or two if he could. Another from Birm^m. to join the W : Hampton Canal I dare say you have heard of, & the Loughbor°. scheme I think is in the House. Mr. Brindley has been with them lately, & he is going to Scotland & Ireland in a few weeks. I am afraid he will do too much, & leave us before his vast designs are executed, he is so incessantly harrassed on every side, that he hath no rest, either for his mind, or Body, & will not be prevailed upon to take proper care of his health.

I most cordially join in your benevolent sentiments respecting Projectors, but do not allow either of your exceptions, for I think Mr. Brindley—The *Great*, the *fortunate, money-geting* Brindley an object of Pity! & a real sufferer for the good of the Public. He may get a few thousands, but what does he give in exchange ? His *Health*, & I fear his *Life* too, unless he grows wiser, & takes the advice of his friends before it is too late.

The other Projector you are pleased to compliment with an *exception*, is very sensible how much he owes to your partiality, but he is in no danger of making a *Plumb* or what wo^d. be esteemed a *fortune* by any other than a little *Country Manufacturer*, & as to his projections those at least that are *sacred to Mammon*, he

wo^d. rather not hear them named *seriously.*
Do you think my friend that the *outline* of a
Jug, even a *Bolingbroke,* or the *fine turn* of a
Teapot are synonims to *Creating a River,* or
building a City. No, no, my friend, let us
speak softly, or rather be silent on such Frib-
ling performances, your friend shall endeavour
to please the Ladys, for the good of his—
Family & friends, but he must not be vain of
such *trifles,* & mistake them for *great actions.*

I like the middle sheet of your last letter
extremely, full of business, & Concise, & then
it was put up so smugly in the middle of the
sheet that the Postman was outwitted, which
alltogether has a very thriving look I can tell
you, & I cannot help congratulating myself on
the visible, & early effect of my late lessons to
you on that subject. Go on & prosper, & I
shall Greet you an Alderman of Liverpool in a
very few years.

Pray has D^r. Priestley made any more experiments relative to gilding by Electricity?
I did not understand what you meant by the
Battery he had some thoughts of attempting,
was it for a Copper work?

—" Why do you trouble me with your musty old
Wills & Testaments, unless I were a Legatee?
—Is this acting agreeably to your late doctrines of *money geting*? so soon to employ me
in business from which I can expect no *pecuniary* advantage—I thought— "

Gently—Gently, my good friend & Pupil—
you mistake the matter totally! This is not
given you as *business*, but as a *diversion*, a *temporary relief* from it.—A Cordial, to invigorate &
encourage you in the prosecution of schemes
of *mere business*—A kind of assurance that I
do not expect my Pupils to divest themselves
of Humanity, to make, or amplify a fortune.

My friend Peter Ducket is an honest, inno-
fensive, tame, domestick Animal, too weak &
poor to oblige R^d. Scarrot the Executor to do
him justice, he therefore calls upon me, & I
am willing to indulge you, by way of reward,
as you promise to be very good, with the
pleasure of assisting my friend Peter, & as this
favour is granted to you in preference to all
my other Liverpool friends I need not tell you
that I shall expect you to be very thankfull.

You'l see by the Will that the Testator has
left to my fr^d. Peters children *TWENTY
POUNDS !*—A much greater sum than you

may imagine at first sight. Wo^d. you know
how much it is, then reduce the pounds into
shillings & the shillings into pence, multiply
the pence by seven the No. of his family, &
then by the *rule of comparison* say, As a *pound*
is to my Neighbour Mr. Wealthy the Batche-
lor, so is a *penny* to honest Peter, & the amo^t.
is £33600 which you are employ'd in the
recovery of.

The Executor lives in your Town & I think
is a Glover or Breeches maker & came from
Macclesfield*   He hath rec^d. the Mortgage
money mention'd in the will, but refuseth to
pay the Legacy to Peters children or to pay
interest for the money, but I have heard one
Party only, you will hear what Scarrot has to
say for himself. If any point of Law sho^d. arise,
& you have ever an attorney, worthy to be
employ'd on the same terms with yourself take
his opinion upon the premises, but if none
such are found, I shall be very willing to pay
any expences that may arise in this business.

. . . .

Ducket can have an undeniable Bondsman
if required by Scarrat in paying the money.

* *Note by Wedgwood :*—He is a Weaver or dealer in silk Hand-
kerchiefs, shaggs, etc.

KNOW ALL MEN BY THESE PRES-
ENTS that wheras I am now situate, lying,
standing, & being, in a place where no other
than this crossgrain'd paper is to be had, that
I am thereby firmly held, & bound to these
lines, & can in no case depart from them, without incuring the penalty of a certain interuption to the fluency of my writeing thereupon.
WHERFORE &c. &c.

Forgive this foolish trifleing for which we
have neither of us any time to spare, & permit
me to thank my dear friend for his most wellcome letter which I have this moment rec^d., &
(it being Sunday) shall have time to answer if
no unexpected Visitor breaks in upon me.—I
thank you most sincerely for the trouble you
have taken in poor Peters affairs, for which
you will have a much higher reward than my
poor thanks, or any returns we can make you.
Enjoy, & be happy in, the natural result of
these acts of Humanity & beneficence to your
fellow Creatures, which employ so great a
share of your time & attention, & whenever
you can afford me an opportunity of assisting
you in these delightfull labours, you will make
a real addition to my happiness, which I know
will be some inducement for you to accept of

126

my services when you apprehend they can be made usefull in any respect.

I am rejoyced to know you have ship'd off the Green & Gold—May the winds & seas be propitious, & the *invaluable* Cargo be wafted in safety to their destin'd Market, for the emolument of our American Bretheren & friends, & as this treasure will now no longer be locked up, or lost to the rest of the world, I shall be perfectly easy about the returns, be they much, little, or nothing at all.—The demand for this s^d. *Creamcolour*, Alias, *Queen's Ware*, Alias, *Ivory*, still increases. It is really amazing how rapidly the use of it has spread allmost over the whole Globe, & how universally it is liked.—How much of this general use, & estimation, is owing to the mode of its introduction—& how much to its real utility & beauty ? are questions in which we may be a good deal interested, for the governm^t. of our future Conduct. The reasons are too obvious to be longer dwelt upon. For instance, if a Royal, or Noble introduction be as necessary to the sale of an Article *of Luxury*, as real Elegance & beauty, then the Manufacturer, if he consults his own inter^t., will bestow as much pains, & expence too, if necessary, in gaining the former of these advantages, as he wo^d. in bestowing the latter. I had with me yester-

day an East Indian Captain & another Gent[n].
& Lady from those parts who ordered a Good
deal of my Ware, some of it, *Printed & Gilt*, to
take with them for presents to their fr[ds]., & for
their own use. They told me it was allready
in Use there, & in much higher estimation
than the finest Porcellain, the Capt[n]. said he
had dined off a very complete service just before he left India. Dont you think we shall
have some Chinese Missionaries come here
soon to learn the art of making Creamcolour?

Yesterday I return'd from our Navigation
Committee who were in the highest spirits at
the great & successful progress made in the
works in so short a time. They are in a very
good way & there does not seem to be any
doubt of their Continuing so. Mr. Brindley
was there & assur'd the Gent[n]. that he could
complete the whole in five years from Xmass
next, & there being a Gent[n]. present (not one
of the Committee) who doubted of the possibility of its being completed in so short a time
& seem'd inclin'd to lay a wager upon it, Mr.
B. told him, that it was a challenge he never
refused upon anything which he seriously
asserted & offer'd them to article in a Wager
of £200 that he perform'd what he had said.
A second subscription was then mention'd by
some of the members, but Mr. B. advis'd them

not to open one 'till they saw a little farther
whether they sho[d]. not like to fill it up themselves, at the same time he assured them that
whenever the subscription was open'd he
would subscribe £2000 more, which was all
the law wo[d]. permitt as he has already 2000 in
the present subscription. The stocks upon
the Wolverhampton Canal was I think he s[d].
30 ℔ C[t]. above Parr, & he was very certain
that *THE GREAT TRUNK* was a more substantial, & better security, than the Wolverhampton, or any other branch could be, as
everything w[ch]. Communicates wth. must
benefit us, & no parellel Navigation can ever
be made to injure ours. What effect these
assurances from a man of Mr. Brindley's
known integrity may have upon our stocks I
do not know, at present it is, as it ever has
been at parr, & if you at any time let me
know what sum your friend wo[d]. wish to in-
vest I will endeavour to do it for him at
Parr, but will not promise *long* to do it at that
price.

And so you have a *plate-Glass Grinder* seting
in Mahogany for me.—Well I hope he is
eminent in his way, & worth the framing, &
then send him as soon as you will & I will
endeavour to find him employment. I am
often wanting a Lapidary, & hope I shall now

I

be fitted, but if he sho^d. happen not to be already jumped into his Mahogany jacket, I can fitt him full as tightly in a plaister one. —Better Modelers in London than in Paris— I am very glad of it, but can your friend prevail upon any one who is thoroughly Clever to settle 150 miles north of the great Metropolis?—such an one is essentially necessary to our new work, & if I had him six months or longer before we begin, I could be preparing him & other matters for our purpose in that time, to make us so much forwarder in our business when we do begin.—You do not in your last say a syllable of our interview, but permit me to tell you that we must see each other often for a thousand reasons, so pray contrive your matters & let me know where we shall meet, & when.

I have had a letter from D^r. Fothergill not long since who tells me he has a fr^d. who has lately been at the place where the Cherokee earth is got, that he could easily procure me a few hund^d. pounds of it for tryal, but it will unavoidably come so dear that unless the finest Porcel can be made of it, it cannot answer. I have thanked the Good Doct^r. who indeed wrote me a very friendly letter, but have refer'd him to our next meeting for a farther discussion of these matters, wch. you will easily imagine as I am circumstanc'd I do not care to say much about.

Well nobody comes to interrupt me, & so I have continued Chatting with you 'till you see it must be a double letter. I believe this may lie safe enough anywhere let it contain what secrets it will, as it wo^d. be taken for some rough Draft of a Deed, or too long a letter for anybody in their right mind to think of reading, however you'l perhaps take some opportunity to see the end of it in a week or two, so I shall proceed with telling you what concerns me just as if you were at my elbow, & what follows you may consider as a P. S. as I shall now bid you farewell & assure you that I am &c. &c.

J. W.

———

This building of houses my Friend so far as we have hitherto gone is very near akin to *Building Castles in the Air.*—The old Mansions are all swept clean away! & you see a totally new one erected in their stead. Survey & admire this *last* & *perfect* work of your fr^d. but do not presume to alter a line, or angle in the whole Fabric, for I have sworn not to waver any longer & so help me—Bentley to create new Vases for the payment of my Architect.

This Plan will be executed for 5 or £700 less than the former, wo^d. be nearly as good a house, more in the Modern, & I think *true* taste, & much better adapted for the situation. The north wing of the other Plan could not be made bearable without giving the house a very wrong aspect, therefore I determin'd to have none at all but shall throw the Stables &c. into the Stone Pitt, & instead of filling that immense Chasm with Earth, I shall convert it into a very Populous Colonie of Horses, Cows, Pigs, & Poultry.

I have some thoughts of opening a *Warehouse*, not merely a Pattern Room, in the City, & let the Patterns circulate amongst our Bretheren (you are a Brother Potter now you know) as quick as they please, but I do not know how to manage about the Carriage. I cannot raise the prices in proportion, & if I pay the Carr^e. without altering the prices it will make near £500 per Ann^m. difference in my proffits. Besides some of my Customers (if I sell goods at deliver'd prices at all) will want them deliver'd at all lengths from 20 to 300 miles. Pray consider of it, as you will soon be a Party concern'd, & advise me what to do.

My dear friend

I thank you most sincerely for your last very affectionate letter, & solicitude for my Bro.ʳˢ recovery. He is now got pretty well again, & I did not care to mention his illness to you 'till I could at the same time give you the pleasure of assuring you of his recovery which was the principal reason of my silence whilst he was so very Ill, for he hath been much worse this time than I ever knew him before.

Poor Mr. Brindley was not well enough to attend the Committe & General Assembly, he has now given up a journey into Scotland & Ireland, which he had promised Mr. Garbett & Lᵈ. Hertford to make this spring, & is going to Buxton for a few weeks, which I hope will have a good effect upon his constitution, as his ailments certainly proceed from a too intense, & constant application to business, both with body & mind. I am going to see him this morning, & shall endeavour to perswade him to be idle for a season that his stay amongst us may be the longer for it.

We were honour'd at our General assembly at Stone with the Compʸ. of the D. of Bridgwater & L^d. Gower, who approved much of our proceedings, & L^d. Gower told us pleasantly, he thought we sho^d. be stiled *the Amicable society of Navigaters.* You know that Mr. Randals scheme for executing our Canal with ploughs proved abortive, he had therefore no demands upon us, as we were only to pay him so much per y^d. as he finished his work. However to comfort him und^r. his disapointm^t., & incourage any future attempts of ingenuity, the Assembly have ord^d. him a present of thirty Guineas. I wish it had been more, though some of our Proprietors think it a work of supererogation that they might very well have excus'd themselves from performing. Narrow minds have no idea of paying more money than the Laws of the Land oblige them to.

I was going to thank you for your remarks upon the plans, but a Gent^n. waits for me in the Wareho. however I cannot forbear telling one piece of news I had from a Gent^n. who was at the Committe upon the Carron Navigation. You remember what plauge & trouble our good fr^d. Mr. Garbett gave us with his limitation scheme of 10 ℣ C^t. in^t. on the Nav^n. Capital. That very plan is now urged upon him & the intended proprietors of the Navigation sorely against their wills, & he is now reduced to the dilemma of proposing & defending a plan which he was before so vigorous in opposing & depreciating. However his efforts avail as little now as they did before. The Parliam^t. will not pass the Act without the limitation, & the subscribers will not have it with that clause, so that the Gent^n. from whom I have my information believes this bone of Contention will prevent their having any act at all.

How justly may we exclaim—The wicked have digged a pitt for us, & are fallen into it themselves! Adieu.

P.S.—Our good wives here are informed that Malaga Raisins are extremely cheap, & desire me to ask you what they can be bo^t. for per hun^d.w^t. at Liverpool, *good, rich fruit.* They are 18/- at London. We shall be glad to know as soon as possible, that the season may not slip us, for we are to have an inundation of Raisin wine this year.

BURSLEM, *28th Apr^l., 1767.*

My dear friend

I have seen our friend Peter to-day, &
he repays you with tears of joy, & gratitude
when I told him what you had done for him :
but I cannot with any tolerable convenience
go to Congleton on Monday next, as I hope to
be seting out for London about that time.   I
know you will be bound for me to Skarret, or
rather for Peter, but can you get another
Bondsman ?   I will discharge you of your
trust the first opportunity I have of doing it.
If you can manage it this way it will be a
great convenience to me, but rather than
Peter shall risque the loseing his money I will
meet the Gentⁿ. at Congleton or allmost anywhere else, so pray let me know in time, & at
what House in Congleton if it sho^d. be necessary to meet them there.   .   .   .

Pray let me know if I can serve you in anything in London.   Y^r. taste is condemn'd !
Printed Table services *are much liked !*

Dear Sir

You see what shifts poverty will reduce
a man to, I hope you will lend me your kind
assistance in winding up my bottoms a little
with these Gentry, & I hope as other sturdy
beggars promise, never to trouble you any
more—*with the same 'Gent".*

You see I have got my secretary* again, he
hath been at Chester & Hollyhead in his way
to Dublin Theatre, & met with one of the
Managers at Chester who offer'd him [a birth.
He soon found that there were too many difficulties in the way, & a letter] from Mr. Cliffton
of Chester overtaking him at Hollyhead de-
molished the Player & hath reduced him to
the humble state of a Potter again, he is to be
very good—never do so again &c. &c.

Vases with high Crown'd hats!—Have you
ever thought seriously, as you ought to do on
that subject. I never think of it but new improvements Crowd in upon me, & allmost
overwhelm my patience, so much do I long to
be ingaged in that delightfull employm'. which
I have every day fuller assurance of makeing
as profitable to the purse—as it must be pleasing to the mind—but you know what sort of

* Tom Byerley.
137

a Partner it requires, either resolve quickly to join me yourself, or find me out another kindred spirit.

I have agreed with a brickmaker & shall work away like fury next year, but must not adopt your plan for my Cottages. What, cut "*this fine [estate] into fritters*" by a thousand foot & horse paths—no, no, it must not be. My time is elapsed.

LONDON, *May 20ᵗʰ, 1767.*

Your most acceptable letter of the 15ᵗʰ. gave me the highest pleasure in seting before me a nearer prospect than I have yet had, of a union that I have long coveted, & which I do not doubt will be lasting, delightfull, & beneficial to us both, & as to the time & manner of leaving Liverpool, make it the most agreeable to yourself in every respect, & it will be perfectly so to me. At present indeed I am not in possession of the land you know to build you either a House or Works, but am in treaty with the Old Ladys Steward, & you

have furnished me with a very strong inducement to comply with allmost any terms they
shall propose.

I am in search of the Town where the Steatites grows, & I believe I shall learn every
particular about it.   One D^r. Mitchel has just
published a Map of N. A. price a Guinea &
half on Cloth, wch. map I have purchased & am
to visit the D^r. who is a Naturalist, Fossilist, &c.
& has resided long in South Carolina.   I find
the Town in his Map to be Hyoree, & the same
in a Map in a Committee room at the H. of
Commons.   The mistake of a l^r. as the sound
is not very different was easy to make either
by Mr. V. or myself, & as the situation answers
the description he first gave me I am pretty
certain it is the place.

Our friend Mr. Griffiths has a Bro^r. who hath
resided many years in N. A., & is seasoned to
the S. C. Climate by a severe fever he under-
went at Ch^s. Town & has had many connections with the Indians.   He is now a Proprie-
tor of a third share of 3000 Acres of Land near
Crown point, but was obliged to abandon it to
the other two Proprietors for want of money
to advance along with them in the prosecution
of a scheme he (Griffiths) had planned of making sugar from *Maple* which secret he had
learned from the native Indians.   But though

he left his partners he did not give up his
share of the Lands to them. He is now at T.
Green & offers his service to me for the Voyage. He is on many acc^{ts}. very proper, but I
have some objections. Supose he sho^d. like
your friend who purchased the Island, take it
into his head to redeem, with my money, his
share of the improvements his partners have
made on their grant of land! Do you think
there is not some probability of his doing so?
As a salvo to his conscience, he may be fully
perswaded (being I apprehend a sanguine pro-
jecter) that he shall be able from his plantations to remit me the money he shall in that
way borrow. And suppose I sho^d. have his
Bro^r. bound for him, I sho^d. hardly take the
forfeiture if made. It goes much against the
grain with me to surmise anything of this sort,
but I have known such instances of Persons
changing their sentiments, & principles with
the Climate, & totally forgeting their connections with the friends they have left behind
them, that there is more reason for caution
" *dan good men wo^d. tink.*"

I shall wait your advice before I conclude
upon anything in this affair.

Mr. Greenville & his party seem determin'd
to *Conquer England in America* I believe. If
the Americans do not comply with their

demands respecting the quartering of soldiers,* the Alternative, I am told, is to be, The suspension of the Legislative power in America. I tell them the Americans will then make Laws for themselves & if we continue our Policy—for us too in a very short time. But I have very little time at present to bestow upon Politicks, if we must all be driven to America, you & I shall do very well amongst the Cherokees. Vid.—the Basketmaker.

I understand your drawing of the salt, a shell is a very pretty device for the purpose, but is rather too much hackneyed. Novelty is a great matter in *slight* articles of taste.

LONDON, *23 of May, 1767.*
Saturday morning Early.

My dear friend

I rec⁴. your kind letter of the 21 last night & am very thankfull for it. Your letters allways rejoyce & entertain me, & therefore do

---

* A clause in the Mutiny Act required the colonists to provide for English troops. Grenville, who had carried the Stamp Act, continued to maintain the right of the Government to tax the colonies.

me good *as a Medicine,* as an old Author observes upon a merry heart, but that is only a small part of the advantage I recieve from them, & I must have more interesting employment even than this great Metropolis can afford me, to prevent me reading them many times over, without taking the opportunity you recommend to me.

You see I set out upon a large plan in writing to you, & in truth I have many things to say, if I am not disturbed but some of the subjects I do not care to trust in writing for fear of accidents—not even if I was to keep the lʳ. myself. . . .

[*Passing through Birmingham he saw an ingenious engine lathe at Mr. Bolton's.**]

He is I believe the first—or most complete manufacturer in England, in metal. He is very ingenious, Philosophical, & Agreeable. You must be acquainted with him, he has promised to come to Burslem, & woᵈ. attend our congress (we are to have one immediately on my return remember on many accᵗˢ.) but this year he is too much immers'd in business to indulge he says in anything else. There is a vast difference betwixt the spirit of this Man

---

* The Birmingham manufacturer, afterwards in partnership with James Watt.

& the Great Taylor,* though both of them have behaved exceeding liberally to me in offering me every improvement they could furnish me with.

Never my good friend did I stand in so much need of your company, advice, & assistance, as at this juncture. I am in pursuit of so many objects, beside what my current run of business furnishes me with, & not a soul—a *congenial & intelligent* soul to advise with that I am allmost at my wits end. A Patent or Exclusive property in the Cherokees, is business eno of itself to sollicit & prosecute in the best manner. I had a Conference with his Grace of Bridgwater yesterday morn^g. for an hour, & hinted the matter to him but the famous Brown was with him, & I could do nothing to purpose. The D— rec^d. & convers'd with me just in the same affable, familiar manner as usual, when he first began to know us, by *ourselves* in Propria Persona, & not from his *go betweens*. I intend to attempt another oppertunity of taking his G—s advice.—Mr. Brown has promised me the honour of a Visit at Burslem, says he has often intended it, merely from the Character the Ladys had given him of me. I told him that my Life was devoted to the service of the Ladys, as his was to that

* A Birmingham manufacturer of buttons, buckles, &c.

of the Noblemen & Gent^n.—He assured me
that they were not ungratefull, & intimated
that I was nearly as famous amongst the
Ladys as he was amongst the Gent^n.—we had
a good deal of Chatt on various subjects & are
to have another interview in Town. He may
be of much service to me, & I shall not
neglect to cultivate what chance has thrown
into my way.

After my Visit to his Grace I spent a great
part of the day in search of a Room for my
repositary, what I have is too small & not the
most convenient situation. It will not do at
all when the Vases are added to my collection.
Pall Mall is the best situat^n. in London. It is
convenient for the Whole of this Great Town,
the avenues to it open, & everybody comes
there some time or other. There is now to be
Let in this Situation an Auction Room, now
Occupied by the Artists for their Exhibition
room, 40 feet by thirty—a room adjoining to it
24 by 17—below but backward two Parlours
(too dark for shew rooms) with Closets large
eno. for a couple of beds, below them a Kitchen,
Brewho. & other Conveniences. Above the
Auction room, a room 24 by 17 (this is too
high) & a bed Chamber. The whole for abo^t.
£250 Taxes included per Ann^m. What shall I
do abo^t. it? your advice would just reach me

before I leave. We must have an Elegant, extensive, & Conven^t. shew room, with store rooms, & some conveniencies for two servants at least. One of them perhaps a married Man, & I cannot anywhere find another tolerable place. Abo^t. £100 per Ann^m. may be let off I believe.

I have spent an hour or two with the Stone Manufacturer & am really sorry for him. He has a Partner who I find is weary of the scheme, & is now seeking for another partner. I am afraid the Concern is, & will be a losing one, —*as it is at present conducted* but think somthing might be made of it. He is beginning upon Vases! What do you think of that? Do not you tremble for our Embryotick Manufacture. He might certainly rival us but from my slight knowledge of the Man I think he will not hurt us. He is about taking the rooms I mention^d, & so is an Auctioneer. The Person who has them to let is a very good old Gent^n. has a young wife, & to her I am making my Court. They are both of the Virtu' species & have a fine Collection of Raphael, Etruscan & other very Curious Earthen wares, one sort is Glazed with a Colour like the Gold on a Pidgeons or Pheasants neck.

Wo^d. you think it, I am this morning going by Comm^d. to visit your old friend

K

G— G—* You may make yourself easy abo^t. America, we will settle their affairs whilst his Lady is giving her ord^{rs}. for Crockery ware. Adieu for the present.

Since I wrote the above I have had the honour of a long Conference with his Grace of Bridgwater on the subject of the Cherokee. I laid the whole case before him without any reserve, & found the confidence I had placed in his honour, & advice was not disagreeable. He does not think a Patent will stand for an exclusive right to the Cherokees, & upon the whole advises to send a Person over immediately without applying for grant, Patent or anything else. Chas. Townsend he says as Chancelor of the Excheq^r. might be applyd to to grant it me Duty free & to lay a duty upon all imported by others, but that must be a Parliam^t. affair, & must be done another Session, & very probably wo^d. not pass, but wo^d. inevitably lay the whole affair open. Besides he says Mr. Townsend is a fr^d. of Garb-ts, so is L^d. Shelbourne, & if it is ment^d. to the L^{ds}. of Trade his Grace says he knows G—t who is a Potter in Scotland is sure to be advis'd of it. So he gives his advice as above & I have some thoughts of following it. I am inform'd they have got the Cherok to a Pott-

* Presumably George Grenville.

work at Cha⁸. Town. It lyes 300 Miles up the Country, & at some distance from water Carrᵉ.

LONDON, *27 May, 1767.*

Dear Sir

I spent yesterday afternoon & Evenᵍ. with two or three Gentⁿ. who had resided long in South Carolina, one of whom gave me a small sample of the Cherok Earth, by way of Curiosity, not knowing who, or what I was, for I kept in Cog. I find the E. must be carrᵈ. near 300 miles by Land Carrᵉ. which will make it come very heavy. I have had a long Conference with Mr. Griffiths, & am inclin'd to employ him, but shall be glad to contrive some restriction to prevent his doing too much mischief if he shoᵈ. be so inclin'd.

I was with Mr. Bagot this morning & we had a good deal of chat upon political affairs, particularly American, in which I told him my sentiments very freely. That our Policy* had a tendency to render the Americans indepen-

* Townsend's proposals for taxing America.

dent a Century sooner than they wo^d. be in the common order of events, if treated agreeable to sound policy.

The Ministry* were run very hard yesterday in the House of Lords. They Carried their point by a Majority of three only. The Dukes of York & Gloucester came to vote for the Ministry, otherwise they had carried it by one only, so that a Change is looked upon as inevitable. But that is nothing to you & I, for whoever is in they will make the most of us they can, so my friend let us unite our forces, & endeavour to do the same by them but in *honester mode*.

Mr. Pennant has bo^t. a very full Table service of Cream colour, otherwise I sho^d. not greatly like him to represent you in Parliam^t., merely because he married the Daughter of an Idolater, for I know no other harm by him. He never can be hearty in the Runkhorn Gap scheme, his Father-in-law, General Warburton being one of the most Zealous worshipers of the Goddess Weaverina so that I shall despair allmost of that great project being carried into execution, at least in any moderate time.

I am glad to hear Crates sell apace with you. I have no reason to complain here. Vases sell, too, even in the rude state they now

* The Grafton Ministry.

are, for such they appear when I take a view of what may be done.

The Alderman is well & sends his sincere respects to you, so does our frᵈ. Griffiths. Adieu I am call'd away.

BAPTIST HEAD COFFEE HOUSE
Sunday morning.

My dear friend

I am so tumbled about, & variously employd in this great Metropolis, that I do not know what I wrote you last, & therefore may very probably say the same things to you again in this sheet, if I am not called away too soon by a party we have formed to spend the day at Greenwich—Mr. & Mrs. Blake—His Aldermanship, & I do not know who are to be of the Corps. But the few moments I may spare you now, must be employ'd in business, only permit me to thank you in this Lʳ. as I do most Cordially in my heart, for your last most instructive & wellcome epistle. The sentiments are just, & perfectly appropos,—such as I have often proffited by, from your lips & pen, & I shall not lose the advantage of them in this instance, as I have done nothing in the business of fixing upon Rooms at present, & shall stay two or three days longer in Town than I expected. The reasons you have given against my fixing upon an Auction Room, or any other which has been a place of public resort, are solid, ingenious, & more than sufficient, & there is another nearly as strong as any of them. At present the Nobility, & Gentry recommend one another to my rooms, & they never meet with any other Company there, but every body wo^d. be apt to stroll into an Auction room—one that they had ever had free access into, & that wo^d. be the most effectual method I could take to keep my present sett of Customers out of it. For you well know they will not mix with the rest of the World any farther than their amusements, or conveniencys make it necessary to do so.

I find I did not sufficiently explain to you my reasons for wanting a *Large* Room. It was not to shew, or have a large stock of ware in Town, but to enable me to shew various Table & desert services completely set out on two ranges of Tables, six or eight at least such services are absolutely necessary to be shewn in order to *do the needful* with the Ladys in the neatest, genteelest & best method. The

same, or indeed a much greater variety of setts
of Vases sho^d. decorate the Walls, & both these
articles may, every few days, be so alter'd,
revers'd, & transform'd as to render the whole
a new scene, even to the same Company, every
time they shall bring their friends to visit us.
I need not tell you the many good effects this
must produce, when business, & amusement
can be made to go hand in hand. Every new
show, Exhibition, or rarity soon grows stale in
London, & is no longer regarded after the first
sight, unless utility, or some such variety as I
have hinted at above continue to recommend
it to their notice. A Lady, or Gent^n. may, out
of Complaisance to their friends, come with
them a few times to see a shew wth. wch. they
themselves are satiated, but of this they will
soon grow weary, unless they likewise share
in the entertainm^t. & will much sooner carry
their friends to a scene which is new to them all,
than to one where their eyes have allways met
with the same objects & the same arrangment
of them. This may be avoided by us with very
little address, when we have a Room proper for
the purpose. I have done somthing of the
sort since I came to Town & find the immediate good Effects of it. The two first days
after the alteration we sold three complete
setts of Vases at 2 & 3 Guineas a sett, besides

many pairs of them, which Vases had been in
my Rooms 6—8 & some of them 12 months, &
wanted nothing but arrangment to sell them.
And besides room for *my Ware*, I must have
more room for *my Ladys* for they sometimes
come in very large shoals together, & one party
are often obliged to wait till another have done
their business.

New difficultys spring up as I proceed in
the business of the C. C.* A Grant must pass
through the hands of the L^{ds}. of Trade &
Plantations, amongst whom are Fitsherbert,
Member for Derby, a L^d. somthing Clare, Member for Bristol, at both which places are China
& Pottworks, so I dare not come there. An
intended Patent must be made Publick, such
a time, before it can pass, & as so many are
interested that their fr^{ds}. or constituents sho^d.
share the advantages of such a discovery endless oppositions & difficultys wo^d. probably arise
from that mode of proceeding, & if I did not
succeed, I sho^d. raise up a whole swarm of
Competitors.

I waited upon L^d. Gower on Saturday last &
laid the whole of my difficultys, & designs before him, & he told me he had many *Personal*
but no *Political* friends in the Administration,
but if I could wait for a Change he sho^d. per-

* Cherokee Clay.

haps be able to serve me. I told his L^d.ship the danger I apprehended from delaying, as several Persons had seen the C: He then told me that he had got the Attorney General of S: C. the place he enjoy'd, that he was a sensible Man & *everything* with the Governor, who is—amongst fr^{ds}. s^d. his L^d.ship, a mere *nobody*. The result was that his L^d.ship advis'd me to send immediately to S: C., & he wo^d. put my Agent under the protection of the Attorney General, to which I assented, & am now preparing matters for Mr. G. to embark as soon as possible. I have a thousand things to say to you which will require an immediate Congress if you can possibly make it convenient, but pray come alone, for if you bring all Liverpool with you, we shall not spare them an hour of our Company, I shall not be able to finish Mr. G.s written instructions before I get home, & shall be very thankfull to you for any hints that may occur to you, which please to forw^d. to me at Burslem. God bless you my dear fr^d.

You will wonder at my dating from this great Metropolis still, but so it happens, & I cannot leave it of two or three days more without leaving the principal parts of my business undone. I have not yet met with a House in every respect agreeable to me, but have several friends, as well as myself in quest of one for me, & have great hopes of succeeding to my wishes in a few days.

Another thing which detains me is L^d. Gowers leaving Town before I have got his L^r. to put Mr. Griffiths, my intended Agent under the protection of the Attorney General of South Carolina & his L^d.sh^p. does not return 'till Tuesday next. I have several other matters that cannot be wound up this week, & which require my Personal attendance.

I have agreed with Mr. G. for him to sail in the first ship, & am to give him £50 per Ann^m. besides his Maintenance, & yesterday Mr. Hodgson waited upon a Merch^t. here who has a partner in Chas. T. to fix a Credit there for Mr. G : & to be a cheque upon him, for which reason it was necessary to make a confident of the Merch^t. When Mr. Hodgson had made known his errand the Gent^n. told him the E. wo^d. come excessively dear. That he had abo^t.

154

seven years ago got a Cask of it for a China
maker here, & wo^d. against monday next, when
we are to have an interview, collect all the
particulars he could concerning it, so that
there is a Chance of its not being necessary to
send an Agent there at all.—So far this morn^g.
—now farewell for the day.—Evening—Too
late to say anything, & quite weary,—have
rode abo^t. 20 miles in search of a House, & believe I shall sit down in the entrance to Scotland yard opposite the Admiralty. I can have
three floors, Viz Celler, Ground floor, & Chamber story, 30 feet by 20, the Chamber story to
be in one room, & lighted by a Lanthorn at
Top, so that there will be all the sides of the
room clear for Vases &c. It is all to build, so
that I can please myself with a design, & have
the whole for abo^t. £70 per Ann^m. exclusive of
the Taxes, the passage is wide enough for two
or three Coaches to pass, & I shall have a foot
way flagg'd very broad before the door. This
situation is the best that can be as a Central
point betwixt both ends of the Town.—Both
Houses of Parliam^t. must pass by it, & there
is a most spacious street betwixt Scotland y^d.
& the Admiralty. We are to conclude this
matter on Tuesday next, & on Wednesday
I hope to set off for Burslem.

I am picking up every design, & improvement

for a Vase work, & am every day more & more convinced that it will answer to our wishes.

BURSLEM, *13ᵗʰ June, 1767.*

Last night I got safe to Burslem & found everything agreeable to my wishes here. I have now about some five hundred things to do, & then shall have time to say a word or two to you. Messrs. Brindley & Henshall are in the house, & I must go to them, but first let me tell you that Mr. G. will sail for S(outh) C(arolina) in about a fortnight, in wᶜʰ. time I am to get his instructⁿˢ. &c. ready, pray assist me, my good friend with a few lines—you know the subject & everything about it. I am preparing designs, Models, Moulds, Clays, Colours &c. &c. for the Vasework, by which means we shall be able to do business *effectually* 12 months sooner than we could without those preparatory steps, & I have no fear but it will answer our utmost wishes. Adieu 'till I have more leisure to talk with you.

Sunday Morning, 14 June, 1767.

It was but yesterday I wrote to you with a heart, perfectly at ease, & rejoicing with my family & friends at our meeting together again in health & safety, after a Months absence from each other. But alass! what a Change did the next hour produce! The post which took your L^r. from me, brought me the meloncholly account of the death of a much loved Brother. Your friend, & my poor Brother is Dead, is no more, is no longer the warm, & benevolent friend, affec^te. Bro^r., or chearfull Companion, but is now a lifeless, insensible Clod of Earth. A sad reverse. And what has greatly heighten'd the shock to his surviving friends is the circumstances attending this Meloncholly event.

On Wednesday Evening he went to see the fireworks at Ranelagh, & afterwards came to the Swan at W^r. Bridge where we used to dine & got a little refreshment & staid 'till about 12, asked for a bed with which they unfortunately could not accommodate him, so that he was obliged to go see for one elsewhere, & in passing the River side, tis supposed he slipped in, he was found the next morning about 5 & the Acc^t. bro^t. to Mr. Hodgson, & these are the particulars he has wrote me, & in his own words for I scarcely know what I write myself.

My Bro'. Tho'. is going to London, & my Bro'. in law will accompany him to perform the last kind offices of Humanity to their departed Brother. My Wifes circumstances will not permit me to think of leaving her so long, otherwise I should have gone with them.

As a small Testimony of the Esteem my poor Bro'. had for you, he hath left you five Guineas to buy a mourning ring. I know he allways wished to be remembered by you, & I doubt not but you will comply with this his last request. I know you will sympathize with me in my distress, & I need not tell you how doubly wellcome a few lines will be at this time from a real, affectionate & sensible friend, such a one as you have ever been to me since I had the happiness of being known to you. Let us now be dearer to each other if possible than ever, let me adopt you for my Bro'.—& fill up the chasm this cruel accident has made in my afflicted heart.—Excuse me my dear friend, the subject is too much for me.

I am your miserable friend.

I have several of your kind & friendly letters which I have not yet thanked you for, but I know you will not attribute the neglect to want of gratitude in me. You have my heart, & share my warmest affections, but a kind of listlessness which has for some time hung about me, has prevented me doing many things, which I otherwise should not have omitted. Your very kind & affectionate letter was such a Cordial to my afflicted heart, as it stood greatly in need of, & such a one as few, very few indeed, could have administered to its relief. I thank you most Cordially for it—for the place you allow me in your esteem & affections, & for the daily new instances you are giving me of your partiality in my favour. I have just reciev'd a most kind letter from our friend Mr. Griffiths for wch. I shall love him better if possible than ever.

I am sorry you are to set out so soon for London, had it been in the begining of Augt. instead of July I wo^d. if possible have gone with you, for I want very much to spend a week or two with you there, pray let me know when you set out, & where I can write to you, but cannot you come this way, it is only taking y^r.

place for N:Castle, & you may go from hence
any day.

I have not yet thought much about Mr. G.s
instructions, pray inquire what they have for
a passenger from Liverpool to Cha⁸. Town
they ask 25 Guineas from London ! . . .

To Mr. R. Griffiths

Burslem, *4ᵗʰ July, 1767.*

My dear friend

I am very thankfull for your most
friendly & affectionate letter, it has answer'd
the purpose you kindly meant it to do, that of
comforting your friend in distress. I read it
over many times a day, & esteem it as a pledge
of the most valuable offer you could make me
—a larger share in your Generous, & Benevolent Heart. And will you then admit me into
that circle of your friends, who are the fewest
in number, but who have the greatest share of
your affection? No other will now content
me, or do anything towards repairing that

breach, the late Melancholly event has made
in mine. I know you will—you would not
have offered it else. Our worthy & amiable
friend Bentley too must be one with us in the
closest bonds of amity. Let us be nearer &
dearer to each other than ever, & Cultivate
that esteem & affection for each other, from
which alone we can derive that consolation, &
comfort in distress we poor mortals so often
stand in need of in our Pilgrimage thro' this
Vale of Tears.

The loss of a Brother, a sensible, Benevolent,
& truly affectionate Brother, such an one as
you well know your late friend was to me, is
very afflicting to a heart rather too susceptible
of grief. And indeed I had long grieved for
him as for one who from an unhappy combination of circumstances could enjoy or relish
very few of the comforts of life, & but little
hopes, alass! of .   .   .

I was so near meeting you at Derby that I had my horse saddled for that purpose but the hazardous state of my health at that time, join'd to the uncertainty of the weather prevented my having that pleasure, but I did not come to a resolution in time to have a letter meet you there.

This return of my Complaint sunk my spirits, & dishearten'd me greatly in the prosecution of my schemes, but it is happily gone off without my being very ill, & I have now begun of a course of Exercise which I intend to continue, & consists in riding on Horsback from 10 to 20 miles a day, & by way of food & Physick, I take whey, & yolks of Eggs in abundance, with a mixture of Rhubarb & soap, & I find the regimen to agree wth. me very well.

Whenever you can spare a few days I shall be glad to meet you at Knutsford, having a thousand things to say, & concert with you.

Mrs. Ashenhurst has wrote a most violent letter to her agent, complaining of my ill usage in not returning a proper answer to her proposal by Mr. Hodgson 6 months since, & threatens, if I do not immediately comply with her demands (wch. is only double what she ever made of her Estate) she will let her Estate to

some other Person, & has had advantageous
offers from Staffordshire for that purpose.
She scolds & huffs away at a large rate, &
seems to be in a good way for making me a
hard bargain.

I have wrote to Her by Mr. Hodgson, &
instructed him to treat with her. If he succeeds, I hope yet to be able to build a Vase
work at the latter end of this summer.

BURSLEM, *5ᵗʰ of Augᵗ., 1767.*

I wrote to you by mondays post wᶜʰ. I hope
you have recᵈ. since which I am favour'd with
your very kind letter of the 3ʳᵈ inst., & thank
you most cordially for your obliging invitation
to Liverpool, with the anxiety you express, &
I know you feel, for my health & happiness.
The former is in a good state at present, & the
latter will be greatly increased by the pleasure
you give me reason to expect of seeing you in
a little time at Burslem.

I woᵈ. gladly accept your invitation to Liverpool or meet you half, or any other way, for so
we do meet, I am very easy about the place of

our coming together, for I cannot do much longer without seeing you : but I am at present disabled for traveling far from home by a sprain of my bad knee, which though I hope it is in a fine way of recovery, will I fear confine me sometime near home.

Your intended Tour to Paris &c. gives me great pleasure, as I know it will be a delightfull relaxation to the mind of my friend from his severer studies, & application to business; & yet may at the same time be made subservient to his commercial views, for which purpose, at our next interview we may form a sheet of hints &c. Mr. Hodgson I have a notion wo^d. like to make one of the Party, & few things sho^d. keep me out of it, was I qualified for such a journey.

I expect a sett of Works will be to be let in a few weeks, with a tolerable smart house to them; & ornamentals of various forms & for various uses are much wanted. Creamcolour Tyles are much wanted, & the consumption will be great for Dairys, Baths, Summer houses, *Temples* &c. &c. This Article will come under the Ornamental Class, & you may be looking out for a sober Tyle maker amongst your Potthouses to bring along with you.

I am going on with my experiments upon various Earths, Clays, &c. for different bodys,

& shall next go upon Glazes. Many of my experiments turn out to my wishes, & convince me more & more, of the extensive Capability of our Manufacture for further improvements. It is at present (comparatively) in a rude, uncultivated state, & may easily be polished, & bro^t. to much greater perfection. Such a revolution, I believe, is at hand, & you must assist in, proffitt by it.

BURSLEM, *10th Aug^t., 1767.*

Well, now I have read your letter another time or two I am more at leisure to thank you for it, & to tell my dear friend that I like these double letters of his of all things. The very feel of them, even before the seal is broke, chears my heart, & does me good, & I am as eager in hunting out a corner to hide myself in, that I may devour my delicious morsel without being molested as—as—hem—no, now I have it, as an Alderman of—wo^d. be to find out a vacant seat at a Turtle feast, & your *kaolin* & *petunt-se* are my *Callypach* & *Callypee.* If I sho^d. not spell these hard words very exactly, you will attribute it to the true cause—my ignorance of the subject, as you know my *meaning* is good.

Seriously, & sincerely, my good friend, I do from the bottom of my heart thank you for your last friendly & entertaining epistle, I have only one fault to find with it—The subject matter is good—The Type is tolerable —*But a pl-gue of all little paper say I*—I think your stationer does not use you well. If you are disposed to change him I can direct you where you may buy your paper as large again, & two of those sheets, well fill'd wo^d. be a Princely meal, & fit to meet a Patagonian Appetite, such an one as I have got for everything which falls from your pen. But you promise me the honour of a visit to Burslem, & intimate that it must be before Mr. Stamford comes to see you, that is, you must be at home again before the 20th.

Pray now if this finds you at home, how long do you think of staying with me here? I beg you will not think of coming for a day or two only. If you do, I am not at home. That time will do nothing for us. The plot thickens as you justly observe, & I hope when you come here we may settle a plan to abide by.

Your French Dictionary is an Orthodox book, & you sho^d. if possible bring it with you, at least the Porcelane part of it. . . . .

You may be thankful that I must now stop my hand for I have wrote such stuff, as I often do to you, that I do not care to let my Clark have the inspection of it, so must reserve the other side & write you an inv°. myself.

BURSLEM, *24ᵗʰ Augᵗ., 1767.*

My dear friend

I am glad to know you were lost *& are found again*, it looks as if what you had heard & seen in Staffordshire had got some hold of you, & I hope it will sink still deeper into your mind.

After the pleasing Holydays you have given me, I am now sunk over head & ears into business again, & have now, at this present time of writing, a Warehouse full of Gentⁿ. & Ladys, & it is full post time so I must say a word or two to the business part of your letter & bid you farewell 'till more peaceable times.

I have but just time to thank you (as you may observe by my paper) for your last kind letter, & the trouble you are taking for me.

"Whether your l^r. will find me at home or at Buxton"—Why you never knew so busy a Mortal as I am,—Highways—surveying Ridge House Estate—Experiments for Porcelain, or at least—a new Earthenware, fill up every moment allmost of my time & wo^d. take a good deal more if I had it—besides all the Hands in the Country are not hired but are still coming to me— "*to know when they must begin.*"

Comfort yourself my good friend with your Cold, that nobody scarcely escapes it, Sally & I have had it pretty severely, & have only Neighbours fare, however I shall be very thankfull to know you are perfectly recover'd & that Miss Oats is got well of it, for She must not expect to escape it.

Pray give your fr^d. G : G.* a triming in some of the most Public papers, he richly deserves it, & I am sure that nobody can do it better.

Mr. & Mrs. Brindley are return'd, he had little more rest there than he has at home. Such a Man is known everywhere & cannot retire. He is a good deal better, but his

* George Grenville.

constitution requires more than a fortnights rest.

They are working mines he tells me near Mattlock & throw all the sparr &c. &c. into a brook wch. washes away all the Dirty & light parts & leaves a great variety of ponderous bodys behind. I long to be Fossiling amongst them, pray tell me when you will see me there.

Y^{rs}. Ever
J. W.

Burslem,
Sunday Even^g., 27 Sep., 1767.

I mean now only just to thank you for [to-] days fine entertainm^t. May my friend throw *doublets* for all the *good* things of this world & *deuce Ace* at the *bad*, for the pleasure he has afforded me with his pair of most friendly letters by this days post. I say I only mean to thank you runing, & to tell you a piece or two of news if you are not in the secret before me—First then

Our friend Griffiths is in good serious, sober, sadness going to take unto him a *Wife*. His

Study is hoisted up into the Garret, & the Parlour newly cleared of its learned lumber is fitted up in the most modern & Elegant fashion; so prepare the Epithalamium for your friend, his Marriage feast will be celebrated in less than a week!

Secondly. Our friend Whithurst of Derby has promised to answer my last letter at Burslem, face to face on Tuesday or Wednesday next, & as I told him my business wo^d. take up a good deal of time, I expect him to spend a week with me here, & at Etruria.— What do you say now to a Congress of three? Burslem is but just beyond Knutsford. You'l recieve this on Tuesday morning. I allow you to eat your dinner before you set out, (provided it be a spare one for riding upon a full meal is not so well) & you will be here to dinner on Wednesday, therefore in full expectation of that happiness we will not dine 'till towards three.

Do not tell me of your shoulders—they want shaking, & your whole habit wants exercise & fresh Air, so once more remember that we expect you. I have some tryals that will do you good to look at them, & make you an Etruscan, allmost before your time! Leave off trimming your old skiff, come & assist in puting a new one upon the Stocks. Her name shall be the *SPEEDWELL*. We will make a *NEW RIVER* for her & *COMMAND SUCCESS*.

Monday morn^g.

Mr. Willett is going to publish a small Pamphlet on—*The importance of Faith.* It will be about the size of our Pamphlet on— *The importance of Inland Navigation,*— & he wo^d. be glad to know what you think 2 or 300 wo^d. Cost Printing, including paper &c. &c.

A Charriot of Ladies Call me away.

———————

I do most sincerely condole with you & your worthy friend, on the loss of his cause; which besides all pecuniary considerations, must have given him many anxious moments, & much trouble & waste of time in the prosecution of it. You have both of you too much sensibility to pass over such an event, without feeling it more severely than many others wo^d. do, in the same situation. I know it must be so; & do most truly share with you in your disappoint-ment, but at the same time, I am sensible that you have too much Philosophy, too many in-ward resourses of consolation, to be deeply, or too long affected by a mere accident; for in that light it appears to me ; & I have not the least doubt but that if L^d. M— had *happened* to interest himself in your cause, as he did in your antagonists, you wo^d. have come off victorious with as little trouble as they did. To be *hasty, partial,* & *overbearing*, is perfectly Characteristic of your Judge. At least they are attributes which are allmost universally given to him, & I am very apt to believe the *Vox Populi* to be just in most cases ; this & many other instances I have of late had an opportunity of knowing, confirms me in the belief, & I shall not easily depart from it.

On this unlucky turn of your affairs, I have given up the thoughts of your coming this way home. Go along with your friend, comfort & assist him, & if possible, do not leave him 'till you have infused into his bosom a portion of that chearfullness, & flow of good spirits, you are so largely possessed of yourself. I cannot conclude this subject without congratulating Mr. Stamford on his happiness in the Company of a friend, so able, & ready to administer every consolation he can stand in need of. And I daresay it will afford some comfort to him, to have this ugly business over at any rate, & his mind thereby deliver'd from a state of suspence, often the most painfull of all others, as there is some satisfaction

in knowing the worst of a bad thing, & now
the desicion is made & anxiety can be of no
farther use, I know you will endeavour to
make your friend forget what is past—look
forward—& be happy.—All I can do is to wish
you success, which I do most sincerely, in the
Humane, & friendly offices you are employ'd
in.

I have for some days past been threatned
with a return of my bilious complaint. If it
sho^d. go off I have some thoughts of meeting
you at Derby, if you can let me know certainly
when you will be there, & that you can stay a
few days there, or if you will return with me
to Burslem, I will bring a spare Horse with
me, & we can make Mattlock in our way, &
visit the Lead mines which I want much to
do, being in the midst of a course of Experiments which I expect must be perfected by
the *Spath Fusible* a substance I cannot at
present meet with, but I will bring Pott along
with me who will direct us in the pursuit of
it, & I am very certain we sho^d. neither lose,
or repent our—labour I will not call it, for it
wo^d. be the highest entertainm^t. to us both.

If it happens that I cannot have the pleasure
of seeing you at Derby, I will write more
particularly on this subject & direct my l^r. for
you at Mr. Stamfords. In the mean time pray

let me know as exactly, & as soon as possible,
when you shall be at Derby, & how long you
can stay there.

Mrs. Wedgwood & her Wedgwoodikin are
both well, she sends her thanks, & respects to
you. I send mine most sincerely to Mr.
Stamford & am at all times your gratefull &
affectᵉ. friend

P.S. I had with me all yesterday afternoon a
Gentⁿ. who claims the honour of your acquaintance. He is a Navigater,—a Tanner *without
Oak bark*—a—in short a Gimcrackarian, & is
come all the way from Twickenham Common
to view our *Harecastles*, our *Tunnels, Grand
Trunks, & Navigations.* He shewed me a piece
of his Leather, & here it is—no—I will bring
it with me. Do I need to tell you his name
is Geo. Merchant, & the scheme of bringing
water from Uxbridge to London is of his own
projecting.

I rec^d. your kind Epistle & thank you for it —but first I ought to thank you for your most friendly visit, which sort of favours I need not assure you allways give me the truest pleasure. This Visit indeed was not of half the value it might, & ought to have been, we were most sadly interupted & I fear we allways shall be whilst we meet at either of our own houses, therefore I shall vote for our next Congress to be at Knutsford, or anywhere rather than at home.

I have been all morning 5 hours in writing so much to you having had about 50 People with me & now I have wth. me Mr. Willett & a builder from Birm^m.—Mr. Copeland & another speaker of the Ho. of L^{ds}., so that my long L^r. which I intended you to make some amends for the delay you will think me guilty of, is broke to pieces. Therefore with the utmost Laconecity I must desire you to send for a Copy of the Patent let the Cost be what it will. . . .

My tryals turn out admirably, & will enable us to do such things as never were done before let *Solomon* or *Whitehurst* say what they will. Farewell 'till more leisure.

I am allways so much better satisfyd in my own mind, & pleas'd with everything about me after spending a few days with you, that I long more & more for the time of your settlement at Hetruria, when I may feast every day upon what I am now permitted to taste of only two or three times a year or so—your chearfull & instructing conversation. I thank you most cordially for the regale you have lately afforded me, & shall be very happy to know that your good Ladys have reciev'd you again safe & sound, uninjured by the inclemency of the weather, or any other cross accident on the road. If you did not stay too long at Warrington, & the weather was as good in Lancashire, as at Burslem, which by great chance might so happen, you would get dry to Liverpool & I hope you so far improv'd the season before you.

I am at all times

D^r. S^r.

Your affect^e. fr^d. & h^ble. Servt.

J. Wedgwood.

Inclos'd are Engine Turning, Antiquitys,
Plans &c, & first, of the first, Engine Turning.
I think you will meet with nothing very curious
'till you come to part the third, but I suppose
you will skim the other part over. I hope you
will read with a pen in your hand, & some
sheets of blotting paper before you to enter the
memorand^{ms}. as they occur to you & let me
have the Identical sheets on which such me-
morand^{ms}. are made. You will readily concieve
which of the Machines may, or may not be
applicable to a Potter. . . . . .

You will as easily imagine what may be of
any use to me in the Antiquitys if you find
time to dip into them. The colours of the
Earthen Vases, the paintings, the substances
used by the Ancient Potters, with their
methods of working, burning, &c. . . . Who
knows what you may hit upon, or what we may
strike out betwixt us ? you may depend on an
ample share of the proffits arising from any
such discoverys.

[*He suggests alterations diminishing plan of
house.*]

As I have room in the box I have put in a
sheet or two which Docter Darwin favour'd
me with & which I think contain some good
hints. Only one word more on these subjects
& I have done. Remember that none of these

M

things require haste, & I beg they may not
encroach upon any but your hours of leisure,
over a pipe or so, when you will have the
advantage of your good sisters thoughts upon
the subjects as you go through them, which
is no inconsiderable advantage. I speak from
experience in Female taste, without which
I should have made but a poor figure amongst
my Potts, not one of which, of any consequence, is finished without the approbation
of my Sally. I have given your love to
her which she rec^{vs}. very kindly, & in return
hath sent you a watch, by way of a love token
I suppose, she says it is a little out of order,
but one Docter Wyke of your Town perfectly
understands its constitution and Complaints,
& wo^d. set it to rights again if you will be kind
enough to send it to him.

The Alderman greets you kindly, he is very
well, but I fear his habit of writing hath well
nigh left him. You'l find your spurs in the
box which you'l please to exchange by bearer,
& he wo^d. be glad to rec^{ve}. the books he bo^t. at
Liverpool by same conveyance if they are at
Liberty.

Mrs. Wedgwood will be very thankfull to you for eight pounds of good Cotton wool by Morriss next week, & will forgive your lapse in omitting to send her watch.

Have I ever told you of the wonderfull & surprising curiositys we find in our Navigation? sometime last month was found under a bed of Clay, at the depth of five yards from the surface a prodigious rib, with the vertebre of the backbone of a monstrous sized Fish, thought by some connissieurs to belong to the identical Whale that was so long ago swallowed by Jonah! Another bone found near the same place in a stratum of Gravel, under a bed of Clay of a very considerable thickness, is of so singular a construction that though I have shown it to several able anatomists, they cannot decide whether it is the *first*, or *last* of the vertebre of some monstrous animal, nor whether that animal was an inhabitant of the *Sea*, or *Land*. Perhaps by the skill you have lately acquir'd in Anatomy, you could throw some light upon these matters, but then another difficulty arises,—*Whether you sho^d. be carried to the bones or they to you.* The latter wo^d. be very expensive by Land Carr^e., & if they come upon the *Weaver* the Boatmen are sure to pilfer them, if it is only to keep their hands in use. These with many other curious Phenonema are met with on the south side of Harecastle. Others of a different, but not less curious nature are discover'd on the north side of the same Hill. A sandstone in which are inclosed small bits of Coal, with various other mineral & heterogenious substances. This stone is so hard that they are obliged to blow it up with Gunpowder.—Great variety of impressions from vegetables, such as Fern, Vetches, Crowfoot, Hawthorn, yew, Withy, & many other kinds, with roots & trunks of Trees, some of them two feet diameter, & all of them converted into a kind of soft stone which moulders, or shivers to atoms in the open Air. What surprises me most is that these vegetable substances or rather impressions should be found in a bed of Metal as the miners call it, that runs und^r. a stratum of Coal, but this I must observe to you, that when this stony stratum gets to be actually under the Coals, then no impressions are found.

I sho^d. be glad to know from some of you Gent^n. learned in Natural History & Philosophy the most probable theory to account for these vegetables (as they once were) forming part of a Stratum, which dips into the Earth to our knowledge 60 or 100 y^{ds}. deep, & for aught we know, to the Centre! These strata, the Coals included, seem from various circumstances to have been in a Liquid state, & to have travel'd along what was then the surface of the Earth, somthing like the Lava from Mount Vesuvius. They wind & turn about, like a serpentine River, & we have one great Hill, *Mole Cop*, which seems to have been formed entirely by them, as the mines are all turned by it, some to the East, & others to the West. But I have done. I am got beyond my depth. These wonderful works of Nature are too vast for my narrow, microscopic comprehension. I must bid adieu to you for the present & attend to what better suits my small capacity, the forming of a Jug or Teapot.

My dear friend

I am sadly in arrears to you! so much that unless you will compound the matter with me & take so much per sheet for the whole, I must really become a Bankrupt. One thing I will promise, that what I am short in writing, I will make out in Gratitude, Goodwill, & affect^n. to my Benefactor.

Your sentiments respecting T(om) B(yerley) are a true Copy of your Humane & Benevolent Heart. I have wrote to let him know how much he is oblig'd to you & shall send you his answer so soon as I recieve it.

I have not yet seen Peter but I am sure you have his warmest thanks.

Count De Lauraguais Patent limit us! Why sure you have forgot who we are!—I will not swear, but you know what Uncle Toby— Honest Uncle Toby—said when he was told L'fever must die—however I am very impatient to see a copy of the Counts P^t. that we may know the worst.

I like your Plan extremely & think you will not mend it much, but have very little idea what it will cost nor do I think it worth considering much about.—You must have conveniencys, & there does not seem to be any more, but if you will have an Estimate, you must, & Sally says it will cost £250 at least—an Authority which I very seldom care to dispute.

The Infantry are pure well, Sally is not quite clever, she has got a little cold but I hope it is going off again. She joins me in best Comp^{ts}. to the Good Ladys und^{r}. your Roof.

Novr. 8th, 1767.

My worthy friend

I like the description of your friends Penzacola Clay, if he sends for a sample let it be a Ton or two, the expence cannot be a great deal, if it is, the clay can never answer for Potters use here, & I will risque paying a reasonable price for that quantity, whether I make anything of it or not.

And now what must I say to your polite, most friendly, & obliging epistle of the 1st

inst. I sho^d. begin with chideing you for the extravagant partiality you so often take occasion of shewing in my favour, but as I wo^d. not doubt your sincerity, or believe that you wo^d. wish to render your fr^d. either vain or ridiculous, I must therefore lament the weakness of your understanding, which I have often observ'd to be warped *occasionally* by the *strength* of your *social* & *friendly* affections. Witness in the first instance nine-tenths of the whole of your pursuits through life, & in the latter, I have in my possession *a cloud of witnesses*, to testify against you under your hand & seal.

But proceed we now to downright serious business.—I have read your letter many times over, & find several of the objections to our nearer approach may be surmounted, & I shall speak to those you have mention'd in the order you have stated them. The first is, "Your total ignorance of the business."—That I deny, as friend Tristram says to St. Paul.— You have taste, the best foundation for our intended concern, & which must be our *Primum Mobilie*, for without that all will stand still, or better it did so, & as for the rest, it will soon be learn'd by so apt a scholar. The very air of this Country will soon inspire you with the mere Mechanical part of our trade.

The difficulty of leaving your business in

Liverpool which seemeth now to be altering
for the better, I cannot so easily obviate, this
being a matter of Calculation, in which there
is no data to proceed upon, but probabilities
of future contingencies, which we cannot
investigate, or command with the certainty
that I could wish my friend to have in a
matter of so much importance to his interest.
I have, it's true, a great opinion of the design
answering our most sanguine expectations
with respect to proffit, but if you should
suffer as much on the other hand by having
your attention taken off your mercantile concerns, *you* wo^d. be a loser upon the whole,
though *I* sho^d. not, & to what degree that loss
might be extended, I can have no idea, nor you
any certainty, unless we co^d. divine in what
proportion your absence wo^d. affect the sucess,
or prevent the increace of your commerce.

The money objection is obviated to my
hand, & I doubt not in a way that will be
agreeable to us both. But the leaving your
friends, & giving up a thousand agreeable
connections, & pleasures at Liverpool, for
which you can have no compensation in kind
(indeed my friend I know from experience you
cannot) this staggers my hopes more than
everything else put together, & allways hath
done, for I have often seriously thought at it

before I rec^d. your letter, & as I wish you to see every shade in this checquer'd piece, permit me to ask you—Can you part from your Octogon, & enlightened Octogonian bretheren, to join the diminutive & weak society of a Country Chapel? Can you give up the rational & elevated enjoyment of your Philosophical Club, for the puerile tete a tete of a Country fireside?—And to include all under this head in one question, Can you exchange the frequent opportunities of seeing, & conversing with your learned & ingenious friends, which your present situation affords you, besides ten thousand other elegancies, & enjoyments of a Town life, to employ yourself amongst Mechanicks, dirt, & smoke? inliven'd indeed with so much of the Pastoral life as you shall choose for yourself out of the Ridgehouse Estate.— If this prospect does not fright you, I have some hopes, & if you think you could really fall in love with, & make a Mistress of this new business, as I have done of mine, I sho^d. have little, or no doubt of our success, for if we consider the great variety of colours in our raw Materials, the infinite ductility of Clay, & that we have universal beauty to copy after, we have certainly the fairest prospect of enlarging this branch of Manufacture to our wishes, & as Genius will not be wanting I am firmly perswaded that our *proffits* will be in proportion to our *application*, & I am as confident, that it wo^d. be beyond comparison more congenial, & delightfull, to every particle of matter, sense, & spirit in your composition, to be the Creator as it were of beauty, rather than merely the vehicle, or medium to convey it from one hand to another, if other circumstances can but be render'd tolerable. Let us therefore endeavour to take a more distinct view of the outlines of our project, which may furnish us with some amusement at least, & perhaps it may not be the first time we have pleased ourselves with future schemes that have eluded our grasp, & vanished away like the morning Cloud, or early dew.

The time of coming you may make agreeable to yourself, it will be 12 months at least before the works can be built, & I suppose you wo^d. choose to have a house, with so much of a farm as will keep you a Horse, a Cow & a Pig, with a few other domestick Animals, all which will take up some time to make ready.

If the Alderman wo^d. like to build, I will make him a building lease, if not, I will do it myself for a common rent. So you may be settling the plan of one house for yourself, & another for my Bro^r. unless you can agree to live together.

The articles to begin the work with will be Root flowerpots of various sorts, ornamented & plain.

Essence pots, Bough pots, & Cornucopias.

Vases & ornaments of various sizes, colours, mixtures & forms, ad infinitum

Then proceed to Toilet furniture, & enrich these & other ornaments with gold burnt in.

Elegant Teachests may be made.

Snuff & other boxes.

Fish, Fowl, & Beasts, with two leged Animals in various attitudes.

Ten thousand other *substantial forms,* that neither you, nor I, nor anybody else know anything of at present.

If all these things sho^d. fail us, I hope our good genius will direct us in the choice of others.

Our best affections wait upon the Alderman.

Dʳ. Sir

Since I wrote last I have been thinking about several things which the Modeler, under your direction, might be trying his hand at, or rather we might know what sort of a hand he has by such essays.—A Clever salt is much wanted, or indeed several, single, double, & treble.—A Tall Candlestick.—Some new clever leaves of diffᵗ. sizes.—A new sa. bowle & stand, & if the pattⁿ. was clever, Terrines of all the sizes might be modeled after it.—Pray set him about some of these things, & have him in yʳ. Room that he may be undʳ. your Eye, & let me see, or somehow know the result as soon as possible.

Burslem, *17 Decʳ., 1767*.

Since I wrote to you last, which I think was on Friday, I have recᵈ. the Terrine model & mould, the imperfections of which you describ'd so justly in your last letter that I need only say your accᵗ. of them was not

exagerated, & I fear Mr. Chubbard will not be of
much use to us, which I am the more concern'd
for, as he seems so well dispos'd to do his
best for us & I know you will have a task very
disagreeable to your nature in making him
acquainted with the result of his labour, even
in the mildest manner it is possible to do it.
The plain fact is, that both the Terrine &
mould are so spoil'd in the execution, that
neither of them are worth one halfpenny. But
it wo^d. be a pity to tell Mr. Chubbard so much,
& I wo^d. rather wish you to take any other way
of *dropping* him, that will give him the least
pain.

Suppose you tell him that I am about leaving home for some time, & in the interim have
so many engagements on my hands, that at
present I cannot attend to some alterations
which are still wanted in the terrine but have
desir'd you to pay him (wch. you'l please to insist on doing) & to send me the sketch of the
Candlestick & Escritoire for my farther consideration upon. The Terrine is capitally
defective in point of truth in the form of the
ends & sides which do not correspond at all
with each other, there is the same fault in the
ornam^{ts}. & likewise in the top of the dish, &
the Cover. The carv'd ornaments are not
finish'd, & the whole shews such a want of

that *Masterliness* necessary in the execution of these works, as quite discourages me from thinking of employing him again as a modeler.

At our Committee on Tuesday last we put our broad seal to a Petition to Parliam[t]. in favour of the Coventry Canal, & sent it to London by Express. Several of our Committee Gent[n]. had been made to believe that the Coventry Navigation wo[d]. injure ours but they were soon set to rights & agreed to the motion Nem : Con :

I have just parted with Mr. John Gilbert this morning who has promised to get me a doz. of *Good* black lead pencils, & a lump of the same for shading with, you are to share in this valuable acquisition.

Pray sketch me an Elevation & oblige y[rs]. affect[ly].

J. WEDGWOOD.

To Mr. Griffiths, Turnham Green.

Dec. 21, 1767.

Thank you my dear friend for your affect^e. & very kind letter which I accept in full of all accounts for every fault of omission, Commission & every other peccadillo since the time I had the pleasure of first knowing you to this present good Sunday Evening past seven O'Clock, & now you are newly shriv'd, take care how you sin again. Nay for that matter I am even pleas'd you did not write to me sooner. I have been married myself in the days of yore, & yet remember wishing it had been the fashion of those days for new Married Men to hear, see, feel or understand nothing but their Wives for a handfull of the first months after Matrimony. Nothing was more irksome to me than business & the impertinence of Gossiping friends, but I am now grown a grave old married Man, am pretty well reconcil'd to the former & am very glad to have my fireside fill'd with the latter. Now my dear friend when you can honestly tell me you find yourself a little dispos'd the same way—that you can bear a third person in Comp^y. for a full quarter of an hour, without looking at your watch, or shewing any other signs of uneasiness, when you can assure me of this disposition I say I will then do myself the honour of kissing—your hand, & your Good Ladys some morning at Turnham Green & give you my benediction, that your Manufactory may flourish, & increase for many years, may be an ornament to your Table, & a comfort to your hearts so long as ye both shall live, & though you may not have much faith in these things, yet as the late good old Pope s^d. " the blessings of an old Man can do you no harm."—But now Sir pray turn your Eyes another way—you may direct them to your dear Betsey if you please whilst I address myself to that Good Lady for a moment.— — — Permit me Dear Mad^m. to acquaint you that your Naughty Husband has such a bewitching way of saying, & doing things, that it is a thousand to one he does either good, or mischief by every letter he writes.—In this now before me, he has wittingly, & knowingly said such things of my Wifes Children, as he well knows must go to the heart of any Mother who suckles their own Children as my Wife does ; & now he invites her to Turnham Green. He says it is to see & love you, but I am far from being certain that she wo^d. not love *somebody else* too. She even now desires me to bespeak your first Girl for the Boy she has

N

in her arms, if she is not pre-ingaged, this &
many other symptoms I have observ'd fully
convinces me that my Wife has no small
liking to a certain family at T. G. And now
I have made this discovery do you think
Madam it will be advisable to bring her with
me to Town. No! I am sure you clearly see
the consequences likely to attend so imprudent
a step, & I will leave her behind me 'till I am
farther satisfyed of her inclinations. You see
Mad^m. the Confidence I repose in you. If I am
too free I must beg Mr. G. to excuse for me &
say it is the manner of an old fr^d. of his who
means no harm to his friends but has an odd
way of expressing himself.

Pardon this Reverie my dear Sir, it is a long
time since I saw you, & the next pleasure to
seeing a friend face to face is holding a familiar
Chat with him upon paper, but I forget how
much you are in debt in your literary Correspondence, & will hold you no longer than
whilst I tell you what I have heard about your
good Bro^r. in America which I sho^d. have done
sooner but expected you wo^d. have had a line
from himself.

My Sally says as you have given her leave
to love your Good Lady I must not conclude
without sending her love & best respects to her,
& by her looks, I veryly believe she wo^d. send the

same to you, if she durst, & it was customary so to do. The Wedgwoods, Byerleys & Willetts salute you my best respects wait on Mrs. Griffiths & yourself.

———————

Burslem, 24 Dec^r., 1767.

I have now rec^d. your obliging letter by way of London, & can readily account for mine from Derby being so long on its way to you. I enquir'd about the post at the George where I was in Derby, & they shew'd me the horse just ready to go for Ashbourne, & I took it for granted that your letter must go by that post, & therefore sent it to the office immediately, but was afterwards told to the contrary, that the Liverpool post did not go out of, I don't know how many days, however I left it with them to send it sometime, wch. I find they have done.

The Coventry People have had a narrow escape of losing their bill, I am told, by precipitating it too quick through a *select* Committee, without acquainting or sending Cards to any of the other Members, or even to Mr.

Gilbert who was appointed to report what the Committee had done, to the House, at which he was greatly disgusted, however the storm is blown over, & I believe they are in a way of doing very well, of which I am very glad, & believe this bill in its consequences will have a very great, & good effect upon the *GRAND TRUNK*, as I apprehend the foundation is now laid for extending it to the *Tideway of the R. Thames!* which extension must double, at least, the value of our stock, & the Publick you know will be serv'd in a fourfold proportion as, agreeable to our Axiom—*The Proprietors cannot gain one shilling, but the Public will save four by it.*

Friday Evening past ten.

I am this moment favour'd with your well-come epistle of yesterday & have only time to just mention a few particulars to you, the principal of which that Mr. Pickford will be here in a few days, & I sho^d. be glad to have your plan of a House to lay before him as I think to agree with him to do all my building,

for so much money, as I like *the Man*, & that
method will save me a deal of trouble. If you
could send me an estimate along with it, there
wo^d. be no harm in it, but do not let that
prevent you sending me the plan in time, you
may send me the estimate afterwards.

Mr. Pickford & I soon settled my plan, &
have made it somthing (140 sq^r. feet) less than
what we chalked out here when Mr. White-
hurst was with us. I was only one night at
Derby & lay at Mr. Gisbourns, whose house
pleases me much, but not entirely.

Mr. Henshall & I have spent yesterday &
to-day at Hetruria, in seting out the Canal
through that district, & on Monday next I
shall begin to make it. The fields are unfortunately so very level that the Canal will run
in a straight line thro' them, at least so it is
set out, for I could not prevail upon the in-
flexible Vandal to give me one *line of Grace*—
He must go the nearest, & best way, or Mr.
Brindley wo^d. go mad.

I have two of your favours which I have not reply'd to, & first of the first—I thank you very Cordially for your kind enquirys after my little Boy who is perfectly recover'd from his late disease*, & a Charming Boy he is, his Mother tells me. . . .

Do not think of trying Mr. Chubbard any farther. I admire his *disposition,* but his *head,* & *hand* wo^d. require a seven years apprenticeship to make them of any use to us.

I have just taken a Boy apprentice for seven years to Model, & am begining to teach him to draw, he has serv'd three years to handling &c., has good fingers, & is a pretty active wellbehav'd Lad. We shall want many of this branch to work festoons & other ornaments upon Vases, free, without moulds which Boys may be taught to do at a moderate expence, & they will look infinitely richer than anything made out of moulds. Mr. Pickford has a Plaisterer who can do this sort of work in miniature (the size we shall want) & he will lend him to me to instruct some Pupils when I have any for^d. enough to put und^r. him. In a little time your Boy and mine may be ready & then he may come to Burslem for a month or

---

* He had been inoculated for smallpox.

two. I sho[d]. be glad to see a specimen of his drawing by post, & afterwards Dan[l]. might bring some with him for my Pupil to copy.

Your *punch bowl* is a *Winter flowerpot*, not to be fill'd with *water*, & *branches of flowers*, but with *sand & bulbous roots* & is to those baubles made in Glass for growing one bulbous root, what a *Garden* is to a *flowerpot*, however I must acknowledge, that seeing you did not find out the original intention of the vessell, you have hit upon a tolerable succedaneum, this cold weather, & I beg leave to tender you my best thanks for the honour you have done the maker in remembering him at your festive board.—May your bottles be like the Widows Cruse of Oyl, & your Viands gratefull as the fat of Lambs, & may they convey health, & Longevity to every partaker of them.

My hands are so cold I can scarcely hold the pen, & a tinkling of Knives, forks, & Crockery ware invites me from the paper, but before I conclude I must desire that youl prepare to visit the mountains of Wallachia by the time they are uncovered again. I am trying your Derbyshire minerals & shall send you an acc[t]. of them soon. . . . . .

I cannot now stay to answer your objections about your *Coasting Trade, Out Ports* & trum-

pery, & must therefore for once beg the privi-
ledge of a Divine, & tell you very dogmatically
—*they all stand for nothing.* I am your cold &
Cordial fr^d.

J. WEDGWOOD.

BURSLEM, *3rd Jan., 1768.*

I wish you wo^d. send me half a doz. of 6d.
penknives by the bearer for I cannot get a pen
to write with, & have no Mr. Swift to-night
to mend them. I have just now rec^d. a letter
from you which Joseph Unwin had pocketed
since Sunday. The contents shall be complyd
with (I hope) by Danl. the next journey.
Though very unwilling I must acquiesse in
the Presidents opinion of the *double polish'd*
vases—Sally is of the same opinion & there is
no withstanding two such powerfull antagonists, but I cannot forbear polishing some
more of them, but will endeavour to lay it on
as thin as the fumigat^r. & then this experim^t.
will be accomplished. . . . .
Mr. John Wedgwood sends the Comp^{ts.} of
the season to you & begs you'l be so good to

enquire the price of the Ropes he mention'd to you for fence.

We are making sagars at Etruria, building the steps, Glazeing the Windows & geting forw^d. as fast as possible,—your house is tiled & the sash frames come, we keep fires in it & the work shops to prevent the frost from injuring them.

There is much *sin* to be committed in the Marble way, as you will guess by the patterns. L^d. have mercy upon our old stock say I !

Farewell, & may many, very many happy returns of the season attend you & y^r. houshold prays y^r. affect^e. fr^{ds}.

J. W. & his Wife.

The elevation for the works which you send me is very pretty & I wish they were built in the form you have drawn them.   .   .   .

Will not the Gothic Battlements to buildings in every other respect in the modern taste be a little heterogeneous ?

BURSLEM, *23rd Jan^y., 1768.*

Mr. Pickford is with me as the inclos'd plan
witnesseth, he sends his compt^s. to Mr. Bentley & begs the favour of him to enquire the
price of Jamaica Mahogany & write to him at
Derby. The inclos'd is laid before you for
your aprobation as Mr. P. has many objections
to that you sent me. The Chimneys cannot
be made tolerable nor the Elevation, nor many
other things, & he says this will be built as
cheap as the other notwithstanding the stone
work, & Elegance of the Elevation. The
brewhouse & stable may be added several ways
if you approve of the rest.—We have now
settled my plans for the house and works, &
Mr. P. takes them with him to make the
Estimates.

BURSLEM, *22 Feb., 1768.*

It gives me great pleasure to know you had
a safe & pleasant journey to Liverpool, where
I hope you found everything agreeable to your
wishes.

We have an ingenious & indefatigable smith amongst us, who has ever since Engine Lathes were first introduc'd here, been constantly employd in that business, & he promises me very faithfully that whatever improvements I may instruct him in, he will make them for no one else, but that you know is a superfluous engagement, as we have renounced those narrow, selfish views & are to let our improvements take a free course for the benefit of our *Bretheren & Country*. . .

It is very cruel in you to convey your raptures at the *Man of Nature* to me unless you intend to favour me with a sight of your translation by the very first conveyance, & on no other conditions shall I forgive your imprudence.—However I can make my boasts of reading a *man of Nature* sometimes though not so often as I could wish, & have my raptures too. Mr. Brindley & his Lady call'd here in their way home, lay with us & are just left us this morning. We are to spend to-morrow with them at Newchapel, & as I allways edify full as much in that mans company as at Church I promise myself to be much wiser the day following. It is an old adage, that a Man is either a *Fool*, or a *Physician* at fifty, & considering the opportunitys I have with the Brindleys & Bentleys of this Age if I am not a very wise mortal before that Age I must be a blockhead in grain.

———————————

BURSLEM, *25th Feb.*, *1768*

I have but just time to thank my dear friend for his last kind letter, & to tell him how sorry I am that I cannot employ the young man he recommends to me. At least nothing occurs to me at present in which I durst employ a painter, as our schemes of that sort are scarcely *ripe* for execution, & to do a *little* & not *pursue* it wo^d. only be retailing my brains to those who wo^d. not make a proper use of the invention.

If I think of anything farther will write to you on the subject, in the meantime it might be no improper step to know farther the value of his hand, & head too if possible, if you think him capable of heading a Class in that branch. If he wo^d. choose to article for a numb^r. of years, & what his expectations are in respect to wages.

[*This letter contains a detailed description of a windmill invented by Dr. Darwin, of which a model was to be seen at Lichfield.*]

This Windmill is to grind colours (if it sho^d. happen to grind anything) for an intended ornamental Manufacture at Hetruria. This I think is a fair call as far as Lichfield, & might easily satisfy a conscience of any reason in it for taking such a journey. And if we do not then prove it necessary that you sho^d. proceed to London, why you can return by Derby, & do some business in the Peake, or amongst the mines you know, & it is only laying sixpence apiece more upon the V—s. But if this Tour sho^d. not be convenient I shall expect *writton instructions* what books I am to buy, & what B^{ks}. I am to see at the Museam &c : &c.

I am much oblig'd to you for the trouble you have taken in your inquirys about the Slate. Mr. Pickford says the light Gray is of the right sort, but not the best of the kind, which is 40s. or more per Ton at the Pitts, & is what I suppose they call *London slate*. Pray be so kind to ask the price of this London, or best slate per Ton at Liverpool & what a Ton will cover.

I admire the manner, & ingraving of your card vastly, but hope the Cards themselves are to be stronger than this I have rec^d. If you sho^d. have another Edition let me recommend it to you to study Mr. Wyke's headpiece, the head piece to his Shop bills I wo^d. say, & I beg you will contrive to see it somehow, but if possible without asking for it. It is the very Pink of it's kind, & you will proffitt by looking at it.

The Boxes with the sugar, Books &c. came here open'd both of them, & both the tops were off when they were deliver'd to us. I sho^d. be glad to know if you sent anything in the Slate box besides them, the turn^g. book, y^r. translation of the honest Man, & things from Wykes, & be so kind to cord the next parc^{ls}. you may send by our clumsy Carr^{rs}.

I am endeavouring to make Slate for both our roofs, (what colour sho^d. they be for red & what for white brick walls) & Stone, or Marble Quarries for our floors. We go on very prosperously. The sun shines & it is a very fine day with us in Staffordshire. Have just found another mine of white Clay & sand. You'l pray for our farther success in the completion of all our schemes, & believe me ever

Your gratefull & affect^e. friend.

BURSLEM, *5ᵗʰ March, 1768.*

My dear friend

I have your acceptable favʳ. of the 3ʳᵈ inst. & from your accᵗ. of Wyat, I woᵈ. not wish you to agree with his mother, on any terms, he will only be a constant plague to us. A spoil'd boy seldom makes a good servᵗ., & I am every day more fully convinc'd of the justness of our frᵈ. Brindleys Maxim that where application is expected,—" *Half bred things are the best.*"

CHARLES STREET, GROSVENOR SQᴿ.,
15ᵗʰ March, 1768.

My dear friend

I left home on Wednesday, & got to Lichfield that evenᵍ. where I spent the next day in settling matters with Mr. Pickford & surveying the Doctʳˢ. Windmill, which I think a very ingenious invention & have some hopes that it will answer our expectations. If you can understand anything of it by the accurate drawing* below well. If not I believe you must come & see it. Well, as I was saying I spent all Thursday at Lichfield, & on Friday morn^g. I arriv'd at Soho, & spent that day, Saturday, & half of Sunday with Mr. Boulton, where we settled many important matters, & laid the foundation for improving our Manufacture, & extending the sale of it to every corner of Europe. Many of our ornamental articles will be finished to great advantage with works of metal, printing upon them with purple & gold &c, &c which he will undertake to execute, & shew'd me some specimens of his printing with Gold which are really admirable, upon creamcolour as well as Enamel. He prepares the gold himself, & lays it on without the loss of a grain in the very mode I recommended to Sadler. This improvem^t. will certainly be of importance to us, but it sho^d. not be mention'd at present.

Mr. Boulton tells me I sho^d. be surprised to know w^t. a trade has lately been made out of Vases at Paris. The Artists have even come over to London, picked up all the old whimsical ugly things they could meet with, carried them to Paris where they have mounted & ornamented them with metal, & sold them to

---

* A rude sketch of the mill, with representations of Eolus blowing upon the sails.

the Virtuosi of every Nation, & Particularly to Millords d'Anglise, for the greatest raritys, & if you remember we saw many such things at L^d. Bolingbrokes which he bro^t. over with him from France. Of this sort I have seen two or three old China bowles, for want of better things, stuck rim to rim which have had no bad effect but look whimsical & droll enough. This alone (the combination of Clay & Metals) is a field, to the farther end of which we shall never be able to travel.

I have very little to send you in return for your news, only that poor Tristram* lies a dying, they have bled him I think twelve times in a day or two & there is little or no hopes of his recovery.

We lay last night (my Bro^r. Jack join'd me at Soho) at Mr. Griffiths's & I sho^d. tell you how happy our host & his Lady are in each other, how happy they made us—what healths we drank after his Majestys and your honours, but the time wo^d. fail me, & my Eyes begin to twinkle, this being the sixth letter this even^g. so good night my worthy friend.

* Lawrence Sterne, author of *Tristram Shandy*, died March 18, 1768.

O

CHARLES S^r.,
          Thursday Evening, Mar. 24, 1768.

At the Close of the Poll here* my attention
was so much engaged with other objects that
I did not think at all scarcely about Election-
eering, & therefore did not send you the first
intelligence of who were in, & who were out,
at the Hustings, & now it is too late to send
you the intelligence *as news* so shall say no
more about it.

One of the objects refer'd to above was seeking after a house, or rather Warehouse in
which I have at last succeeded to my wishes, &
quite beyond my most sanguine expectations.
I have a lease assign'd over to me for forty
years, of a house near the bottom of St. Martins Lane, Charing Cross, which will be quite
convenient for Westminster, & within a 12d.
ride from St. Pauls Ch.y^d. I think of making
habitations for a Colony of Artists—Modelers,
Carvers &c. I have already agreed with one
very usefull Tennant, a Master Enameler, &
China piecer,—he joins old valuable pieces of
China, not with Rivits, but a white glass, &
burns them till the glass vitrifys, & they are
as sound as ever they were. I have long had
connections with this Man, who is sober, &

---

* The general election when Wilkes was returned for Middlesex.

210

steady, he is just come out of Yorkshire to
settle here.   He paints flowers, & Landskips
very prettily, prepares a pretty good powder
gold, & has a tolerable notion of Colours.   He
has an apprentice & another hand, I have set
him to work upon Table & desert ware, & shall
get his rooms ready in St. Martins Lane immediately.   The having such a man as this
under the same roof with the Warehouse, to
do Crests, or any other patt^{ns}. by ord^{r}.—to take
sketches &c—is the most convenient thing
imaginable, & nobody but ourselves will know
what he is doing.   A Modeler in the same y^{d}.
too will be very clever to send to any Ladys
favourite Antique for a coppy.

I have spent several hours with L^{d}. Cathcart
our Embassador to Russia, & we are to do
great things for each other.

My dear friend

I have hired a Modeler for three years, the best I am told in London, he serv'd his time with a silversmith, has work'd several years at a China work, has been two or three years carving in wood & marble for Mr. Adams the famous Architect, is a perfect Master of the Antique stile in ornaments, Vases, &c, & works with equal facility in Clay, wax, wood, Metal or stone.

I have met with another house which pleases me better for situation than that I have taken. It is at the top of St. Martins Lane*, a Corner house 60 feet long, the streets wide which lye to it, & carriages may come to it either from Westminster or the City without being incommoded with drays full of Timber, Coals, &c. which are allways pouring in from the various wharfs, & making stops in the Strand, very disagreeable, & sometimes dangerous. The rent of this last ment^d. house is 100 Guineas a year. My fr^{ds}. in Town tell me it is the best situation in all London for my rooms. I am quite at a loss what to determine & you can hardly help me out without seeing the places.

* Great Newport Street.

I thank you for your kind & ready comply-
ance with my request & can better tell & shew
you here what I want assistance in, than
write you by letter,—you partly know w^t. is
going forw^d. here, & how I shall be distress'd
to leave them all at work, & nobody that I
can depend upon with them, whilst I go to
Town again as I must do in about a fortnight.
Think of this & you *will feel* how charitable it
will be to spend a few weeks in the plains of
Etruria this spring, & I hope it will be con-
ducive to your health & good flow of spirits.

Mr. Brindley is now in Earnest at sharing
Brindley Bank with you. Dont you think we
shall set the Trent on fire amongst us?

Burslem, *10th Apr^l., 1768.*

I am this moment favour'd with both your
letters, & am greatly concern'd to hear of Miss
Oat's indisposition but I hope the means
proposed to be made use of, with the salutary
Air of Derbyshire will restore to her again
those most valuable of all blessings, Health &
good spirits. Attend your Good Sister my dear

friend to Buxton, your affect^e. regards, & chearfull, enlivening company will soothe & cheer
her spirits, & double the efficacy of every other
help for the recovery of her valuable health.

I shall not go to London again so soon
as I expected, it will be the first of May before
I can set out, though it is a very disagreeable
ousiness which will keep me so long at home.
Some of my good Neighbours have taken it
into their heads to think that I shall have too
pleasant, & valuable a situation by the side of
the Canal as it is plan'd and executing thro'
my estate.   This has raised a little envy in
their breasts, & as they are Proprietors they
have represented to the Committee that the
Canal ought to be made along the meadows,
as that is the shortest, & most natural course
for it.   That it will recieve more water, & retain better w^t. it does recieve as the upper
course is over sloping banks & sandbeds.   The
consequence of this representation has been
a survey of the two roads by a select party of
the Committee, & they seem convinc'd in
favour of the lower path, but have ord^d. Mr. Jas.
Brindley to survey, measure, & make an accu-
rate calculation of the two roads & lay them
before the Committee at Trentham the 20th
Inst. for their final determination.   This Cloud
has been gathering for some time, & no pains

are spared by the Party who have blown it up,
to make it light as heavy upon me as possible,
but notwithstanding all this bustle, I am in
no fear for the event. I know my cause is
good, & feel myself a match for them all. I
am preparing a little ammunition for the
battle, & I know you will come in time to
assist me to give it its full force. Mr. Brindley's Bro^r. is at the head of this affair, but that
circumstance does not alarm me at all, as I
know *Brindley the Great* to be *an honest Man*
& that he will give in a true state of the case
let the event be what it will.

BURSLEM, *20th June, 1768.

I did intend writing to my dear friend by
this post, to tell him how thankfull I am for
his last most kind & affectionate letter, & how
great,—but that is impossible, to measure the
obligations he has laid me und^r. is a task I cannot perform, but I am perfectly easy under
them, knowing a gratefull heart is the most
acceptable return I can make him.—I say I
purposed to write this morn^g., but L^d. & Lady

Vernon, & their son & Daughter, with Mr. &
Mrs. Sneyd & Miss Sneyd, with other matters
& things have prevent^d. me, & I must send
this to Talk o' th' Hill just to let my good fr^d.
know that I proceed in the good way he left
me.* Have been at the Workhouse, & had
two Airings in a Chaise—have left off my
laudanum & do bett^r. without it. The skin on
the upper part of the wound is healed, & got
down to the bone, which I tell you to confute
all those who deny the present to be an Age of
Miracles.

Mrs. Wedgwood says you are a sad flattering
Mortal. I deny its being flattery, & have
reconcil'd her so far, that she sends her love &
respects, I need not say *best* respects, as
nothing short of *best* is sent to you from
hence, with your most gratefull & affect^e. fr^d.

J. WEDGWOOD.

---

* Wedgwood's leg was amputated May 31, 1768, Bentley being
with him at the time.

I shoᵈ. like to have an estimate though Mr. Pickford promis'd before he left to send me the particulars, he sᵈ. he thought it not right to give such things to Noblemen, or Gentⁿ. as it hurt the Neighbourhood, for the Gentⁿ. woᵈ. afterwards expect his Tennants &c to work for him as low as they did for the undertakers, wᶜʰ. was not reasonable, as a Gentⁿ. will not consider, & allow for a mischance, or bad bargain like a workman, & seldom pay so well. At the same time he assur'd me that he shoᵈ. do my buildᵍ. upon very different (much lower) terms than he did for Gentⁿ.—however there can be no harm in havᵍ. a counter estimate, & then I shall see more clearly how he befriends me.

I am pleas'd with yʳ. feeling so much for the poor Morter maker, & will endeavour to set his mind at rest. Mr. P. has much of the Bashaw in his treatmᵗ. of workmen, & does not seem to consider their havᵍ. any feelings at all, I have seen a great many instances of it, & may perhaps sometime or other find out a mode of conveying a lecture to him upon a proper treatmᵗ. of our inferiors, & to prove that, *our humble friends* as somebody beautifully calls them, have like passions wᵗʰ. our

selves, & are capable of feel^g. pain, or pleasure,
nearly in the same manner as their Masters,
—but this must be done obliquely, when a
proper occasion offers to introduce it.

The Green & Gold Captn. well deserves his
Commission indeed, oh that he had had some
more of it, when does he come again to Liverpool? Suppose you give him the proffitts, or
take them yourselves, for I desire none.

I think the inclos'd card cannot be much
mended, I have struck out *Mr.* & intend to do
the same in the advertisem^t., & have added—
his Warehouse, that the *Queens Arms* may not
be thought to be a Tavern, as I thought in
hear^g. it read it sounded somthing like it.

Danl. has been very good, & stopped whilst
I have wrote all this business, but is now going, so I must bid you farewell.

I have many, very many most kind & affect^e.
letters to be thankfull for to my dear friend,
with a thousand other instances of his esteem
—but that is too cool a term to express the
feelings of my heart by; permit me to call it
Brotherly love & affection, as such I do, &
ever must regard you, & though I may be

prevented telling you so, as often as I should wish to do it, yet I trust you know my heart too well, to think that I could for a moment cease to love, & be gratefull to you. Now I am recover'd so far as to be able to write, I find myself over head & ears in debt in that way, & every post is increasing the heavy load. It is this which confines me to the house, & retards my perfect recovery more than anything else, & though I put as much of this business off me, as I decently can, yet I have very many letters which, *when I am able, & at home*, must be wrote by my own hand, or they wo^d. give offence. With you I know I can take the liberty of a friend, & Brother, I have done it, both now, & often before, & I know you will forgive me ; so you see I am in a state of assurance to you-wards, & do you be so too respecting my health & wellfare when you do not hear from me of a few posts, for whenever anything runs crooked, either with my body, or mind you may be assur'd of my asking for your advice, or sympathy. At present I am well even beyond my most sanguine expectations, my leg is allmost healed, the wound is not quite 2 inches by one & ½, I measur'd it with the compasses this morning when I dress'd it—yes, *when I dress'd it*, for I have turn'd my surgeon adrift & Sally & I are sole managers now, only we give him leave to peep at it now & then, when he lifts up his hands & eyes, & will scarcely believe it to be the wound he dress'd before.

My Nephew T. Byerley is now going to Philadelphia & will want to recieve seventy pounds when he comes there, for which I must beg of you to settle with some good house in Liverpool, to give him a letter of Cr. for so much upon their Correspond[ts]. there, & I will remitt you the Cash whenever they demand it.

You will be able, & I am well assur'd of your goodwill, to give the bearer such advice on this occasion as may be of great use to him, & if he will hearken to council from any one, I am sure it will be attended to from you. If he has a mind to take a few pieces, or 3 or 4 pounds worth of my Ware with him, you may let him have so much on his own acc[t]., & pray advise him to ship himself in the cheapest way for America, as he may there come to want a Crown, or even a shilling, & know not where to have it.

The buildings go on but slowly this bad weather (I hope it rains at Liverpool), the *white* bricks are *brown*. Pray wo[d]. you advise me to get my house built of *red bricks this year* or wait 'till the *next* for *white ones*, for that I believe must be the Alternative.

I have many things to say to you from the good folks at Newcastle &c, and somthing of the inclos'd Nav^n. l^r., but Sally says "give over Joss, and tell our fr^d. B. that I command it," so I have done, only I must just add that if Mr. Hustlet is well assur'd of his Estimate, & a £200,000 Subscript^n. I sho^d. vote for the larger boats.

BURSLEM, *6th July, 1768.*

I am very glad Tom does not go in the Steerage, I had no idea of its being so disagreeable a birth, although the difference according to the Captains L^r. is £5 to £20. I suppose Tom will be sailed before this reaches you, I have a very sensible letter from him by Mrs. Lloyd, in which he expresses his obligation to you with the warmth wch. he ought to do, & must retain so long as he has a spark of gratitude left, he promises to be very good, & I hope for his own sake, as well as his friends, that he will perform his promises, my best wishes attend him, & that is all I can now do for him.

I have been rambling into Cheshire two or three times, have left my Wife behind me, & am to go to her again to-morrow, & bring her home again on Saturday, 'till then farewell.

BURSLEM, *14th July, 1768.*

I have accidentally met with another Artist who is like enough to stick by me if you can send me a good sober honest account of him. He is a Mathematical instrument maker, a Wooden-leg maker, a Caster of Printers types, & in short a Jack of all trades. His name is Brown & he wears a wooden leg, at present he is making me some legs, but as he can forge Iron & file extremely well, & cast in various metals, I sho^d. employ him in making & re-pairing Engine Lathes, punches, & tools of various sorts. I wish you wo^d. be so kind to inquire his character & let me know it as soon as possible. If that proves good, he is in other respects just the very hand I wanted.

The building goes on slowly, for the weather will not permit us to make brick for it. Your house and mine stand at Plinth height, and there I intend mine to remain 'till next spring, yours will be got forward in about ten days.

Mrs. Wedgwood begs the favour to know how raisins sell at Liverpool.

GEORGE, DERBY, *Sunday Evening.*

My dear friend

I have wrote to Coventry & promis'd to do all I could for them with our Proprietors, Committee &c, but told them I could not think of leaving home to attend Parliam^t. for them, however Mr. Brindley has represented their Cause & danger so strongly to me, & the consequence their design is of to us, both as Manufacturers, & Proprietors of *the Great Trunk*, that I might say to him as Felix said to Paul—allmost &c.—Besides all these motives I have another which is far from being the least. The pleasure of spending a month with you in London wo^d. overballance many difficultys & obstacles with me. And I hope our being so long together—in such a place—at such a time—& in such company as we shall keep, or see at least, will have its weight with you.

I have wrote Mr. Lloyd my real sentiments —that I do not know a Person in the World so capable of serving them as you are if you can be prevail'd upon to leave your business so long, & sure I am that I have told him nothing but the truth—& for myself I have determin'd not to enter the lists without you. If you ask why, I shall only say read your Bible, turn to Genesis where Moses is recieving his Commission to go to plauge the Egytians—Exodus I believe it must be in though, but being at an Inn I have not the Book at hand, & wo\u1d48. not set them a staring by asking for a Bible!

Well without more adoe, in full expectation of meeting you in London, you must not be surpris'd if my next sho\u1d48. be dated from that place.

You tell me what a bustling World you are in.—Pray my good friend how do you steer? Are you a P— or a G— * for ever? or both, or neither — are you — can you be neuter? I never envied your situation less than I do at this time, & hugg myself that I am not a *Free-man* of *Liverpool*. But be it remembered that I do not mean this as any reflection upon the

* Probably Pittite or Grenvillite.

worthy Electors of your Borough, my thankfullness arises from my particular situation
(hang these pens) which you are not unacquainted with.

The Post horse hangs at the Door, just going
away so must bid you adieu.

BURSLEM, *30ᵗʰ of Augᵗ., 1768.*

I believe Danˡ. will have Dᵈ. you 12 Crates
before you recᵛᵉ. this, & along with them a
basket containing 2 Etruscan bronze Vases
full of my best compliments to Miss Tarleton,
which you'l be kind enough to deliver along
with the Vases to that ingenious Lady, &
beg her acceptance of them as an offering of
first fruits. There are 3 other imperfect ones
to shew you a little into the *light of our imperfections* in the manufacturing of these delicate compositions, & the disappointments you
must expect to meet with when you become a
Potter so that if you can be picking up a little
patience & storeing it against a time of need,
there may be no sort of harm in it.—Every

P

Vaze in the last Kiln were spoil'd! & that only by such a degree of variation in the fire as scarcely affected our creamcolour bisket at all.

We have got the Etruscan works nearly ready for Roofing, & then we found that no timber was ord^d. for them, or if it was the Timber man had lost it wch. accident I fear will retard us some time.

You sho^d. have been here at the Rearing of your House which was completed so far yesterday—(The Brewhouse, I mean, & Stable), but as that could not be we shall postpone the solemnity 'till y^r. Arrival at Etruria, which I hope you will make as soon as your business will permit.

———

BURSLEM, *Wednesday Evening.*

To-morrow the Liverpool Coach goes through Newcastle, & takes up there two antique Vases, one is of the *Holy Door* Marble, & the other *Jaune Antique*, they are both in one box, & directed for your worship, much good may they do you. That is, may they keep up the

disorder which it is thought you have lately
been a little, or perhaps, not a little, infected
with. I confess this is my kind intention in
sending them, & if they have not the desir'd
effect, it is no fault of mine.

You'l see the polish is not complete, but
you will form from them as *they are* some idea
of their capabilitys, & I co^d. not bear that you
sho^d. wait another day before you feasted your
eyes with such *fine things.* But you'l please
to remember that none of them can be made
for sale of some time, Ergo, no Man, Woman,
or Child, but your own hous-hold, nor scarcely
them, sho^d. see these things at present.

Pray return them by Danl., & return yourself as soon as possible to help me get all
things ready to proceed with these Vases. It
is with the greatest difficulty imaginable that
I restrain from indulging my fancy in making
more of them, & if I am not indued with the
Continence of a Scipio, & you do not come &
prevent me in my doings, I shall never hold out
another week. Farewell.

One of the Fumigations is a most exelent
Enamel colour, so fine a yellow that I have
some hopes of the *GREAT WORK* being
perfected, & that we shall be able to turn even
the dirt under our feet into *Gold.* I will leave
off at a good word so once more good night.

BURSLEM, *8th Sept^r., 1768.*

You have inclos'd Mr. Pickfords *new* Estimate of your house amo^t.—I dare not tell you all at once, & therefore have not cast up the several long columns of figures you'l please to look over.

I am much displeas'd with Mr. P. & have stopp'd his men from going on with y^r. house & sent an express for him to meet you here on Saturday or Sunday for I know he must be at Derby Races on Monday or Tuesday, & I beg you will meet him here as much depends upon it, & I have a thousand things to tell you besides wch. I have not time to put down here.

BURSLEM, *15th Sept^r., 1768.*

I sent you a packet by Saturdays Coach which was to have gone by Thursdays post but an accident prevented it. I hope you have rec^d. the packet & yet I can hardly think you have or I sho^d. have seen or heard from you before this time. The contents were

an estimate of your House by Mr. Pickford &
his Clerk amounting to upwards of eight
hundred pounds ! I dare not put it into figures
least you sho^d. think I had made some mistake
in them. They have given me all the particulars & I sent you a Copy of them that you
might have an opportunity of shewing them
to Mr. Brooks or some other of your friends
who are acquainted with such matters before
you saw Mr. P. You were intended to have
had this Estimate in Liverpool on Friday &
at the same time I wrote you that I had settled
with Mr. Pickford for him to be here on the
Sunday & Monday following, & hoped it
wo^d. be convenient for you to give him the
meeting here. Mr. Pickford came accordingly,
& stayed here till Monday afternoon. I talked
a good deal to him upon the subject of his
two estimates, & told him the difference
betwixt them was the most extraordinary
thing of the kind I had ever known, nor could
I concieve how he could answer it to you, even
supposing his present Estimate was ever so
moderate, which he assur'd me it was. I then
pointed out several articles to him which were
extravagantly charged, & told him I believed
you wo^d. not have anything to do with the
House upon any such terms, & assur'd him
that I wo^d. not if I could avoid it. He ac-

knowledged he had been guilty of an Error, was sorry for it, & wo^d. do everything in his power to make the House agreeable to us both, that he wo^d. make us a present of the survey- ing & desire only to be p^d. barely what it cost him.

BURSLEM, *6 Nov^r., 1768.*

" Mr. Pickfords comp^{ts}. & if I am not engag'd will wait upon me "—Now for a battle with him about your habitation, but 'till he makes his appearance I will be telling you what we are doing there. The works are cover'd in, & they are begining upon the Cellar Arches, & the Chamb^r. & Gr^d. floors, so soon as any of these are finish'd I shall order them to be fitted up & put some men into them to make sagars, prepare Clay, build ovens &c, &c, that we may begin to do somthing *in earnest* as soon as possible. The Partnership books sho^d. be open'd on Monday the 14th inst. as some hands (Potters) will begin there at that time & if you can leave home—Liverpool I wo^d. say, for I must now consider Etruria as your

home—I think it will be absolutely necessary
for you to be here the preceding Saturday at
farthest.

Upon mature consideration of the premises,
for & ag^t. taking the new house, my humble
opinion is, *that you sho^d. take it*—you will not
repent, we shall fill it well, & well become it.

I have lately had a vision by night of some
new Vases, Tablets &c. with wch. Articles we
shall certainly serve the *whole World.*

Never give yourself any pain abo^t. Mr. Watt
or the blue neck Vases you apprehend are
traveling this way. We are far enough before
our rivals, & when ever we apprehend they
are *treading too near our heels,* we can at any
time manage them better than L^d. B—te can
manage the Merch^{ts}.—to compare great things
with small.—Well—here he comes, so farewell
at present.

We have a L^r. from T. Byerley, he is got
safe to America & likes it vastly but as the
packet was just coming away as he arriv'd he
had not seen anybody to do business with.

To Mr. Thomas Bentley, at Mr. Josiah
Wedgwoods, Burslem, in Staffords.

Newport St., *21 Nov*., *1768*.

My dear friend

We got safe to Town yesterday in time
for dinner, which I mention as a feat, considering the badness of the roads, & *worseness*
of the horses kept to travel in them. We met
with no accident upon the road, unless having
three very fine sunshiny days may be call'd an
accident.

I suppose you will lift up your eyes & say you
have no such accidents at Burslem! well, dont
be over envious! we have rain here, even in
this fine City all day long.

Mr. Boulton is still in Town, & has not done
half his business, nor shall have time he says
if he stays a month longer. He has seen so
many pretty things that he has sent for his
Artist to come up to him, & we have been alltogether, the Ladys and all, at Harraches this
afternoon, where we have amongst us spent
near twenty pounds. Do you remember what
Harrach asked for the Raphael bottles? I
think it was 10 Guineas. They now ask
twenty-five! Harrach is just return'd from
Paris & has bro'. a great many fine things

with him. I bid £30 for 3 p^r. of Vases, they asked £32 & wo^d. not abate a penny. There's spirit for you!—must not we act in the same way?

Mr. Boulton is picking up Vases, & going to make them in Bronze. You know how old China bowles, Jarrs &c are mounted in Metal, he proposes an alliance betwixt the Pottery & Metal branches, Viz, that we shall make such things as will be suitable for mounting, & not have a *Pott* look, & he will finish them with the mounts. What do you think of it? Perhaps you wo^d. rather he wo^d. let them alone. Very true, but he will be doing, so that the question is whether we shall refuse having anything to do with him, and thereby affront him, & set him of doing them himself, or employing his fr^d. Garbett. If we join with him in this scheme, I apprehend we can allways bind him to us by making him such things as nobody else can, & thereby make it his interest to be good. We can make things for mounting with great facility, & dispatch, & mount^g. will enhance their value greatly in the eye of the *purchacers*. Pebble in particular will in this way scarcely be discover'd to be counterfeit. Bass reliefs will have a most fine effect too, & will fetch *Guineas* instead of *shillings*. These things will do for the East India

Co. & they give any price for *fine things*, 20 or
£30,000 a piece for Clocks I am told is a common price with them to give. One of this sort
we have seen to-day, though I believe not of
that price, but it is the finest piece of work I
ever saw in my life. The maker is to visit me
& I expect to have some traffick with him in
the ornament way.

Mr. Boulton & I go a curiosity hunting all
day to-morrow, we begin with a Visit to L^d.
Shelbourn* & shall then proceed—the Lord
knows where, for I cannot yet tell you.

Mr. Cox is as mad as a march Hare for
Etruscan Vases, pray get a qu^{ty}. made or we
shall disgust our good customers by disappoint-
ing them in their expectations. But raise no
dust at home though about them, for that will
make our antagonists open all their eyes, &
ears too, & push them forwarder than they
wo^d. perhaps move at their own natural rate.

Mr. Boulton has not sent any of his things
to St. James's. He soars higher, & is schem-
ing to be sent for by his Majesty! I wish him
success,—he has a fine spirit, & I think by
going hand in hand, we may in many respects
be usefull to each other.

We have just now rec^d. your very agreeable
epistle & will endeavour to follow your advice

* Prime Minister, 1782-1783.

& make ourselves as happy as we can, & we hope you will, nay we conjure you to do the same, 'tis a pitty but we could be alltogether in this fine world here, we want you much to help us see, & enjoy the many fine things we see, & are plotting to see every day, but it cannot be, somebody must take care of the Etruscans & prepare *vessels* of *honor* at home. And pray do not forget to take care of yourself —keep a good & hospitable house & make much of your friends who have goodness enough to visit you. My love to Mr. Rhodes for his friendly call & to Mr. Willetts. Our love & respects wait on all our friends & your fellow Labourers Messrs. J. Wedgwood, Swift, Unwin &c. This L^r. is for yourself *only* to see, farewell.

Dec., 1768.

"Urns a better name"—very true, call them so, I have consulted Mr. Chambers upon the difference between *Urns & Vases*, he says there is a real difference in the characters, but

could not stop to tell me all about it as he was
going to wait upon the Queen, & he was so
obliging to take a piece of my ware with him
—a cover'd dish enamel'd after his own drawing. So much as he told me of the difference
betwixt Urns & Vases I will now put down in
writing that we may not forget it. The
character of Urns is simplicity, to have covers,
but no handles, nor spouts, they are monu-
mental, they may be either high or low, but
sho^d. not seem to be Vessels for culinary, or
sacred uses.—Vases are such as might be used
for libations, & other sacrificial, festive & culinary uses, such as Ewers, open vessels &c.—I
hope Mr. Bakewell has made drawings of the
Vases wth. Numb^{rs}. to sell them by, & he must
do the same to be sent here for the same
purpose, or it will be impossible to avoid confusion. They may be done in the same sort
of a book, all the N^{os}. we have hitherto made,
& the book sent up as soon as may be, the
new ones may be sent on half sheets, along
with the Vases to be pasted in the book here,
these may be done pretty accurate, as they
will be looked over by our customers here, &
they will often get us ord^{rs}., & be a pretty
amusem^t. for the Ladies when they are waiting, wch. is often the case as there are somtimes four or five diff^t. companys, & I need

not tell you, that it will be our interest to
amuse, & divert, & please, & astonish the
Ladies.

——————

I have been turning two or three sorts of
faithfull copys from Etruscan Vases & am
quite surpris'd both at the beauty of their
forms, & the difficulty of making them, especially in pairs.

A Card will be very necessary.—" Vases,
Urns, & other Ornaments after the Etruscan,
Greek, & Roman models." I like the best—
It sho^d. be in French certainly as well as
English.

——————

BURSLEM, *26th Dec^r., 1768.*

I am much oblig'd to my dear friend for so
early a testimony of his kind remembrance
upon his arrival at Liverpool (I scarcely know
which to call y^r. home now) & rejoice with
him in finding everything there agreeable to

his wishes, may they continue so, & then you will leave them again with less regrett.

I have been at drawing two Kilns this morning, a bisket & a Gloss one. The latter is a bad one especially for vases. Our old fireman is ill, so I ord^d. the new one to bring the tryals to me as he went on with the fire. He fired however two hours too long before he bro^t. me a single proof. I stop'd the fires immediately but they were so hot as allmost to melt the Etruscans & this misfortune prevents me sending you two or three bass relief ones as I intended, they are all gone awry. The bisket oven is a good one. The small marbled Vases look delightfully, but the Gloss oven is the Purgatory, or somthing worse, which I am just now too polite to name, of these colours.

The Etruscans which I dipped & put into the Gloss oven before you left us, are so perfect & Clever that I cannot forbear sending you a sett of three of them. But how shall I prise them? put a price to them for sale I mean. I am quite at a loss. If somthing extra is not put upon them for this fine polish, they will think it easier put on than the other; nay, may even be wicked enough to think of *black Potts* whilst they are looking at them.—Well I will sett them down somthing, but alter it as you think proper, after calling

Miss Oats to the Council, or rather make her President, if she has no objection to being a Place-Woman.

I have had many *Visions* since you left us, some of which are so *strange, & fore-bodeing,* that I have even been so weak as to write them in a book.—Farewell, God bless you my friend, & your good sister & family, & send you every good thing prays your affect^e. fr^d. & his wife

J. & S. WEDGWOOD.

I don't believe you can read it, but I cannot help it.

NEWPORT ST., *Tuesday morning.*
[Jan., 1769.]

I will not trust to writing in the evening any more, for I find it impracticable, engagements of my own, or the Ladies allways filling up those hours, indeed we are under the necessity of incroaching upon regular bed time, to have an hours rest, or enjoym^t. of ourselves in peace, & tranquility, & notwithstandin

every moment is employ'd, & we are in a
constant bustle, I have for my own part got
very little done yet, & the Ladies have business
enough cut out for them to employ them a
month longer, but they are leaving a thousand
visits unpaid, & over runing as many which
are to be return'd to them, & are resolv'd to
set their faces homewards on sunday. About
this time I shall be begining to get somthing
done amongst the artists, & but *begining*, however I shall leave all, to conduct them home,
where we hope to arrive on Thursday next but
one.—Farewell for the present my Coach is
waiting to carry me to St. Mary Axx where I
must be (for the fourth time) soon after nine.

Well, now it is evening & we are favour'd
with the company of Mrs. Blake, Mrs. Hodgson
& a room full of Ladies, & I have Mr. Sparrow
to write to about his money matters, that I
can only thank you for your goodness in writing to us, & to tell you that an epidemical
madness reigns for Vases, which must be gratified. I have five or six modelers & carvers at
work upon different branches, & a moulder
constantly in my house. I have seen the
Italian Vases & like them vastly—have seen at
S^r. Henry Chairs some better prints of vases
than any I have, particularly for Bass reliefs
& he has promis'd to lend them to me, & I am

in a fine channel for good things if I could stay here awhile. I am sent for, adieu, you cannot write to us again here.

BURSLEM, *16ᵗʰ Janʸ., 1769.*

I am much rejoiced to know by a former letter of yours, that the Liverpool Gentⁿ. are in earnest about the Bridge over Runcorn Gap, & most sincerely wish them unanimity & success in the prosecution of that Noble undertaking.

With respect to the probable Tonnage over Runcorn Bridge I think it will be too great for any pre-calculation to come near the truth. In looking over my old Nⁿ. papers I find the following articles.

Raw materials for the Pottery from your Port 4000 Tons per Annᵐ.

Goods manufactur'd return'd from hence, including the coarse wares made of our own Clay, which will be greatly increas'd by the reduction of Carriage to your Port, the carriage being at present nearly equal to the value of the goods—3 or 4000 Tons per Annᵐ.

The Cheshire Cheese ship'd at Liverpool

my Bro^r. Cheesfactor says will nearly all come over the bridge.

Slate, Deals, & Mahogany into this Country will be very considerable Articles, as well as Wines, spirits, & all sorts of Groceries.

Oak Timber for Ship building to Liverpool.

I might mention Iron Stone to the North, & red mine in return, the Birm^m. trade, with a great many other articles, & the vast circle of a rich & populous Country which will pour their Produce & manufactures into your Port, & be supplied with your merchandice in return, every ounce of which must pass over the Bridge at Runcorn. But you know the whole much better than myself, & I will not take up any more of your time than to wish you, & every promoter of this noble design, *spirit & strength* to execute it.

My best respects to Mr. Tarleton, we will be prepar^g. some *Etruscan* Earth to make his Statue, with that of Brindley L' Grand to grace the most conspicuous part of this tremendous Fabric.

Decend we now to Vases & Crockery ware.

To Mr. Bentley, in Burslem, Staffordshire.

London, *6ᵗʰ Febʸ., 1769.*

I intended a corner of my last letter for you, but the post surpriz'd me, & I was oblig'd to conclude abruptly; since then I have inquir'd a little more minutely into the state of our Vase trade here, what sorts are best liked &c. &c., & I find there is not one of the large blue sprinkled Vases, with double snake handles sold yet. Marbling with Gold is hiss'd universally, so we must have no more done in that way. Etruscan Vases are the run at present, though the others go off by degrees, & serve very well to make a variety, & prevent that sameness which must be rather disgusting if we confin'd the shew to one sort only. I shoᵈ. be glad to have Lady Gowers flowerpots up as soon as may be consistent with their safety, as she is now gone to her new house— & the Duchess of Bedfords Vases, as I scarcely dare see her Grace without them.

Tuesday afternoon.

I have been warehouse-man to-day, whilst Messrs. Cox & Swift have been collecting, & they are now return'd with *six shillings & sixpence*! I

have been more successfull hav^g. sold about
ten pounds worth. My last, & best chap was
L^d. Bessborough, a fine old Gentleman, a very
fine old Gentleman, admires our vases &
manufacture prodigiously, says, he sees we
shall exceed the Antients, that friezes & many
other things may be made, that I am a very
ingenious man (theres for you now, did I not
tell you what a fine old Gent^n. he was) & that
he will do me every service in his power. He
has given me four Guineas for three vases,
one of them the large blue wch. I ment^d. Mr.
Cox had not sold one of, the other two Etruscans at a Guinea each. I hope he will set
these large blue ones a going. I have made
two or three promises to some Ladies & Gent^n.
since I was Warehouseman which I shall mention in the business L^r. & beg you'l enable me
to perform them.

If you sho^d. happen to see my wife pray
give my duty to her. I don't know but I may
write a line to her before I leave Town.

To Mrs. Wedgwood, at the Brickhouse,
Burslem, Staffordshire.

15 Feb., 1769.

I thank you my good friend for the noble
treat I have just been enjoying. They do me
good to see 'em, but alass, the whole four
packages are not a mouthfull, not one days
sale, I could sell I am fully perswaded 1000
worth such Vases if I had them before I come
home. Large, very large ones are all the cry,
& we must endeavour to satisfy them. You
sho^d. set both the mills to work at grinding &
with two setts of hands, one for night, & the
other for the day.

I must thank my dear Sally for her last
favour, though she did not conclude it so
meekly as one might wish, but with a Toss of
her head crys, I shall not trouble my head &c
—Oh Fye Sally Fye, wilt thou never mend?
you are a naughty Girl, & fill but half a sheet
with your letter, whilst I scribble by the Quire.
Oh I had quite forgot to send you a copy of
the Advertisem^t. I intend for next week. Let
me have y^r. Criticisms by Saterdays post & it
may save me some shame perhaps.

Queens Ware & Ornamental Vases
the manufacture of Josiah Wedgwood Potter

&c, &c—are sold at his Ware-house, the Q^{ns}.
Arms, corner of Great Newport S^t. Long Acre,
& at no other place in Town. Orders are
executed on the shortest notice as above, or at
his Manufactory at Burslem in Staffordshire.
He does not now charge Carr^{ge}. to London,
sells for ready money only, & the lowest price
is mark'd on each Article.

Card for Direction
WEDGWOODS WAREHOUSE
for Queens Ware and ornamental Vases
at the Queens Arms
the corner of Great Newport S^t.
Long Acre

NB.   His goods are not sold at any other
place in Town.

Goodnight love.

To Messrs. Wedgwood & Bentley,
Newport Street, London.

Etruria. *Sunday morn^g., 17th Feb., 1769.*

Josiah Wedgwood Potter to Her Majesty
being honor'd with the continued patronage &
support of the Nobility & Gentry of these
Kingdoms, constantly endeavours to give to
his manufacture all the variety & perfection
he is able; & with this view he has lately
model'd & finish'd, at very great expence, all
the Articles necessary for a complete Table &
Desert service of a new pattern, in which he
has endeavour'd to unite beauty of form, with
the greatest simplicity: & by means of this,
& several improvements the Public may now
be supplied at his Warehouse in Great Newport St. London, or from his works at Burslem
in Staffordshire, with a great variety of usefull
services, adapted by the addition & alteration
of various articles to the Oeconomy of Foreign,
as well as English Tables.—The Goods are
deliver'd safe & carr^e. free to London, for ready
money only, as usual: or if order'd from the
works to any other part, the Carr^e. is paid
so far as the first Carrier takes them, whether to Derby, Nottingham, Leicester, Sheff^d.,
Manchester, Warrington, Liverpool, Chester,

247

Shrewsbury, Bridgenorth, Wolverhampton, Birmingham, Lichfield, Coventry, Daventry, &c, &c. And as a farther acknowledgement of the obligations Mr. W. is under to his good Customers, (or, And in order to put his business upon the most equitable plan for the Purchacers of his Manufacture) & to remove every fear of the goods being broke in Carriage & all objections to ordering them at any distance, he (Mr. W.) engages that every piece shall be deliver'd whole at their houses in any part of England, provided they are not order'd to go upon any River Navigation, or if any of the goods are broke the deficiency shall be made up either in goods, or by deducting so much from the bill, at the option of the purchacer, who shall likewise be at liberty to return the whole, or any part of the goods they ord^r. (paying the carr^e. back) if they do not find them agreeable to their wishes.

NB. Some of Mr. W.s friends have intimated to him that it was generally thought his attention had been too much ingross'd by the Ornamental branch, to the neglect of the usefull ware, but he flatters himself, that as there is not *in reality* any foundation for such a surmise, so there will be none *in appearance* to those who do him the honour of viewing his new assortments of usefull wares.

I sho^d. be glad to know if my dear fr^d. has any new objections to my advertiseing at all, & if not, what he thinks of something like the above. I am aware that the insure^g. the goods to their own houses, & giveing them the liberty of returning them will be an addition to our trouble & expence; but I think the disadvantage will not be equal to keeping a £5000 stock; nor indeed, so great as we might at first imagine; for at present my Customers do return their goods if they do not like them, & they are out of humour if the breakages are not made up to them in some way or other; but this advertisem^t. will acquaint thousands who at present know nothing of it, that they run no risque at all (except paying a little carr^e. of the goods back) by ordering goods from me, & I make no doubt will induce numbers to order services who, without such intelligence wo^d. not think of doing so. You will see my ideas in the above draft & as to the form, & diction, I must trouble my dear friend to put them in order, & shall be oblig'd to him for a copy when he has settled it to please himself—& Mr. Griffiths, if he sho^d. have an opportunity of seeing that good Gent^n. soon.

To Mrs. Wedgwood, at the Brick-house
Burslem, Staffordshire.

Feb. 23, 1769.

I have settled a plan & method with ———
to Tinker all the black Vases that are crooked,
we knock off the feet & fix wood ones, black'd,
to them, those with tops, or snakes want^g., are
to be supply'd in the same way. I wish you
wo^d. send me a parc^l. of these Invalids by *Sundays* Waggon, as he wishes to have w^t. we can
furnish him with of each sort together.

Some of the Ladys say the same thing that
occur'd to you & me abo^t. the sug^r. dish Vases—
that they are like the things on the tops of
Clock cases, or Beds heads. They certainly
are not Antique, and that is fault enough to
D—n them for with most of our customers.

My love to you all, share & devide it as you
please, you have my heart though my bodily
Tabernacel is confin'd here at present.

J. W.

It will be of great importance to have the
service for *my friend* Barclay as neat and fine
as possible, the Quakers have for some time
past been trying my ware, & verily they find it
to answer their wishes in every respect, they

have now ord^d. this full sett, & my future re-commendation to the bretheren must depend upon their usage in their sample. A word to the wise is enough.

Pray say *Double only*, upon y^r. double l^{rs}.—we p^d. 2s. 8d. for the last double one, thank Morgan for it.

LONDON, *28 Feb., 1769.*

The Freeholders of Middlesex are determin'd to have Wilks or nobody to represent them* They will choose him again, & if he is not accepted, will petition the K, first upon parchm^t. & next in proprie Persone if the first is not efficaceous—This at least is the news of the day, & they say that Wilks's int^t. in the City gains ground very fast, & that every expulsion must increase it vastly. They begin to see *his cause* to be their own, & it is thought will soon act accordingly. But all are not Wilks's friends, for a bold Champion the other night

* Wilkes was expelled from the House on February 3, 1769, and re-elected for Middlesex, February 16. The following day the House voted that having been expelled he was incapable of sitting in that Parliament.

when the Populace was shouting round His Majestys chair as he was going to Covent Garden house, A pardon for Wilks!—A pardon for Wilks! put his face to the Glass of the Chair & cryd out D—n Wilks, & Liberty too!

LONDON, *2 March, 1769.*

Why now you are all good folks, I have three letters by this post to thank you for, & first thank you good sir for your agreeable epistle,—thank my Wife, & thank my cousin Thos.* but I have very little time to say farther at present, only I must acquaint you that customers come in apace in consequence of the advertisem^ts, & we are sadly short of ware, as the Cargoe is not yet arriv'd.

We continue collecting, & collecting, but we get in very little money, Mr. Swift has rec^d. but about 250 in all & he has done nothing else but collect since he came to Town, but he is now in a way of doing business, & I can-

* Wedgwood's partner in the Useful Ware at Burslem.

not think of taking him from it at present as
it wo^d. be losing one half of w^t. he has done,
for he has now many promises on hand. I
hope Mrs. Swift does not want him, for I
must either collect in my debts, hire money,
or take my place amongst the whereas's.

I must conclude, & am my dear fr^d. & my
dear Wife, for this belongs to both,

Your faithfull & affec^{te}. fr^d. &c, &c.

J. WEDGWOOD.

BURSLEM, *23 March, 1769.*

Mr. Cox makes a great outcry, in every
letter, for marble, & blue pebble Vases, & even
threatens in his last, to sell every old shop-
keeper he has, if I do not send him some immediately. He has patched up some, and
bronzed others of the invalids, & *sold them,*
& serves the old creamcolour, & Gilt ones in
the same way, by which means they are
gradually diminishing, & we have doctered, I
wont say Tinkered, near £100 worth of what

we deem'd reprobates here, & by the next weeks end I believe shall not have a single waster left. I have got an excellent cement, which we can even mould into ornaments, which grow nearly as hard as the ware, & scarcely to be distinguish'd from it, with this we have done the Vases over again which were stopped with the wax cement, & intended to be sold as seconds, & have converted them into best. In short we are arriv'd to such a degree of perfection in the Art of V: *making* & V: *mending* that we have not had two seconds in the three last ovenfulls, nor even a single one that I know of! We are making some Marble, & Pebble Vases, & will send you some of the first we finish, with a sett or two of good Etruscans.

––––––––––

BURSLEM, *9ᵗʰ of Aprˡ., 1769.*

My dear friend

I had a piteous letter last night from Mr. Cox—not a Vase scarcely of any sort to sell, Blue Pebble, & Marbled, all gone. Mr.

Du Burk* had Pack'd £50 worth of Vases, & he was quite broke down, Mr. Cox, I mean. To assist him a little, I have sent him this week end Vases to amo^t. of £136 & they are not much more than a good Crate full! But they are large ones, & he is now distress'd for the smaller sizes to make up setts, I am making a few of these sorts, but two or three hands make little progress on fine goods, & if I take my hands from my other works, such I mean as can do anything at Vases, it will all-most put a stop to my completeing the orders on hand, or supplying my Warehouse, for we are as much at a loss for desert ware, & the finer articles which employ these hands, as we are for Vases, & without those finer articles, we cannot sell the other goods. What shall I do in this dilemma? not a hand loose in the Country to be hired, this s^d. Creamcolour has made the Trade in general so brisk. The hands at Liverpool, if there sho^d. be any loose, wo^d. I doubt be of no use to us, unless by any great chance you could find out a presser, or finisher of China figures, we shall want a few of them immediately.

Our last Kiln of Blacks turn'd out extremely well, we had a fine cargoe of Medallions, wch. Mr. Cox writes, are much wanted. Seven

* Wedgwood's agent in Holland.

large Urns, *all good*—The Bedford Goats heads
the same—we can now make them with the
same certainty as other goods, & several sorts
which I have now in embrio may be made with
tolerable dispatch if we had but a modeler to
form, & a few hands to execute them. And
these must be had somewhere, for such an
opportunity as we have now before us must
not be lost, or trifled with.

I am geting things forw^d. at Etruria as fast
as possible. The slip Kiln is nearly finish'd
upon our fr^d. Whitehursts Plan, the Sagars
are got ready to fire, & I have sent some fired
ones from hence to support the new ones in
the oven. Two mills are nearly finish'd, &
your house is going on as fast as the works.
The joiners have left mine to finish yours,
which Mr. Pickford assures me will be completed in seven weeks at farthest.

I have alter'd my opinion about the turning
room, & unless you think of any objection
shall fix the Lathes in the lower corner room
under that we before proposed. Here the
lights are high enough & a ground floor is
much better for Lathes than a Chamber story,
the latter are so apt to shake with the motion
of the Lathe, & as we shall want so very often
to be steping into the Lathe room, for there
the *outline* is given, it will be more convenient,

especially for me, to have it without any steps
to it. I have thought of another alteration
for the Lathes too, which though it may not
be of much consequence for common things,
will, I think, be a great help to the workman
in turning plain Vases, where a true outline,
free of any irregular swellings, or hollows, are
of the first consequence.—The alteration I propose, is to set the Lathe so that the turner
shall have an *end light* instead of a *front one*,
which they now have. If you hold a Mug
both these ways to the light, you will see the
advantage I propose from this alteration. I
have try'd the experimᵗ. upon Abrams Lathe &
it answer'd to my wishes. On shutting out
his front light, & leaving the Window on his
right hand open, he had much ado to shave a
piece of ware even enough to please himself.

I agree with you in *most* of your sentiments
respecting V—*, & do not intend to have
anything farther to do with him on any accᵗ.—
But where the matter is of consequence, I like
to see, & argue upon it in every light, even
though I may have resolv'd at the time, so far
as I can judge of the subject, what measures
to take in it, for it somtimes happens, at least
it has with me, that after I have been fully
perswaded it was right to do so & so, & have

* John Voyez, a very skilful modeller.

R

acted accordingly, I have found that a little more time, & reflection would have inform'd me I was wrong, & therefore in any future situation of the like kind, I grow more & more apt to say to myself, though the thing for the time appears ever so clear to me, that it is very possible a few days longer, & a little more reflection may convince me that my present resolve wo^{d}. be wrong, & where the circumstances will admit of farther time for consideration, I generally take it.

When I mention'd the affair of V— to you I had been thinking upon the subject in somthing like the follow^{g}. train.

I have got the start of my Bretheren in the article of V—s farther than I ever did in anything else, & it is by much the most profitable branch I ever launched into, 'tis a pity to lose it soon—there is no danger—true, not of losing the business, but the prices may be lower'd by a competition, & if the imitations are tolerable, the demand from us may be diminish'd, for all our buyers are not, though many of them are, qualified to discern nice differences in forms, & ornament. What then do our competitors stand in most need of to enable them to rival us most effectually?— Some Person to instruct them to compose good forms, & to ornam^{t}. them with tolerable propriety. V— can do this much more effectually than all the Potters in the Country put together, & without much Personal labour, as the ornam^{ts}. may be bo^t. or model'd by others. —The next question was how to prevent this, without employing him ourselves which I had fully resolv'd against.—Suppose he had his wages for doing nothing at all, 'tis only sinking six & thirty shillings per week, to prevent this competition from taking place of two years to come, by his means at least.—The selling a single V: say a Medallion, less per w^k. through such competition wo^d. be a greater loss to us than paying him his wages for nothing!—does not this *fact* strike you!—Suppose we sho^d. lose the sale of 20 or twice that No. per w^k. & lower the price of others!—'tis possible, & instead of sinking 36s per w^k. we may lose the getting of so many pounds, aye twice that sum! —I am quite serious.—The facts I build my reasoning upon are true—& the consequences I mention, very probable. But we have it at present in our power to prevent this evil taking place—& is that power think you of no value? or to be lightly parted with? I think not, & as he has near two months longer to stay in Goal, I shall take that time to consider how we can best dispose of him when he comes out.

I know he is vicious, & everything that is bad, & all my *feelings* are up in Arms against even so much as naming him—But to live in this world, as matters, & things are constituted, it is sometimes necessary to make a truce with these sensations, whilst we manage a Rascal, our evil stars have thrown in our way, to prevent repeated injuries which he might otherwise do us.

I know too that he is Lazy, & fickle, & not likely to stay long in any one place.—But revenge may be an antidote to the first, & he may stay long enough with a Master to give him a relish for such a business as V— making, & depend upon it, my good friend, whoever tastes a little of the sweets of it, will afterwards spare no pains, or cost, to have a full meal, at least, I am sure he must be both very dull, & very idle who does.

I just mention these things to you as they have floated in my brain—I like none of the plans, neither to employ him, pay him for doing nothing, nor yet to discharge him.—As I have now explain'd myself more fully to you than I did before, I sho^d. be glad of your advice, but I do not like to write upon these subjects for fear of their being made public. Pray burn this Scrawl when you have read it.

Whenever you come here, we shall begin to move everything relating to Vases from *Burslem* to *Etruria*—& *not before,* as you sho⁴. certainly be upon the spot on many accᵗˢ. at that time, so shape your business accordingly, & I shall be glad to see you here as soon as you can make it convenient.

We have had a lʳ. from Mr. Du Burk the Gentⁿ. who boᵗ. £300 worth of Vases & other Goods for Holland.—He has had a most surprising sale, & ordʳˢ. to amoᵗ. of aboᵗ. £150 more, & shall send he says another order in ten days.

Mrs. Byerley is just return'd from London, & brings a strange accᵗ. of their goings on in Newport Street. No geting to the door for Coaches, nor into the rooms for Ladies & Gentⁿ. & Vases, she says, Vases was all the cry.—We must endeavour to gratify this *universal passion,* though we shall be sadly short of hands for a year or two, trained ones, I mean. . .
. . .

Your kind letter gives me much pleasure as it assures me of Miss Oates's continued recovery, & your safe arrival amongst your friends at Liverpool.

Mr. Cox in his last letter says marble Vases, with black veins & gilt ornaments will sell in London, though he had told me in a letter before that *all* the marble Vases were so paultry compar'd with the black, that he shoᵈ. be obliged to bronze them. I have no marble vases here of any sort, but intend to make some the first ovenfull at Etruria.

Pray make my best compliments to the Criticks, & thanks for their remarks. I hope they will furnish you with some elegant drawings, & we will make the feet as large as they please—nothing, I think, can be said in favour of very small feet but that they are *antique*, & that you know in these things is saying a great deal.

I hope now you are at home, & have so much Genteel company visits your Ware-house you will look it over & see how many fine things you want that I can send you from hence. You must make all the shew you can *to take in the unwary*, or you will never come up to the London Ware-house.

I am sorry for poor Tom Byerley, but much more so for his Mother & dare not acquaint her with this last instance of his incurable madness. Nothing more can be done for him & he must take the consequences of his own misconduct.

BURSLEM, *25ᵗʰ June, 1769.*

Your house is now finished, the painting was completed yesterday & I have got the rooms all clean'd, the walls only want drying & it is habitable, & they tell me the rooms may now be dryed as we please as the plaistering cannot be injur'd.

Danˡ. will be with you on Wednesday & so many Grates as you send by him shall be set up & have fires kept in them to dry the rooms, for though we are so far from thinking you a trespasser at Burslem that your good company is allways a great addition to our happiness yet I cannot help joining with you in thinking that on many accounts the sooner you now become an inhabitant of Etruria the better. Your out buildings are to be begun upon immediately &

will not be long in finishing, & I will endeavour
to get the Pump done at the same time.

Yesterday I hired a man who works at the
China work at Derby, but he has not been
used to making figures. He tells me there are
two very good workmen in that way, who want
to leave their master if they could get em-
ploym^t. elsewhere. He says they are sober &
is to speak to them for us. He likewise told
me that near twenty painters are just now discharg'd from Worcester, several had been at
Derby but were not taken in, some are come
here, one of them I have had with me today,
his name is Willcox, he serv'd his time in
Liverpool at Mr. Christians Potthouse, &
work'd with Mr. Read when he fail'd, could
you inquire his character from better authority
than Bakewell.

This Willcox has a wife who paints & is very
ingenious, she is at present finishing some
work at Worcester, Willcox says she is an excellent coppyer of figures & other subjects, & a
much better hand than himself. He shew'd
me two heads of her doing in indian ink which
are very well done. She is daughter to that
Fry who was famous for doing heads in Metzotinto which you have seen. Willcox is at present employd. by Twemlows but not ingaged,
he wants much he says to be fixed & wo^d

article for any time. I like his appearance
much, he seems a sober solid man, & has
nothing flighty or Coxcomical in his dress, or
behaviour of which most of this Class are apt
to contract a small tincture. His wife & he
have got very good wages he says at Worcester,
better he believes than he must ever expect
again, they wo^d. now be content he says both
of them at 25s. per week which is low enough
if they will be tolerably dilligent. If we get
these painters, & the figure makers we shall
do pretty well in those branches. But these
new hands sho^d. if possible be kept by themselves 'till we are better acquainted with them,
otherwise they may do us a great deal of mischief if we sho^d. be oblig'd to part with them
soon. I have had some thoughts of building
steps to the outside of some of the Chambers
for that purpose. What think you of it ? We
cannot avoid taking in strangers & shall be
oblig'd sometimes to part with them again, we
sho^d. therefore prevent as much as possible
their taking any part of our business along
with them. Every diff^t. class sho^d. if possible
be kept by themselves, & have no connection
with any other. But of this more when we
meet.

July, 1769.

I rec^d. a very agreeable present today at Newcastle in the form of a packet from my dear fr^d. for which I thank him the length of two full sheets, & tomorrow everything in my power shall be done towards supplying his many, & very urgent wants for the season. Mr. Cox too, though one would imagine his *high season* was over continues to make as great complaints as ever, I believe London will, like Bath, extend her season through the whole year !—You both want Vases,—you both want flowerpots, & you both want *Engin'd ware* of various kinds, & we have but two turners & an half for both our works, & for all these things which would employ six or eight. Abram is turning flowerpots at Etruria, but we cannot fire them 'till we have a whole Bisket ovenfull, which circumstance has run us out of that Article & disappoints us sadly. . . . . I hope to set in Bisket this week at Etruria, & Gloss the next. I wo^d. fain have your Comp^y. at the *Christening of the oven*—a ceremonie of great weight & importance. Your pump well is finish'd, & a very fluent spring it is. The water is near seven feet deep & springs allmost as fast as two men can draw it out. Your windows are set open every day, & the sun & wind dry the walls faster than all the fires we could make in it wo^d. do, so we have made none at all, & I think you may buy your Grates better at Liverpool than at Newcastle.

Burslem, *17 July, 1769, past noon.*

I have many of your good letters to be thankfull for, & my conscience smites me every day for leaving undone what I ought to have done. This morn^g. I intended to have said a good deal to you, & just as I was sitting down for that purpose comes a German with his interpreter who has kept me 'till now, though I told him he might buy much cheaper of other Potters, & that I had very little or nothing to spare. He has bro^t. drawings with him of my goods, & must have the same sorts. They have several excellent Fayence & Porcelain manufactures he says in Germany. But the English *forms*, & *Glaze* are so much superior to any of them, that the *English Manufacture* he says sells before them all. I have promis'd to let him have *a little* in a month or six weeks for wch. he is very thankfull.

I have rather too much business upon my hands, especially now you have left me, for when we have been together some time I feel but the half myself when we are seperated, but I am much comforted with the thoughts of having you here *for good & alltogether*, we shall then do somthing to be talked of.—You know we have a spare bed 'till little Joss comes, & then what do you think of Newcastle if your own house is not dry, which I think it will—we keep the windows open, & the rooms dry apace. . . . .

Poor Ben, I hope he has repented, & is forgiven by this time.—Love has very different effects upon different subjects, but all follies arising from that cause will meet with every possible indulgence from you who have the justest, & most elevated notions of that sublime passion which leads us, even the strongest of us, captives at its will.

*13ᵗʰ Septʳ., I think Wednesday,
however I am certain it is.*

I now write to my dear frᵈ. from Etruria where I am settling a plan to make Vases more systematicaly than we have hitherto done, & will acquaint you with the result as we proceed.

I wrote to you concerning Warburton a Painter, but have since learn't that he will do us no good he is so poor a hand even at common India pattⁿˢ. All these matters I leave to yours & Mr. Crofts better management. I have enough to do to make the Potts, & manage the Pottmakers though I woᵈ. rather, man for man, have to do with a shop of Potters than Painters.

I must tell you whilst I remember that we have had great Lamentation for the Microscope which is not come either in the Waggon or by the Coach, & poor Jack Wedgwood is very Ill, & nothing will satisfy him but the Microscope—he sent his Pappa down to me after other Messengʳˢ. to know *for certain* if it was not come, or when it woᵈ. arrive.

BURSLEM.

Whilst I have been at Etruria, here they have had Lady Gower, Lady Pembroke, Lᵈ.

Robt. Spencer &c to breakfast. This is the second time the Trentham family have been here whilst I have been abroad—Well, it cannot be help'd—I was going to say when I left Etruria that I liked much your plan of hav^g. the Bronze figures from Rome, provided they are fine, & have not been hackney'd here.

To MR. BENTLEY at the Queens Arms,
    Newport St., Longacre, London.

Sept. 16, 1769.

Trouble me indeed—you cannot think how happy you make me with these Good, long affect^e. & instructing letters. They inspire me with taste, emulation & everything that is necessary for the production of fine things & I hope in a few weeks to shew you some of the effects of your excellent lectures. I go to Etruria every day allmost, but it will not be sufficient to spend an hour or two there in a morning as I do at present, I intend to go & live there if you will lend me your house, &

take Mr. Denby with me, whom I shall not spare you at present, he will be very usefull to me & will help me to keep them in order with respect to forms which I am convinc'd with you is the principal part.

I give you leave my dear friend to find fault with me as fast as you please—*The more & the oftener the better*—& I will endeavour to proffit by it. Your letters I must own are a little troublesome to me for I cannot read them to my satisfaction without a heap of books by my side—the Etruscan order book—the Burslem order book, & one I have just made for hints, memorandums &c, so that it is the work of an hour or two to read one of your packets a single time over. Indeed they are now become my Magazines, Reviews, Chronicles, & I had allmost said my Bible.—But do not let this discourage you my friend,—go on—I will tell you when I have enough.

I think we sho^d. have some of the casts from Antique gems from Rome as well as the figures, I hope by means of the Gent^n. you mention that you will be able to settle a correspondence with some of our ingenious Gent^n. or Artists at Rome yourself which I think will be very usefull to us.

There is a book-seller on the left hand side of the Haymarket tow^{ds}. the bottom as you go

from Piccadilly but he does not make any shew
of his business to the street. He is a foreigner,
& was recommended to me by L^d. Clanbrassil,
I ord^d. from him a book of Lamps publish'd at
Rome, & I imagine the same you mention. I
wish you could find him out, he has often good
things by him in our way.

I have sent Boot to Etruria today to begin
upon Terra Cotta figures, but I have only a
Sphynx, Lyon & a Triton for him to begin
with. I have been oblig'd to threaten to discharge him for being loose & wild, but he
promises to be very good, & will bring up
hands to figure making or do anything that
we please for our advantage. What do you
think of Terra Cotta figures of the same composition with the Fox heads? they wo^d. have
the appearance of Models, & make an agreeable variety with the black, both figures and
Vases. Oh! what a feast have I by this post,
thank you for it my dear & well-beloved friend,
I will do everything possible about the orders
& will simplify, & hire hands, & send you Vases
&—what will I not do for such packets as
these? farewell & believe me y^{rs}. evermore

J. W.

My dear friend

I am fully satisfyed with your reasons
for the *Virtuosi* of France being fond of *Elegant
Simplicity*, & shall, more than ever, make that
idea a leading principle in my usefull, as well
as in our Ornamental works.—But Modeling is
so slow a process that *great* alterations cannot be made in a *little* time.   My baskets
are, I think, the simplest & best I ever saw,
much better than the Chelsea ones.—They are
old—& new ones may be made, but I fear not
better.   You are in the midst of Artists, be so
good to try if you can strike out anything in
that way & let me see the drawings.   I have
two new ones carv'd by Mr. Coward in the stile
of the Princes compotiers, but they are heavy
& bad.   I have some drawings likewise of his
which I will send you if I get a frank or two.
I know there wants something *new* in the
basket stile, & I shoᵈ. be glad to have it *Good*
at the same time.

We think so much alike about the flowers
being *allways stuck in the wrong place* that—
no more flowers—was one of my first ordʳˢ.
when I came home, & I have converted Dame
Flora into a spoutmaker.

You have a most agreeable way of flattering, but I beg it may be mixed with *Quantum suffìcit* of fault-finding, least the dose taken simply sho^d. be too much for my weak head. One Antidote indeed I have generally before me, which is a kind of *second sight* of the great things that *may* & I hope *will* be done. A Prophetic view, or if you please a reverie of these things passing in review before my imagination make anything I have hitherto done appear sufficiently diminutive to keep me as humble as I wish to be for I wo^d. not have too much of that good Xⁿ. virtue.—I think Pride, a certain kind of it, & to a certain degree, is productive of a world of good amongst us Mortals, who stand in need of every incentive to great, & good actions.

I now understand the Tree-chests very well, they are model'd, both sizes, & a pair or two made, & we have made the Pott-pouris & to-morrow begin to turn the other Vases for Mr. Baumgartners orders, but they are so many sorts, & finish'd in so many diff^t. ways that it will be a tedious affair to complete the orders exactly.

I wrote to Mr. Cox a long time ago to know if I sho^d. send him a Boy, but rec^d. no answer. If you can get one from Liverpool or Derby-shire upon moderate terms, who will come for some time, it will do very well, otherwise I must try what can be done here for you sho^d. have one up in time to know somthing of the Town before winter for there are somtimes near fifty parc^ls. to be carried out in a day. We must pay the same for the board of a Boy, as for a Man—his wages therefore sho^d. be very small or it wo^d. be better to have a Man.

You want plain Etruscan Vases for painting immediately. I am glad you are begining to paint & will supply you with some as soon as possible, but Mr. Baumgartners two orders & others we have on hand will serve us at Etruria, in the state we are in there, a month or six weeks, & I know you will be very impatient if you have not some plain Vases in London in a fortnight. On rec^t. therefore of your l^r. on Saturday I sent Moreton immediately to the Wheel for Black Vases though it was near six & made him stay & throw a qu^ty. We have dry'd them this good Sunday ready for the Lathe tomorrow morning & I hope to have some doz^ns. fired this week. If I succeed you will have them per Haywood on Tuesday sevenn^t.—On any other plan than this I have adopted you could not have had any in less than six weeks or two months. I was in hopes I had done making Vases at Burslem,

but necessity has no law, & I am convinc'd of
the *absolute necessity* of your making a shew of
Encaustic Vases this approaching season.

I hope you have taken the house at Chelsea
& are ingaging some Painters. Mrs. Willcox
is loosing time here as she might as well
paint figures upon *Vases* as upon *paper* as I
am perswaded you will be convinc'd from the
drawings I sent you. If she does such things
of herself, what may not be expected of her
under the tuition of a Bentley & a Crofts?
Pray let me know when I shall send her &
her Goodman for whilst they continue here
there is 18s at least per week sunk out of 24.

Burning the Gold in upon Vases wo⁴. no
doubt be a capital improvement & I think the
sooner you begin upon it the better. Upon a
plain surface there will be no difficulty, but to
cover the ornaments over thick enough to bear
a polish will take an immense qu⁷. of Gold &
be extreme tedious to polish as you will percieve by a bare inspection of the snakes &
other ornam⁺⁸.

Brown Gold, as they prepare it in Worcester
is better than Shentons *Metalic Gold powder*
& I doubt not but it may be easily made. I
will make some tryals at Gilding here & let
you know the result. Mr. Bradley of Worcester sold one Vase abo⁺. 14 inches high for 100

Guineas—the Gold was rais'd in bass relief Flowers thicker than a Crownpiece! & finely chased. This by way of encouragem^t. to us for burning in Gold upon our Vases.

I want to talk very seriously to my Dear friend about *Encaustic Vases*, pray sit down, take a pipe, & compose yourself. If our potters once make the black body they will mimick the painting as soon as they see it, this shews the necessity of doing a quantity in as little time as possible. I will engage to supply you with Vases enough for all the *good* painters in England. You say you can sell a Waggon load a week, if you sell that quantity in the Season, you must have ten Waggon load of painters to finish them. One Vase per day, with a fine subject, will be as much as one painter will do upon an average. I repeat it again that you shall not want Vases, & it must be your & Mr. Crofts care to collect & make the painters, perhaps you may get some better hands from the Fan painters if that business is carried on now, or from the best Coach & House (Fresco) painters than from amongst the China men. If you think Holland will be a necessary hand for you I must endeavour to bring up one in his stead.

I have sent to Liverpool to enquire after a Tile maker that article being very much called for for dairys baths Temples &c. Lady Gower will build a dairy on purpose to furnish it with Cream Couler if I will engage to make Tiles for the Walls, & many others I make no doubt will follow her example.

I am to wait upon our good friend S^r. W^m. Bagot at Blithfield in a few days to take his order for some large Vases to furnish the Niches in an Elegant room he has just built, & I intend at the same time to wait upon Mr. Anson who wants, & says he will have, some black Vases with White Festoons; he has some excellent Figures & other Antiques very suitable for our purposes which I intend to signify my longings after.

18th, Monday.

We have had S^r. Harry Mainwaring this morning, he came on purpose to ord^r. a sett of Vases for a large room, amo^t. £13. 4. all Etruscans. I have taken 6 weeks to complete them in.

To Mr. Bentley, at the Queens Arms,
Newport St., Longacre, London.

Burslem, *20ᵗʰ Septʳ., 1769.*

I hope the inclos'd will not come too late to
go along with the goods to St. Petersburg,
indeed I shoᵈ. have wrote sooner, but I have
had so much business upon my hands, & hate
writing to great folks that both together have
prevented me till just now. You'l see you
are to write with the Vases. There seems to
be difficulty how to *deliver* these Vases to Lady
Cathcart. They must not be *presented*, & we
must not pretend to charge them, so that
they must neither be *given* nor *sold*,—but we
must borrow a pair of her Ladyships chimney
pieces to shew them upon. I think your
letter and mine shoᵈ. be wrapt up in two
seperate cases. May not you give Lᵈ. Cathcart
a hint that we are preparing to paint the
Etruscan Vases after Mr. Hamilton's Book ?*
I have not yet mention'd to Mr. and Mrs.
Willcox our intention of having them to Town,
but I asked Mrs. Willcox this morning about

* Sir W. Hamilton had made a valuable collection of Greek
and Etruscan vases, &c., which were described and engraved by
D'Hancarville in a book entitled *Antiquités Etrusques, Grecques,
et Romaines, tirées du Cabinet de M. Hamilton* and published at
Naples 1766-1767.

279

her living in London &c & how she sho^d. like
to live there again. She s^d. she sho^d. not like
it at all, she had much rather live in Stafford-
shire. I must talk to her again.

Boot is making Tritons* & Sphinx's,* & does
them very well, better than I expected.

I hired an ingenious Boy last night for
Etruria as a Modeler. He has modeled at
nights in his way for three years past, has
never had the least instructions, which circumstance considered he does things amazingly
& will be a valuable acquisition. I have
hired him for five years, & with Denby & him
I shall not want any other *constant* modeler at
Etruria. Palmer, & several others wo^d. fain
have hired this Boy but he chose to come to
me.

Medallion to match the Sacrifice—We have
none & I am not in the way of geting such
things here. If you can send me one I will
put it upon the Vases & think it will be a
great improvem^t.—you have several subjects
in y^r. books that will do & you are in the only
place in the world for artists.

---

* *i.e.*, candlesticks.

My dear Cousins, for if my letter must
follow my affections it must not be address'd to
one , or two only, all three share in them very
largely, & that you may be convinced of more
fully in due time by the frequency of my Calls
at Wattleton, & I shall trust to your letting
me know when they become troublesome
with as little ceremonie as——as——as you
please, no similie offers to me at present, but
the less ceremonie the better. This being
premis'd I intend never to go by Oxford, to, or
from, London without treating myself with a
cordial shake by the hand, & a kind look with
a kiss from my cousins. All these good
things I know may be had at yʳ. house for asking, & it shall be my fault if they are not
sufficiently claimed. You may call this assurance if you will, I care not. I am apt to fall
into that state with my frᵈˢ. & I like it too
well to be easily cured of the malady—if it be
one.

Was ever such a chattering Impertinent
Mortal—I know my Cousin Polly thinks, &
she may as well speak out, I shall love her the
better for it.—But do you hear my sweet little
cousin I will be even with you, I know that

though you seem'd to like me well enough
when you were here, young folks are so slippery
& fickle that there is no hold of them, so if you
sho^d. change your mind, I am beforehand with
you in my revenge, & I'll tell you how.—Nay
do not look so inquisitive, you shall know all
about it immediately. You must know then
that a vast number of People in these parts,
simple enough to be sure, took it into their
heads to think they had not seen so good
a Girl (L^d. help 'em) as Miss Stringer, they
could not tell when, & this report gain'd more
and more ground daily after you left us, inso-
much that, such I confess was my weakness,
I could not help falling in with the prevailing
opinion, & what do you think was the consequence of all this, why. . . . But I am call'd
to breakfast, good bye for a bit I'll talk to you
again just now. . . . What was I going to say
——No, I have it——Why, having so good
an opinion of our Cousin Stringer, & most of
us having Children of our own whom we wish
to be as good, aye & better too if it was possible than our Cousin Polly what was so natural
as to fix upon her as a pattern, & example for
them to copy after. This we have done, &
now the young Husseys, I warrant you, wo^d.
be so glad to hear of any little slips or Peccadillo
in their Cousin Polly, to be an excuse for their

own faults, nothing could be like it, so that it behoves you to take care of treading awry, I assure you. Nay they talk of sending a little bird we have in this country call'd *tale fetcher*, to perch & harbour about your house, & to bring them a weekly account of everything you say or do which acc^{ts}. you may be sure they will sift & examine with all the Eyes they have, and if they sho^d. find anything to lay their fingers upon——that may furnish me with matter for another letter, & as I told you before, if you do not continue to love me as well as you ever did, I shall magnifiy a grain into a Molehill, and a Molehill into a Mountain by way of quitting scores with you. So farewell for the present, but let me tell you whilst I remember to desire your Pappa will be so good to order some Carr^r. who comes to Wattleton to call at the Angel Inn in Oxford for a small Crate he will find there directed for Dr. Stringer, to be left till call'd for, & if you sho^d. find anything in it which does not suit for your use perhaps your Mamma will accept them at your hands. There sho^d. have been a pair of salts, but those will come in a parc^l. I am sending to Sherburn Castle.

I hope my dear friends had a safe & pleasant journey home & found all agreeable to their wishes there. I have not heard anything of this sort from my Cousin Rhodes's at present but I hope we shall soon, which will complete the pleasure we rec^d., & that is no little, from the enjoyment of your good Company in Staffordshire. I hope you will pardon the length of this trifling epistle as I can very truly assure you I had no intention of offending so *largely*, & if you will allways think of us, for my Wife will join with me here, as your most affect^e. friends & relations you will add another obligation to your loving Cousins & h^ble. serv^ts.

J. & S. WEDGWOOD.

To MR. BENTLEY, Newport Street.

BURSLEM,
Sunday morning, Sept. 27, 1769.

I wrote a line last night to my dear friend, what the post would wait for, & if these Bratts will let me I propose to myself the pleasure of holding a chatt with him this morning. I told you Mr. Cox came here

yesterday, we have had very little time together yet as Saturday is the busiest of my
busy days—however he tells me he called at
Messrs. Boultons & Fothergills to look at
their Manufacture. They shew'd him how to
make buttons, & watch chains, but wo^d. not
permitt him to see their Vase work, & only
shew'd him a few pairs of finish'd ones. I
find they are affronted at my not complying
with their orders for the Vases to be mounted,
& likewise for a pair of each sort, colour &c
which Mr. Boulton desir'd I wo^d. send him as
I got them up. This they mention'd to Mr.
Cox, & told him, that though I had refused
them they had been offer'd the Vases for
mount^g. by several Potters, but were now
determin'd to make the black Vases (Earthenware Vases, they took care to tell him) themselves, & were building works for that purpose!—If this be true, I expect every day to
hear of their offering some of our principal
hands two or three hundreds a year to manage
the works for them. Mr. Cox thinks farther
from what he heard them say, & the hints
they gave, that they are to be concern'd with
Cox of Shoe Lane, they talked to him in the
stile & manner of Rivals to us, big in their
own conceits, with some mighty blow their
uplifted hands were prepared to let fall upon

us.—So stand firm my friend, & let us support this threatned attack like Veterans prepar'd for every shock, or change of fortune that can befall us—If we must fall,—If Etruria cannot stand its ground, but must give way to Soho, & fall before her, let us not sell the victorie too cheap, but maintain our ground like Men, & indeavour, even in our defeat to share the Laurels with our Conquerors.—It doubles my courage to have the first Manufacturer in England to encounter with—The match likes me well,—I like the Man, I like his spirit.—He will not be a mere sniveling copyist like the antagonists I have hitherto had, but will venture to step out of the lines upon occasion, & afford us some diversion in the combat. A room is taken in Pell Mell, & there they are to exhibit this Winter. Oh what coursing there will be from Pell Mell to Newport St., & from Newport St. to Pell Mell—all as St. Paul said of some other Citizens—to hear, or tell, or see *some strange thing*.

Well, be it so—but if we are to have The Boultons, & the Coxes—The great ones of the Land to contend with, If everything we do, & produce, must first be criticis'd upon so severely by the Nobles, & instantly copied by the Artists, our rivals—should we not proceed with

some prudent caution, & reserve, & not shew
either one, or the other, *too much at once*, to
glut the curiosity or spoil the choice of the
former, or give the latter so large a field to
fight us in.—By every new sort we invent, we
inlarge their field of action, & give them
another chance to rival us more effectually.—
One may succeed with the Raphael ware, who
could not with the *Encaustic*, another may
succeed with the latter who could never
manage the former, & a third may hit off the
true Etruscan manner when they see it done
before them, who wo[d]. otherwise never have
thought of it, & could not have imitated either
of the former.—What then shall we sit still &
do nothing, least others should rise and work
too ?—not so neither, I wo[d]. propose, & I only
mean to propose it, for when you have *smoked
another pipe*, & considered the subject afresh,
I shall very readily submit to your councils
as you are more in the way of learning what is
the *Public taste* & and are more capable of
judging how far it ought to be gratified *at once*
than I am.—I wo[d]. propose then for this win-
ters Sale of Vases *four species* only, Viz, *Blue
Pebble, Variegated Pebble, Black Etruscan, &
Etruscan Encaustic.*—These with the variations
of sizes, forms & Ornaments, Gilding, viening,
Bass reliefs, &c. &c will produce business

enough for all the hands we can possibly get
together, & I think, variety enough for all
our *reasonable* customers. The *Encaustic*
will be imitated as soon as seen, let us therefore when once we begin, *push it with* all
our force.—You shall have plain vases enough,
as I told you before, & it is needless for
me to say, that you cannot get too many
paint^d. Mr. Crofts you say must begin at
home.—If he does get a few done there, pray
do not shew them at all in the sale room, nor
shew them to any but those you perfectly know,
for depend upon it if you do not take this
precaution they will be here in a week after
they are shewn in the rooms. I think you
sho^d. make a point of shewing, & selling these
yourself only, lock them up, do not let Parker
see them, *remember Voyez is in Town*, & the
Warehousemen sho^d. not have it in their power
to shew a pair of these Vases for sale.—They
may without offence tell any customer that
you take that branch of business upon yourself.—They will think them the more *precious*
—you can tell them the history of the piece &
all about it, and let them know that we do not
make good things by chance, or at random. It
will baulk the spies for some time at least
who are daily haunting the rooms, & answer
many other valuable purposes.

I observe what Mr. Crofts says about the white, & believe it all to be true, but wo^d. nevertheless wish you *rigidly* to confine yourselves to the red shaded with black, 'till that is mimick'd, & then strike out into other colours. When this too is pretty well imitated then we may begin with——after this too has had its day, surprised the World, & got into other hands then we have——ready to keep the public attention awake, & then ——& then——to the end of the Chapter, but if we bring out all these fine things in one day, supposing that to be in our power, we sho^d. certainly do so many bad things at once, for the reasons above mention'd, & divide our own attention, & the labour of our workmen too much to get up a qu^{ty}. of anything—we sho^d. beat the bush, & start the Game for others, & though by this means we might make more *sport*, we should in the end perhaps find we had not hunted down game sufficient to regale ourselves & friends in the evening of life agreeable to our wishes.

I shall be glad to have your thoughts upon this subject. You'l easily observe the foundation of my arguments is *money geting*, take that away & they all drop to the ground. Instead of this if you substitute *fame* (& my bosom begins, & allways does glow with a

T

generous warmth at the idea), I say, if instead
of *money geting* you substitute *Fame* & the
good of the Manufacture *at large* for our principles of action, then we sho^d. do just the contrary of what I have been recommending—
make all the Good, Fine & New things we
can immediately, & so far from being afraid of
other People geting our patterns, we should
Glory in it, throw out all the hints we can &
if possible have all the Artists in Europe
working after our models. This wo^d. be noble,
& wo^d. suit both our dispositions & sentiments
much better than all the narrow, mercenary,
selfish trammels—the coats of mail we are
forgeing for our reluctant hearts, to case &
hamper them in their journey through life, &
prevent all benevolent overflowings for the
good of their fellow Citizens,—*all* I mean that
relate to the subject we are now talking of.—
How do you feel yourself my friend ? have you
forgot how *our hearts burned within us* when
we convers'd upon this subject in our way
from Liverpool to Prescot ? We were then
perswaded that this *open, Generous* plan would
not only be most congenial to our hearts, &
best feelings, but in all probability might best
answer our wishes in pecuniary advantages, &
for the time, I well remember we agreed to
pursue it. Do you think when our principles

were known the Nobility would not still more make it a point to patronise & incourage Men who acted upon such different principles to the rest of Mankind? the tradeing & *mercantile* part of them at least. When they are witnesses to our bestowing so much pains & expence in the improvment of a capital Manufacture, nay in creating a new one, & that not for our particular emolument only, but that we generously lay our works open to be imitated by other Artists & Manufacturers for the good of the community at large. This wo^d. certainly procure us the good will of our best customers, & place us in a very advantageous light to the Public eye. We sho^d. no doubt be esteemed as *antique* & as great *curiositys* as any of the Vases we fabricate, & perhaps upon the whole, this skeme might bring us as much *proffit* as *loss*.—With respect to myself, there is nothing relating to business I so much wish for as being released from these degrading slavish chains, these mean selfish fears of other people copying my works—how many new & good things has, & still does this principle prevent my bringing to light—I have allways wish'd to be releas'd from it, & was I now free I am perswaded that it would do me much good in body, more in mind, & that my invention wo^d. be so far from being exhausted

by giving a free loose to it that it wo^d. increase
greatly by such a generous exercise of the
faculty, & with the help of your Genius &
correct taste we could continue to furnish
new, & capital improvments sufficient to engage the Public attention during our lives.—
Dare you step forth, my dear friend & associ-
ate, & share the risque & honor of acting on
these enlarged principles, or do you think it
safer, more prudent, & advisable to follow the
plan laid down in my first sheet? One of
them we must adopt, & to be consistent, abide
by. I have stated them both just as they lay
in my perecranium, endeavouring to forget in
this sheet what I had said in the other, therefore you must not be shocked at seeing such
glaring contradictions in one & the same
letter, consider them as coming from two
distinct beings, or call then if you please the
arguings of my *outward*, & *inward* man, & close
with that which liketh you best.

Now I have said my own sayings I will read
your good letters over again but fear I shall
not have time to say much more to you at
this time & you will perhaps be ready to cry
out—Enough already in Conscience!

L^d. Moreton wants the first Etruscan Urns.
Many have been promis'd some of the first—
S^r. Watkin W^{ms}.—L^d. Bessboro—L^d. Clan-

brasil—Mr. Crew—Mrs. Chetwynd for their Majestys, the first of every capital improvm^t. —These if possible must be deliver'd all on the same day. We want *hands & feet*, Plaister ones from Hoskins, St. Martins Lane to draw & model after.

Pray make the most of Dr. Chauncey & his fine things, we will endeavour to please him.

Real Etruscans I believe may be made.—I know the sort of Vase L^d. Moreton fell in love with & will make some— in due time. Is Mr. *Croze's* name of your own spelling by the pronunciation of the name, or did the Gent^n. give it you in writeing? I know a Mr. *Krauts*, & so do you pretty well, it is Mr. Coopers German Correspond^t. we were so plagued with. —If his fr^d. comes to the rooms & buys & pays for them like other Gent^n. to be sure he is *kindly wellcome*, but no orders or Credit will I accept from that quarter, so you'l know what answer to give & dress it up how you please.——*Sunday Even^g*. Good night, our Committee & General Meet^g. are tomorrow & Tuesday so I shall have no time to write tomorrow. Mr. Cox & Sally & the Good Folks at N: C: join in best respects, love &c to you with y^r. most affect^e.

J. W.

I have two or three of your favours to thank you for & though exceeding busy cannot forbear just telling you that we are all alive & well & all that & shall be very glad to see you here. . . . .

Has Lᵈ. Bessborough sold all his casts from Antique Gems, or the Gems themselves to the Duke of Marlborough? I am, & so are you, much interested to know this as we had leave from Lᵈ. B: to take casts from all his Casts, but if the D. of M: has boᵗ. them we shall have that leave to solicit again.

Though the Gems from Italy may be too small to apply to the Vases themselves, they will make very good Studys & we can have larger modeled by them much better than from prints, we can likewise paint after them. Gems are the fountain head of fine & beautifull composition, & we cannot you know employ ourselves too near the fountain head of taste.

We have nothing proper at all to go along with the Sacrifice Medallion, Mr. Denby has begun to model one, but it will be too much for him.

J^{no}. Wood knows where Bacon lives, but Mon Seu^r. Tassie may be a better hand.

I cannot send any dimention of the Vase 'till it is made. I propose to have it in black, painted & Gilt, the Gold burnt in, so I must polish it to hold the Gold, for a mere dry body will not do for Encaustic Gilding.

We have many orders for Vases, I verily believe they wo^d. employ all the people I have if they could all work at them. I have left myself here but one *Journeyman* handler wch. prevents our geting forw^d. with Jugs, Teapots, or anything that requires any finishing from the Lathe. The truth of the case is that all the hands at Etruria are wanted here, & all the hands here are wanted at Etruria. Hire more you say. Aye but trade is as good with others as ourselves, allmost everybody wants hands. I have ingaged about half a score Journeymen & as many Apprentices, & I think myself very lucky—we will divide them as well as we can. . . .

I shall long to know how you like the plain Vases, in the Etruscan stile. I was oblig'd to put them into the oven before they were dry, in consequence of which one or two of them will want a little stopping which is the case of a few of those sent today, but they will be made good after they are finished.

We have had two days of fine weather which bro⟨ᵗ⟩. us two Coaches & other Company here today (Saturday), Sʳ. Walter Blount & Lady, Lady Throckmorton, Mrs. Throckmorton & her two Daughters, Mrs. Brockholts &c, allmost everybody who comes here are sadly disappointed in not finding a collection of Vases & other fine things which they have heard so much talk of, & some of them have seen in Newport St. The pattern room at Etruria is now finish'd all to painting. I must fit that up as soon as I can but indeed we shall not have much more Compʸ. 'till spring. The post is now come in—very late & I must not detain him.

Thank you my dear frᵈ. for your good packet. I have scarcely time to read them, but perfectly approve of the contents. The two plans I mention'd in my former letter were both in the extreme, perhaps a little *Outree*— first thoughts generally, if they are good for anything, are so. You have pared them down, wᶜʰ. they wanted, fitted them together & consolidated them into one excellent plan which I shall gladly pursue. Your reasoning is just, there is no withstanding the force you have given yʳ. argumᵗˢ. Farewell for the present my good frᵈ.

We are very busy geting up the orders you have sent us, Mr. Cox & J. W. at the usefull

& myself at the Vases, but what with Mr.
Baumgartners orders, those we had on hand,
& such as are now wanted in Lond^n. & Liverpool—Pebble—Candlesticks, plain Etruscans
—Medallions—new Bass reliefs & an hundred
others—Oh my poor head!

The Etruscan Vases are arrived—I see how
the mechanical part of the glaze & painting is
perform'd, all which may be faithfully imitated
at any time*.

BURSLEM, *1st of Oct^r., 1769.*

Be it so, my dear friend, even so be it, let
us begin, proceed, & finish our future schemes,
our days & years, in the pursuit of *Fortune*,
Fame & the *Public Good*.—You will be my
Mentor, my Guardian Angel to pluck me back
from the confines of extravagance, either in
Theory, or practice when you find me verging
that way. I will answer to the friendly call;

* He never did this.

lend a willing ear to your instructions, & most
gladly join you in the Paths you have chalk'd
out for us.   My talents, which your friendship
is so apt on all occasions to magnify, are very
confin'd ; they lie chiefly in *the Potter*.—Such
as they are, think of them as your own, enlarge,
confine, or use them at your pleasure, they
can never make me happier than by contribu-
ting to the use, or comfort of my friend.   We
have now I think nearly fixed the plan of proceedings for this Winter, & with respect to
Rivalship, we will cast all dread of that behind
our backs, treat it as a base, & vanquish'd
enemy, & not bestow another serious thought
upon it.

   We are perfectly agreed that the attention
of our Customers sho^d. not be distracted with
too great a profusion of variety, I shall nevertheless be bring^g. other things in forwardness
to succeed the *encaustic* which I look upon as
our principal article for the ensueing season.
Do you give up the *Gold* along with the *R—l*
& the *vera Etrusca* for the present.—I have no
fear but they may all be done to the height of
your wishes, & the wishes of your customers—
in due time, & I hope to shew you a specimen
soon. . . . .   Strange as it may sound I sho^d.
be glad never to recieve another order for any
particular kind of Vases, & I sho^d. wish you to

avoid taking such orders as much as you
decently can, at least 'till we are got into a
more methodical way of making *the same sorts
over again*, & there is no other way of doing
this but by having models, & moulds of every
shape & size we make. This plan I have been
pursueing some time, & have many models
ready to fire this week, & if you sho^d. not hear
from me again 'till this day sev'nn^t. you may
conclude I am turning models at Etruria, &
ord^d. myself not to be at home, or am gone to
S^r. W^m. Bagots where I sho^d. have been last
week, but cannot find in my heart to leave so
many Folks, & so many things that are wanting me every moment.

I believe *Vases* are much better articles, *for
us*, than *figures* & shall act agreeable to my
convictions especially as I percieve I shall
have your approbation along with me.—
Figures, & other things may come in very well
when we have not sale for all the Vases we
can make, or have hands to spare, who cannot
work at Vases, but the latter can never be the
case with *good hands*, & *bad hands* will not
suit us for anything we shall make at Etruria.

I have no fear at all even from the combination of Chelsea & Soho, if that sho^d. ever
happen, we have got, & shall keep the lead so
long as our lives & health are continued to us.

I am perswaded they are thoroughly in earnest
at Soho. Mr. Fothergill told Mr. Cox that
the Vase trade wo^d. be *inexhaustable,* it wo^d be
impossible to supply the demand for *good
things* in that way. This is a right, just &
true idea, & was not of Mr. Fothergills *own
Manufacture* I am pretty certain. The field
is vast indeed! It seems to grow wider &
every way more extensive, the farther you
advance into it. The Harvest truly is great,
& the labourers (thanks be praised—theres
my outward man for you, he will be stealing a
march now & then upon me) but few.

Pray be so good to get a Crow quill &
write *as fine as I do,* or else some paper that
will not drink in the ink & stain thro' so
terribly. In the next place you see I date my
letter the first thing I do, & make a fine
[mark] for my wafer. I shall be glad to see
you follow a good example, & become a little
orderly. A Margin wo^d. be a good thing, but
that I sho^d. be so much a loser by that I will
excuse it, though now I come to make up my
Monthly Number I am sadly pinched for a little
stitching room. I have read over my whole
number today, made an index, deposited it in a
new portfolio, & am now as *orderly in my head,* &
as finely refresh'd & *happy at my heart* as can
be, so farewell, & thank you for my elegant

treat my good friend. I am most affection-ately your J. W.

Raphael may succeed the Etruscans, in order of time he ought to do so.

Lord Barrington is angry with me for neglecting to send a table service he ord^d. a long time since; he has had a great deal of company and nothing to eat off. I promis'd to have the things sent immediately which I hope may be done.

———————

To Mr. Thomas Bentley at the Queens Arms, Newport Street, Long Acre, London.

Burslem.

My dear friend

If you continue to write such letters as your last there is no saying where our improve-ments will stop. I read it over, & over again, & still proffitt by every repetition of your agreeable Lessons.

And do you really think that we may make

a *complete conquest* of France ? Conquer France
in Burslem ?—My blood moves quicker, I feel
my strength increase for the contest. Assist
me my friend & the victorie is our own. We
will make them (now I must say *Potts*, & how
vulgar it sounds) I won't though, I say we
will fash^n. our Porcelain after their own hearts,
& captivate them with the Elegance & simplicity of the Ancients. But do they love
simplicity ? Are you certain the French Nation
will be pleased with simplicity in their Vessells ? Either I have been greatly deciev'd, or
a wonderfull reformation has taken place
amongst them. *French & Frippery* have jin-
gled together so long in my ideas, that I
scarcely know how to seperate them, & much
of their work which I have seen *cover'd over
with ornament*, had confirm'd me in the opinion.

I left London with a full resolution to
simplify, & you shall soon be convinced I was
in earnest, as a first essay I have discarded
the twiggen and flower'd handles from the
Terrines, & everything except the baskets,
where I think their *apparent lightness*, & *real
strength*, & their similarity to the work of the
vessels will induce me to retain them but I
am not determin'd, & sho^d. be glad of your
opinion.

I have shapen out some models of Cream

Ewers which I hope will be thought pretty
well of, 'till I can make better. They are
simple, convenient, & of an Antique cast.
Half pint mugs come in the next. Porphiry
Vases will be very Clever; but we must proceed with some method, & Mr. Baumgartners
ord^{rs}. wth. plain black ones for your finishing
stand first on my list. . I shall send another
Turner to Etruria on Monday & more finishers
as they are wanted. A Porter has offer'd
himself who I think is likely, he is abo^t. 50,
can write, is a stern morose or rather resolute
Character, & wants a fix'd situation for the
remaind^r. of his days. The worker in Metal I
mention'd to you in my last has try'd various
schemes but never could succeed as a *Master*,
he is pretty well stricken in years & will now
be content with a place that will procure food
& raiment for life. I shall still want a Book-
keeper & head Clerk at Etruria, I wish I may
be lucky enough to meet with them both in
one Person, but allmost despair of it, as he
sho^d. be somthing of a Potter, though that
is not absolutely necessary. Could you get
some such body in London think you for me ?

I hope you will have an opportunity soon of
geting some figures from the Cabinets of y^r.
Noble customers, which have not yet appeared
in the shops. Pray make a push for it when

& where you can with decency & I will endeavour to execute them in Terra Cotta.

We have the best possible patent for Vases
if we can hold it, as I hope we shall for a long
time to come, & as to the black composition
we could not have a patent for it to answer
any purpose on several accounts, which I do
not care to mention in writing.

I have no objection to the Glass cases or
sliders you mention, & think they will have
a good effect, we are perfectly agreed in our
sentiments that much depends upon the mode
of shewing these articles, & you are quite a
Master in that branch of our science, & I beg
you will give free scope to your good taste &
Genius in this, & every other maneauvre which
has a tendency to sell *fine things* at *good prices*.

I am very agreeably flatter'd with Mrs.
Chetwynds disappointment in the Herculaneum, but shall not be quite at ease 'till I
know how my Royal Mistress approves of the
whole, with the price you have fixed upon it,
which I think is no more than it ought to be,
everything consider'd, & hope her Majesty
will think so too.

All fr^{ds}. are well here, I dare not tell them
of their & my loss by your settling in London
all at once but let them into it by degrees as
they can bear it. I hate the thoughts of it

myself, & shall never be thoroly reconcil'd to such a plan of seperation.

J. W.

BURSLEM,
Saturday morning, Oct. 30, 1769.

My dear fr^d.

I have some charming packets to thank you for, but you call me to you, & shall be obey'd. I come my good friend, & hope to present your good Sister to you in a few days for which I know you will thank me well.

Say nothing of the Br—ze *Encaustic* to anybody. It is accomplish'd—I bring it with me, & it will do your heart good to look at it.

Trouble not yourself about the gold powder, that business is finished likewise—You shall have satisfaction in both.

I have been an Etruscan, & dined at the works every day, except monday, this week. I have been turning models, & preparing to make such *Machines* of the *Men* as cannot Err. But more of these matters when we hold the

grand talk in Newport St.—I am going for
Etruria—God bless you prays y^r. J. W.

Upon Mr. Wedgwood going to Etruria this
morning he gave me an order to write to you
to desire the Kiln might be got ready by the
[time] he comes as he should like to be with
you at the first firing.

I have just heard that Miss Oats came to
Newcastle last night and is very well. I hope
to do myself the pleasure of waiting on her
tomorrow, today I cou'd not get time.

I am Sir your very Hum^e. ser^t.

S. WEDGWOOD.

BURSLEM,
Upper house, 11th Nov^r., 1769.

I know my dear friend will be glad to hear
that I got safe home & found all well there.
We met with several accidents on the road,
such as springs snapping, shafts breaking, &c,
which delay'd us somthing in our journeying,

but we had no bodily hurt, & the greatest evils we met with were small Chaises.

We were three days upon the road though we lost no time & travel'd a little by moonlight each evening—but at the last stage—Etruria —I was rewarded for all the risques & pains I had undergone in a tedious long & dirty journey.

I found my Sally, & family at Etruria! just come there to take possession of the Etruscan plains, & sleep upon them for the first night. —Was not all this very clever now of my own dear Girls contriving. She expected her Joss on the very evening he arriv'd had got the disagreeable business of removing all over, & I wo^d. not have been another night from home for the Indies.

Tonight we are to sup 120 of our workmen in the Town hall, & shall take up our lodgings here at Burslem. I cannot tell yet whether we shall send you any Vases, we have some finish'd if we can find plinths for them, but of this you will hear more by mondays post.

We have got another Lathe up (the third)
& I have committed a sad robbery upon my
works at Burslem to furnish it. I have taken
James Bourn to Etruria! The only tolerable
turner of *Good things* I had at Burslem, & he is
far superior to Abram at Vases. I wo^d. not have
parted with him from my works at Burslem for
a great deal on any other acc^t. for we have not
one Engine Turner left there now. Poor Burslem—Poor Creamcolour. They tell me I
sacrifice all to *Etruria & Vases*!

We have now got thirty hands here, but I
have much ado to keep the new ones quiet.
Some will not work in Black. Others say
they shall never learn this new business, &
want to be releas'd to make Terrines & sa:
boats again. I do not know what I shall do
with them, we have too many *fresh* hands to
take in at once, though we have business
enough for them, if they knew how, or wo^d.
have patience to learn to do it, but they do
not seem to relish the thoughts of a second
apprenticeship. I have been but three or four
times at Burslem since my return though
they want me there very much, indeed I have
been confin'd to my room several days Plan-
ning with Mr. Gardner the remainder of my

works here, wch. must all be built, beside a
Town for the men to live in, the next summer,
for I have notice to leave the Brickhouse
Works the next year, my Landlord is married
& will come to them himself.—Heres a fine
piece of work cut out for me ! Where shall I
get *money*, *materials*, or *hands* to finish so
much building in so short a time. It is work
enough for years if I had not one other Iron
in the fire, & must be done in one summer, *&
nothing else stand still the while.*—Collect—
Collect my fr^d.—set all your hands, & heads to
work—send me the L'Argent & you shall see
wonders—£3000 !—" £3000 ?"—Aye £3000 not
a farthing less will satisfy my Architect for
the next years business, so you must either
collect or take a place for me in the Gazett.

I *sell for ready money* only you know, now if
we can but manage that it shall be so *in
reallity*, all may be well & the business done
in due time. When you want a hand I will
send you John Wood, & when you needs must
have another—Mr. Cox, but you'l let him stay
here as long as you conveniently can, but you
shall have him, Mr. Swift, myself, or anybody
else when necessary, for the main point, geting in the Cash.

Oh,—thank you my inspired, poetical friend,
a most excellent song indeed.—What a pity

that the subject was no better, however I love, & thank you for your partiality & have begged the Original of Mr. Cox least any *copies* sho^d. get abroad.

I have no objection to employing Tassie, but the money, & I think we can repair the things as fast as we can make use of them, so you may send us some down from time to time for that purpose. We want several pieces to complete the Apollo & Daphne wch. is highly finish'd.

FIGURE MAKERS.

I have not seen these s^d. black figures which have converted you again to a good Opinion of figure making, therefore if I sh^d. waver a little you will not wonder. My opinion is, that if we can make more Vases than can be sold, or, find hands who can make *figures* & cannot work at *Vases*, then we sho^d. set about figure making, but 'till one of these cases happen I cannot help thinking our hands are better imploy'd at Vases. If there was any such thing as geting one sober figure maker to bring up some Boys I sho^d. like to ingage in that branch. Suppose you inquire at Bow, I despair of any at Derby.

The six Etruscan Vases three handled sent to you a fortnight since were those we threw &

turn'd the first at Etruria, and sho^d. be finish'd
as high as you please, but not sold, they being
first fruits of Etruria.

Has Mr. Cox taken a drawing of the Seve
Vases at Morgans? I think them composed
in a very Masterly stile, & as well put on.
One or two of the forms were poor, the rest I
thought good, that like L^d. Marches not so fine
as his L^d.ships. I sho^d. like much to have
drawings of those Seve Vases, many of the
parts are excellent, & the *whole* has often a very
fine & pleasing effect, though after all I must
confess that the colour^s. has a great share in
their merit.

Must we make pebble Teaware?—When you
send the drawings for S^r. Geo. Young, & I can
make a little time to attend to the forms we
will see what can be done, but I could sooner
make £100 worth of any ware in the common
course that is going than this one sett. It is
this sort of *time loseing* with *Uniques* which
keeps ingenious Artists who are connected
with Great Men of Taste, poor & wo^d. make us
so too if we did too much in that way.

I am glad you go on so currently at Chelsea,
& hope you will soon be settled there to your
satisfaction, pray push them all you can to find
money for the alterations, & take the new
buildings too if practicable.

They must be unreasonable mortals who
want a larger soup ladle than our largest. But
peradventure it may be intended for the Patagonian trade. We are making the Vases
lighter, but our composition is much more
metallic & heavy than the Etruscan earth.

ETRURIA, *1ˢᵗ Decʳ., 1769.*

I have two good letters to thank my dear
friend for, & first of the first with the Portrait
of Mr. Grubb, an excellent likeness, so just that
I see him squeeseing & straining his Phyz
before me, just as he sat for you when you took
the sketch. I hope he was easier when he left
you with the Cash in his pocket. Much good
may it do him, I do not think the Patent dear,
& we must now endeavour to make the best
use we can of it.

I am often giving my people lessons upon
the loss of Clay, & with it the loss of credit in
making heavy ware, but all will not do, I have
boᵗ. them half a doz. pair of scales, but there
seems one thing wanting still which I propose

to have soon—*A Clerk of weights & measures*, whose constant business it shall be to weigh the goods as they are get up—he will save me three times his wages in *Clay*, & ten times as much in *Credit*. The first clever fellow I can spare I shall certainly set down to this business.

I have a very small drawing of a Vase which was dug out of Herculaneum, & I think you told me S^r. W^m. Farringdon gave it to you. I do not see any beauty in it but will make somthing like it if we can manage it without too much trouble.

We find our large Ovens very inconvenient for Vases, I mean in point of time as it is near two months work to fill the bisket oven. I am therefore building a small one of a new construction which is only to hold two or three basketfull, say £100 worth or so of Vases, it is to be a very good natur'd Oven & either bisket, Gloss, or Enamel as occasion serves. We have some Medallion Vases in the Oven, & are making plenty of them which you shall have in due time, I now give myself allmost entirely to *Vasemaking* & find myself to improve in that Art & Mysterie pretty fast. Many fine things revolve daily in my pericranium, some of which I hope will escape as our hands & other matters approach to greater maturity.

I have set two hands down to Lyons,
Sphynx's & figures, & work along with them
myself, we have made a few much better than
Boot ever did as you will see (pray keep one
or two to compare with them) & shall improve
as we proceed in the business.

To Mr. Bentley.

ETRURIA, *Decr. 6, 1769.*

Sir

The complaint in Mr. Wedgwoods eyes
which he mention'd to you in London growing
worse he has consulted Mr. Bent who advises
him to use them as little as possible and not
to write by Candle light at all for which reason
he knows you will excuse his not writing.

The peg leg is much wanted. Mr. & Mrs.
Wilcox set out by the Waggon on Sunday
night please to let somebody meet them at
the Inn on Satturday the less Mr. Willcox
sees beside his own proper business & better

for he will drink and prate with every painter
he meets. . . . .

D^r. Sir

Y^r. very Humble Ser^t.

S. WEDGWOOD.

ETRURIA, *16th Dec^r., 1769.*

I am much concerned to find so many more
blunders in Mr. Cox's Cash acco^t., & as I am
daily suffering in so tender a point, as that of
my Character for Honesty, & all through his
neglect, I cou'd not help reproving him very
severely for it, I shall send him up to Town
immediately, & before he sets out, shall tell
him that I insist on his doing nothing, but
assist in clearing up the Books 'till that is
done, & 'till this work is finished, I beg you
will not send out any more bills, unless such
as you are certain are not paid, for I had rather
hire money at fifty ℔ Ct. interest, than lie
under the suspicions, Mr. Cox's extreme
neglect has brought upon me.—It must appear
as the Gentⁿ. you mention justly observes,
that I must either be wanting in honesty or

have trusted my business to servants, who cou'd not, or wou'd not keep any books, & as you know this latter has been the case, I beg they may be told so without reserve, or any way mincing the matter though Mr. Cox shou'd be present at the time. I acquaint him with what I write to you, & I owe this piece of justice to myself. It is equitable and just, that he shou'd rather lose his Character as a book-keeper which he has deserved to do, than that I shou'd lose mine for honesty, which I have never forfeited.

ETRURIA, *28th Dec*., *1769.*

Keep making such things as these—I wish I had nothing else to do you shou'd see a great deal better very soon, indeed it has been the chief of my business since I came home, 'till within this week or ten days, but thirty hands employed in making Vases, things of which they have no idea when they are doing right, or when they are doing wrong, is alone suffi-cient employment for three of the best heads in the Kingdom to look after them. I shall do the best, but as I am obliged at present to leave them, sometimes for whole days together, many things will escape my attention 'till it is too late to remedy them, & this in every branch that is going forward from the Throwing to the Gilding, most of the faults you mention were noted by me before the Goods were sent off; but I shall nevertheless allways be glad to heare of any defficiencies, as they occure to you, as those I might know of will serve as memento, & those I did not is so much knowledge gained.

I am convinced of the Difficulty of your situation, owing chiefly to the perplexed state of accounts you are involved in, & I have my fears lest your adjournment to Chelsea will not mend the matter, you will then only be able to visit the Warehouse in the busy part of the day, when you will scarcely find time to recieve & examine their Cash & Cash acc^{ts}. which shou'd be done daily, to avoid that confusion or other bad consequences which may ensue, & there are a thousand other things which they will want to consult you about, & which that busy time of the day is Ill calculated for; if it now requires all your attention, which I know it does, when you are the whole 24 hours upon the spot, what will become of those things which you can scarcely keep streight in this time, when you have only four or five hours to regulate them in. I am perswaded you will find it necessary to Continue a bed in the house & stay now & then a night amongst them in the busiest part of the Season. I shall want Mr. Cox here early in the spring, & to stay with me the whole summer, & as he will be chiefly in the Country for the future, I apprehend it will not be convenient for him to be a Housekeeper in London. I have mentioned it to him, & he thinks as I do; he will acquaint you of the plan we have talked of, & either that or some other must be adopted in two or three months.

The plan I have ment^d. to Mr. Cox is for the serv^{ts}. to be at board wages & supposing there is four of them they may afford to give a woman her board for cooking, washing, mending &c for them, & we must pay her wages for cleaning the rooms, stairs & other things. There are some objections to this plan, & so there will be to every one, I wish we may fix upon that which has the least. I only mean to give hints & leave them to be digested by you.

I think Mr. Crofts does not use us very well & I admire in you what I fear I could not have imitated, though I believe it was right—I mean your patience with him—Not pleas'd

with our behaviour to him!—Why if he had
been a Nabob himself we could not have
behaved with more respect, & caution towards
him, & between friends I believe that is the
very thing which has spoiled him, by giving
him an air of more importance than he can
bear.—But does he think it is right in him, or
doing justice to us, to, neglect our constant
employment for the sake of a lucrative jobb?
—If he does, I wo^d. not give sixpence for him,
or his principles, let his professions be what
they will, we never have, nor ever sho^d. have
serv'd him so, & as he knows how much we
want the Vases done for this season, and the
bad consequences of neglecting Mr. Du Burks
ord^{rs}. I shall not easily forgive his deserting
us at this time, & meanly preferring a jobb to
our constant employm^t. He too will find in
the end, as such people allways do, that he is
penny wise & pound foolish. I shall be glad to
know the new proposals he makes to you. I
believe our ingaging him at the rate of £200
per Ann^m. & making a companion of him, has
turn'd his head more than his working for the
Nabobs will ever do, though we sho^d. not have
thought too much of one or the other, *if he
could have bore it.* But enough of this subject,
you will know much better what to do with
him than I can at this distance advise.

I agree with you that it is very desirable that Vases of the *same kind* sho^d. be done the *same way*, but it cannot allways be so. They are done *different ways* to hide *different defects* wch. was the case with the Candlesticks with gilt Listels, & will unavoidably be so with many other things, but you may rest assur'd we shall observe your maxim when we can.

Pray get the Companion to our Triton if possible, but not at 30 Guineas. I suppose you mean the Triton was carv'd from a work of Michael Angelo's.

My good Father is somthing better, but not out of danger, his disorder is a fever, & of a bad kind. He has kept his bed some weeks but as the fever dininishes a little I hope he will get over it. My eyes continue the same.

ETRURIA, *Wednesday Even^g.*,

[*Dec. 29, 1769*].

It is now just dark, & I am absolutely forbid to write, or read by candlelight but I cannot longer forbear thanking my dear friend

for his many kind letters & affectionate concern for my health & welfare.

Mr. Cox wo^d. write you that I was gone to
consult a D^r. Elliot abo^t. my Eyes. I met
with him at home & he told me there was
allways some danger in these cases (Mice
Volanti, I think he calls the disorder) but he
hopes he shall be able to overcome them. I
am this moment return'd from Spen Green
where I left my Wife & her bantling* both
well, my Father is still very poorly, far, the
Apothecary says from being out of danger.

I am very well in health but cannot help
thinking my eyes in a bad way, & I do not
know what to determine about building any
more though I must leave my works at
Burslem the next year.

———

SPEN GREEN, *1st Jan^y., 1770.*

I cannot begin the new year better than by
thanking my dear & worthy friend for his
affectionate solicitude for my health & wellfare with that of my friends, & assuring him

* His second son, Josiah.

X

that whatever relates to his health, ease or happiness is far from being indifferent to his friends in Staffordshire. They lament with me the necessity of your very distant situation, & cannot any more than myself be reconciled to a plan which robs us of the pleasure we had long flatter'd ourselves with the enjoyment of in your company. I often comfort myself with the thought that this necessity may be of no long duration though at present, I must confess, I do not see any probability of our wishes being gratifyed soon —*Patience & hope* are our best friends, we allways need their assistance, & therefore sho^d. make them our constant companions through every stage of our lives.

My Good Father, in whose room I write, has had some comfortable sleep tonight, & is much better for it. His fever has in a great measure left him, & I hope he is in a fair way of recovering, though we must expect it only by very slow degrees. He desires me to send his best respects & thanks to you.

I thank you my dear friend for your kind caution & inquirys about my eyes. The D^r. I apply'd [to] has made these organs his study for many years, & is the most famous in this branch of the healing Art of any man in England. He cured the Duke of Bedford who was with him several weeks, & he was just return'd from attending the Duchess of Norfolk at Bath for a complaint in her eyes much the same as mine, when I waited upon the D^r. at his house. He has cured her, & hopes he shall be able to set me to rights but says there is allways *some danger* in these cases. He has ord^d. me a Collyrium consisting of Elderflower water, Sp^t. of Wine Champorat^d.— Sug^r. of Lead & somthing else which I have forgot & with this I am to wash my eyes three times a day, & use them favourably & see him again in March, but in the meantime I must let him know the effect of his prescription. I have made use of it a week & percieve no alteration. The Atoms which appear when I look at the sky, the line or lines which are pellucid, & the little clouds continue still before my eyes when I look at the sky, or any distant object, as usual, & *sometimes* upon the paper when I am reading or writeing, but not allways. These things do not allways appear before my eyes, & never in the dusk of the evening or by Candlelight, but I can allways find them (in the daytime) by looking for them in the Air, or against a cieling, & sometimes against the floor but not allways there. They are near, or farther from the Eyes in proportion to the distance of the object I am looking

upon. When I look at the sky, or a distant
landskip they seem floating in the air at
twenty or thirty yards distance, allways
descending till I raise them again by a turn of
the eyes. If I look at a Window they are
upon the glass, & float upon the paper (when
they appear at all in that situation) when I
write or read. The little Atoms are lucid,
fill the whole compass which the eye takes in,
& are ever twinkling & in motion. But these
sorts of Atoms I have allways seen from a
Child though not in the same degree as at
present. The D^r. says that both they & the
other appearances are the same disorder.
Both my Eyes are equally affected. The *lines
& clouds* assume various forms but ever appear
like two distinct & different objects.—the lines
allways pellucid, & the clouds dark & more
opaque.

Mr. Whitehurst was at Etruria about a
fortnight since but I was at this place & did
not see him. He told Mrs. Wedgwood he wo^d.
insure my Eyes for 6d.—he had been affected
in the same way, thought he was going blind
immediately & apply'd to D^r. Darwin for
advice. The D^r. told him he was very safe—
that everybody at one time of life or other had
the same appearances before their eyes, but
everybody *did not look at them*, that he wo^d. be

well again in a little time, which he soon was, & says he has no doubt but I shall be so too.

SPEN GREEN, *Tuesday, 2ⁿᵈ Janʸ., 1770.*

I still date from this place, being confin'd here by rainy weather. My Father is not quite so well as he was yesterday, but notwithstanding these little relapses continues to mend upon the whole.

Mr. Cox I suppose will be with you before you recieve this, and I hope he will employ his time solely, as I have earnestly requested of him, in settling the accᵗˢ. that collecting may go forward without the risque of ruining my Character. I have great need of the former, but am much more solicitous about the latter, as *Cash* may be procured on some terms, but a *good name*, when lost, is scarcely redeemable. Mine has been made free with here of late on another accᵗ. A report has been pretty current that I was broke, & run away for no less a sum than Ten Thousand Pounds! This report I believe has been rais'd by Voyez, & I have sufficient ground for a prosecution, but I believe his insignificance, & worthlessness will save him. He is not worth any serious notice & yet I have half a mind to frighten the Rascal a little. It wo^d. be charity to the Country to drive him out of it, but I am aware that it wo^d. be deem'd *revenge* & *pique* rather than *justice* in me to do it. What wo^d. you advise me to do? I shall wait your advice before I take any decisive step in the affair.

ETRURIA., *6th Jan^y., 1770.*

As I have not for some time past omitted writing to my dear friend by every post I was surprised to find by your last very affect^e. letter that you rec^d. no letter from me on monday or Tuesday last. Upon inquiry I find it was not sent off in time to Newcastle which I had intrusted to Mr. Cox & begged the Man might be sent off in time, but he was not.

I thank you my dear friend for the share you take in our afflictions. I know your friendly & affectionate heart, & that you do sympathise with us most cordially, & this perswasion is not without its comfort, though the distance at which we are fixed robs us of a great deal more. I often stand in need of your advice, assistance, & consolation. The great variety, & load of business I am at present ingaged in with the near prospect of a vast increase if I pursue the plan I am already in a manner involved in, & can scarcely retreat from, without giving up business intirely & at the same time being threatned with a disorder which must totally incapacitate me from doing anything at all, & yet it is absolutely necessary that I sho^d. resolve upon, & pursue some one plan immediately—These things altogether, with some other Anxietys I have lately felt, have at times bro^t. on a temporary suppression of spirits which I am not accustomed to & which do not naturally belong to my constitution.

If I carry on my works I must build the next year. If I build I must lay in the Timber & other materials, agree with all sorts of workmen &c immediately, & perhaps may lose both my Eyes (for they are equally affected) before the building is completed. Is not this a terrible dilemma—What shall I do my Good fr^d. But who can advise what is best to be done, when the *better* or *worse*, depends upon an event which we can neither foresee nor command.—But let me turn from this dark scene, & tell you that my good Father continues to recover without much interuption & I hope will be able to come down stairs, & spare me my wife again in a short time which will be a great comfort to me for at present I am sadly forlorn indeed. I hope I shall recieve a good letter from you by tonights post which will do me much good. God bless you & preserve you from every evil Amen.

———————

SPEN GREEN, *10th Jan^y., 1770.*

I sho^d. have wrote to my dear friend on Monday but was two days, Sunday & Monday in traveling to this place, & am now weather bound, & do not know when I shall be releas'd for the Welkin is made of Glass, & the snow comes down most abundantly. . . . .

I hope to send Mr. Baumgartners orders, complete, the next week, but for the future, as we shall certainly have great choice of Vases at the Rooms I wish you could bring it so to pass with him, & he with his correspondents, that he might from time to time choose out of your stock, instead of giving particular orders, which ord^{rs}. must be given by his correspond^{ts}. from some of the first, & worst, & lowest priced things we have made, & our complying with such orders is carrying us many degrees backward (a road I hate to travel) in our manufacture. In my first essays upon Vases I had many things to learn myself & everything to teach the workmen, who had not the least idea of beauty or proportion in what they did, few, or none of our productions were what we should now deem tolerable, & the prices were fixed accordingly; but after so long practice from the best models, & drawings, such a long series of instruction as our workmen have gone through, & so very expensive an apparatus, or rather collection of apparatus's as we are now masters of, & all to enable us to get up *good things*, I think we ought not, & I am sure we cannot without great loss return back again to make such things as we first started with.

Besides, this course wo^{d}. not be doing justice to *our selves* or our *manufacture* on many accounts. The same hands who at first finish'd the serpent & other Vases with white bodys at about 3s. 6d or 4s. 6d. each were content with earning 7 or 8s per week, but they now are improv'd in their *wages*, as well as in their *workmanship*, to double that sum.—

It wo^d. prevent our improvments from being seen or known abroad, & consequently all demand which such improvments ought, & would naturally procure us; for how can any man order what he has no idea of? I observe in the ord^rs. which have come from Paris, that no regard has been had to the *price*, but to the *goodness* only of the articles sent for, & I have no doubt but they wo^d. act from the same motives if they were to have all our improvments laid before them; & I am equally certain that it would be as much for the interest of Mr. B—s correspond^ts. as it wo^d. for our satisfaction, to have the choice of the Vases left to the judgment & good taste of Mr. Baumgartner, & I hope you will be able to shew such variety soon as will give satisfaction to all parties.—Defend me from particular orders, & I can make you allmost double the qu^ty. & accompanied with much greater variety & Elegance.

Though some of the faults you mention in the Vases had been observ'd by me before, do not let that prevent your writing just what occurs to you upon them, let it be good, bad, or indifferent. It is sure to be edifying, & often what may please me better—*Flattering*, when I find myself confirm'd in the opinion I had form'd, by your concurring approbation.

Whilst I have been busied at Etruria & elsewhere, the painters at Burslem I find have had shamefull prices, & done shamefull work for it. I have turned one off & reduced another from 3s. 6d. per doz. to 2s.—& I wish you wo^d. in some way or other let Mr. & Mrs. Willcox know this, as I find they were offended at these people who were inferior hands, geting as much or more than them selves.

ETRURIA, *15th Jan^y., 1770.*

How happy sho^d. I be in spending a few weeks, or even days with my dear friend, his letters comfort, & console me greatly, but his chearfull, & enlivening comp^y. accompanyd with the visible emanations of his sympathize-ing heart wo^d. be a cordial indeed—a Cordial wch. alass I must not expect. There is a gulph betwixt us, which neither one nor the other can pass with any degree of propriety, pru-dence, or convenience. I am sensible what a wrong step it would be for you to quit the rooms at this season, & I am equally ingaged

& tyed down to this spot. The frost is now nearly left us, & we are going to set out the buildings, & I am just upon the eve of agreeing, or disagreeing with Mr. Pickford for completeing them. The prices he has given me in his estimate are much higher than I shall agree to, but he has deputed Mr. Matthews to talk with me upon the subject, we are to try what we can do tomorrow, & this afternoon I must prepare myself a little to be a match for him. I have seen Mr. Bent today at Newcastle, & told him you had sent me to consult with him upon the disorder in my eyes. He says a perpetual blister, or a caustick behind my neck he thinks is *absolutely necessary*, & he believes this wo^d. cure, or relieve them, & prevent their growing worse, but this application he told me with great earnestness & several times over he believ'd to be *absolutely necessary for my safety*. I did not greatly like the earnestness of his manner for reasons you will easily guess at, but I intend to try his prescription, though I must first consult the Doct^r. under whose care I have put myself, & of whom I have a very good opinion.

I sho^d. my dear friend, be under some uneasy apprehensions for your Eyes, if I was not perswaded the crisis was over, & the

danger past. Many I believe are attacked
with this disorder. Some are perfectly recover'd, others remain in the same way with
little variation their whole lives, whilst in
others the disorder hurries on to the last
dismal stage, a total deprivation of sight.
Yours my friend I believe, & rejoyce in it, is
of the middle kind, & there is all the reason
in the world to believe the disorder will not
proceed any farther, but I wish nevertheless
you may believe them in so much danger as
to induce you to use them *gently*. The disorder in my eyes is *recent*, & the event *uncertain*, but I am learning to acquiesce in this,
whatever may be the issue, as I wo^d. wish to
do in every other unavoidable evil. I am often
practising to *see* with my *fingers*, & think I
sho^d. make a tolerable proficient in that
science for one who begins his studys so late
in life, but shall make a wretched walker in
the dark with a single leg.

I have a thousand things to say to you if I
had time & eyes for it, but must not omit to
thank your good sister for her kind concern in
my behalf which induc'd her to consult her
worthy cousin, who I believe is perfectly right
in his opinion & I am under great obligations
to him for so freely giving his advice wch. I
shall pay a due regard to.—My best thanks are

due to Mr. & Mrs. Cooper two worthy souls on the same account. My heart overflows with gratitude to my sympathizeing friends though I am often oblig'd to be short in the expressions of it. Will you my dear friend accept of the same apology for this short, or rather no reply at all to y^r. two last good lett^{rs}. & believe me at all times most gratefully & affect^{ly}. y^r.

J. W.

_____

22^d. Jan^y., 1770.

S^r. Watkin W^{ms}. must have *anything & anyhow*, so let us know as soon as possible what we must provide. I fear I cannot wait upon S^r. Watkin at Blithfield I am so tyed down to this spot of Etruscan earth.

Thank you my Dear friend for your entertain^g. and interesting acc^t. of the debates in the House of Lords, & for a thousand other good things which I recieve by every post but alass, all the return I can make is a gratefull heart, which you have every day & allmost every hour of my life.

I left Spen Green yesterday, & this time
have brought my Wife & Child along with me.
Etruria is now begining to brighten up & look
like itself again, five long weeks of absence
have hung very heavy upon me, but her aid
was much wanted to nurse & comfort an
Aged, & worthy parent, & I was well pleased
that she was able to pay this debt of duty &
affection to him. He is now pretty well recover'd & sends his best respects & thanks to
you.

BURSLEM, *24ᵗʰ Janʸ., 1770.*

I wrote to my dear friend by Mondays post
& I fully purposed writing to Lady Cathcart
today but find it impossible for me to do it on
several acc^{ts}. . . . . I must, my dear fr^{d}. scarcely
use these eyes, or this head of mine at present
—my *life*, as well as my *sight* is at stake, for
I find this disorder with which I am afflicted
nearly as often deprives the miserable patient
of one as the other, of which we have had two
recent instances in this neighbourhood very
lately wch. have come to my knowledge, & many

more perhaps of which I am unacquainted,
for I have made no enquiry after such cases.
If the disorder is seated near the brain w^{ch}.
is often the case, Vertigoes convulsions &c
put a period to life & sight together. I only
mention these things now as a reason why I
dare not make much use of my pen.   Time—
perhaps a little time may effect a change, &
whether it be favourable to my hopes, or the
contrary, I shall endeavour after that resigna-
tion & fortitude which I know my best friends
wo^d. advise, & if possible inspire me with
through every trying occasion in life.

ETRURIA & BURSLEM, *3^d Feb., 1770.*

I thank my dear friend very cordially for his
last most kind & affec^{te}. letters which I read
over, & over again by way of cordial to my
heart when it stands most in need of support.
Your advice to make my business an amusement only is very good, & wo^d. suit me extremely well if I could but put it into practice,
but 'tis very difficult to see things going wrong
without feeling *uneasy sensations* & exerting

the *necessary* force be it *more* or *less*, of the *head* or *hands* to set them right again. I do strive to make things pass on with me as easy as possible, & hope to be makeing some progress in that very usefull Philosophy, but to keep 150 hands of various professions, & more various tempers & dispositions, in *tolerable* order is no easy task even when the mind is otherwise free & in full vigor. I long to see you my dear friend, & I must on acc^t. of the Patent be in Town in a few weeks, but how to leave these works at Etruria, & the Warehouse without any head to look after them I do not know.

Danl. does pretty well when at work, & I am here every day, but he often leaves the works, & drinks two or three days together, & has no taste to direct, at any time, & for the Warehouse I have nobody at all.

———————

ETRURIA, *10th Feb., 1770.*

The last Vases were not, some of them, what they were intended to be, & it will very often happen so in Pebble Vases, but I have

Y

often observ'd that what we have esteem'd a
great fault, has been admir'd by some as a
peculiar beauty wch. makes me easier about
such mishaps. . . .

When you have settled matters in the best
manner you can in London & Chelsea, I could
wish you to be at the Manufactory awhile to
learn the Art of Pottmaking, whilst I am able
to go through that branch with you, which I
shall do with great pleasure & hope you will
carry on to great perfection those improvments which I have been endeavouring to lay
a foundation for, & shall be happy in leaving
them with you my good & worthy friend, who
neither want ability nor spirit to pursue the
task.—May it be a pleasing & successfull one.
—Indeed I have no doubt but it will, & so
long as my eyes & health will permit I shall
gladly assist you in it. Do not think by
what I have wrote that my eyes are worse,
but I am sensible of my danger, & the last
attack may be sudden & not give me an opportunity of communicateing many things which
I wo^d. not have to die with me. I know how
ill you can be spared from the rooms, but I
think it will be better to suffer a little incon-
venience for the present than leave you
immers'd in a business, & not master of the
principal parts of it.

Will Bourn got to London! I need not tell
you by this time that he is a chip-i'th'-porridge
Animal, will neither do much good, or harm in
any situation, he took French leave of us
because pounding plaister blister'd his hands
which is all the Character I can give you of
him, my Workmen call'd him Miss Nancy.

If it is bearable to keep in with Mr. Crofts
we had better do it, he may give us more
trouble in our Patent than anybody else.

I wish you every good thing in y^r. new
habitation & am most affectionately yours,

J. W.

ETRURIA, *18th April, 1770.*

I wrote a few lines to you from Leicester &
Loughbro' which I hope you rec^d. That
Evening I got to Ashbourne, & dined here
yesterday. I found all friends well, Mr. &
Mrs. Willet have dined with us today, we
drank your health & our friends in London.
Mrs. Willet is very well & looks as if nursing

her younge Patagonian was not very preju-
dicial to her health. They are just gone back,
making but a short visit least her younge
Gentleman sho⁴. miss his Mamma.

We have another Ovenfull of Vases for
bisketing which we shall set in the oven
tomorrow. I apprehend we shall make many
more than you can sell in any one place, that
some other additional mode of sale must be
thought of or our dead stock will soon grow
enormous.

I was not surpris'd at learning by Mr. Cox's
note that one of Mr. Rhodes's men wanted
to be rais'd to 24s. per week because I had
expected that consequence from an imprudence I had been guilty of, contrary to my
judgment & settled rules of acting in such cases
—I mean telling Mr. Rhodes in the hearing
of his servants how much we wanted of Enam⁴.
ware & what a number of hands he might
employ &c. My conscience smote me before I
left the room, & I expected the consequence
which has follow'd. Our treatment of the first
appearance of this disorder to which painters
are more liable I think than other men, will
have its consequences too. If we absolutely
refuse this mans demands, & turn him off, or
let him go about his business, & at the same
time instruct Mr. Rhodes to tell the rest, that

unless I can have the usefull ware enameld
upon moderate terms in London, I am determin'd to have it done in the Country where I
can have hands in plenty at 12s or 14s per
week the dissease may perhaps be stopped in
its first stage, but if his demands are at all
complyd with, it is sure to spread & infect
every soul we employ.. It is very probably a
settled plan that this man—this *best hand*—
shall make the first onset upon his new
Masters; if he succeeds, the rest, both those
we have at present & shall ingage afterwards
are sure to follow the example, & there is no
knowing where it will end. I am therefore for
parting with this man at all events, unless he
chooseth to be good, & continue upon the
terms he is at present ingaged for. I believe
I could send Mr. Rhodes two or three hands
who wo^d. soon learn to do flowers, & desire he
will let me know if he cannot meet with
enough to his mind & I will seek after some &
send them up as he can employ them. . . . . .

I wish you could take some opportunity to
call upon Checkaw & tell him, or Mr. Marr,
that I was oblig'd to leave London (my Wife
ord^d. me positively away you know) before
Monday or I wo^d. have sat to him, but it shall
be the first thing I do when I return to Town
again.

I hope to have a peaceable letter from you tonight acquainting me that every body has been very good at the release of their Patriot.* We have had great rejoycing in the Country, Ringing & roasting sheep, Drinking, Dancing, &c, but we are all very quiet again now as I hope you are.

ETRURIA, *29ᵗʰ April, 1770.*

. . . . "We are allways too much in a hurry to do anything right." Who says so? "Things done in a hurry are never done well." *Never?* That I deny as Mr. Yorick says on another occasion for, first thoughts are *often* best, & many things must be done *now* or *never*,—Dispatch is the soul of business—And—Take Time by the forelock or he will slip through your fingers—And—but I have not time for any more old proverbs or I woᵈ. string you as complete a neklace of them as ever Sancho hung round his Masters neck. It was not precipitation in *making*, but in firing the Kiln at Chelsea which blew it up.

* Wilkes was released from prison in this month.

I am told young Stringer of Knutsford is coming to Town to see the exhibitions & draw at the Acadamy. I sent him a direction to you & ventur'd to promise you wo^d. introduce him to the notice of some Painters, who might be of use to him, & hinted at your being able to put him in a way of geting some money to pay his expences in Town if he chose it. You will know I mean by painting Vases so if he sho^d. call you will know how to act with him.

ETRURIA, *4th of May, 1770.*

I thank you for two fine packets by the last post which I must reply to as briefly as possible having just rec^d. a summons from Mr. Baumgartner to meet him at Newcastle where he arriv'd this morning, & from thence by Etruria to Liverpool is our route.

I have this moment ingaged one of my hands to come to London. I have hired him for three years to have 16s per week in London & 13s when in the Country, & I purpose sending him & R. Unwin the next week. I spoke to Mr. Rhodes about Ralph being with him to which he was agreeable & I have promis'd Joseph Unwin that his son shall be there & within a few doors of you.

Mr. Baumgartner is here now (Saturday morning) & he proposes sending four or five boxes of Vases to Italy for his Bro^r. to dispose of & take orders by. He is fully perswaded there may be a qu^{ty}. sold there, especially the painted Etruscans. He will look out the boxes of patterns with you in London.

As I am going to Liverpool I will talk with Mr. Boardman about settling a Correspondence with a good Jewelers shop or two in Dublin, & I think we sho^d. have another in Bath wch. with a City Correspond^t. may perhaps take off as many Vases &c as we can make.

I think the Windsor brick will make a more durable Kiln than composition, but experience only must determine that point. I hope you will have a kiln of some sort up soon that we may drive away like Jehu the son of somebody.

—" Bronze Terrines "—Take the covers off, I think they Terrineify the Vase & spoil it. Do not call them nor the others done here *Bronze*. They will give *bad* ideas of a *good* thing.

You will certainly do right in bringing the painting to piece work but it will require a good deal of knowledge & attention in fixing the price or the hands will all be ruin'd, by geting *too much* in a *little time*. I mean cheifly, flower painters. The fine figure Painters are another ordʳ. of beings, & I suppose must be by piece work, that being as you observe the likelyest way to satisfy them.

The crack'd Vases must be stopped after they are enameld. We have very few crack'd now to what we used to have. We have drawn a bisket oven this morning & scarcely a bad vase in it. We shall send you some Green Porphiry Vases, Gilt, but I hope to make some *true Porphiry*, ungilt Vases soon, if you dare risque their spoiling the sale of your stock on hand.

You certainly judge very right when you
say we must have a 2nd & a 3d. sort of painting, permit me to carry this idea yet farther &
to believe that the bulk of our Vases must be in
that stile or we shall never have very many
done. I woᵈ. have what quᵗʸ. I could get done
in the best manner, to please the nicest eye, &
shew what we can do; but at the same time
I woᵈ. get all I could done in such a manner
as Mrs. Willcox, a Japaner, Coach, Fan, or
Waiter Painter could do them, & I think I
may venture to assert that if all your present
stock of plain vases were done in that way they
woᵈ. be sold in a few days, & more money got
in the same time by these common paintings,
than by the very fine ones, & *no credit lost* to
us, as we shall have *very fine ones* for *very fine
Folks*, & they must fetch a *very fine price* as
they will allways be raritys, few hands, who
will paint potts, being to be had to do them.

What is become of your scheme for taking
in Girls to paint? Have you spoke to Mrs.
Wright? Mr. Coward too said he could tell
you of some Fan Painters.—You observe very
justly that few hands can be got to paint
flowers in the style we want them. I may add,
nor in any other work we do—*We must make*

them. There is no other way. We have stepped forw^d. beyond the other Manufactures & we must be content to train up hands to suit our purpose. Where amongst our Potters could I get a complete Vase maker? Nay I could not get a hand through the whole Pottery to make a Table plate without training them up for that purpose, & you must be content to train up such Painters as offer to you & not turn them adrift because they cannot immediately form their hands to our new stile, which if we consider what they have been doing all this while we ought not to expect from them.

J. Bakewell sets out by tomorrows coach & promises to be a very despatchfull hand.

ETRURIA, *23rd May, 1770.*

The Man I mention'd to you from Derby will do us no good. He told the Man he work'd along with that he wo^d. stay abo^t. a month here, wo^d. then go to Liverpool which wo^d. complete his Tour over all the works in England, & he wo^d. then embark for America.

He has been drinking three days & I have ord^d. him off that he may proceed upon his intended Tour without farther loss of time, so you will hear no more of him.

I observe what you say about the care of the Cash, & have not the least doubt of the integrity of the two you mention. But you know the Cash is a *weighty matter*, it is the Ultimatum of all our labours, & unless either you or I know that the acc^t. is kept right we sho^d. never be easy about it. At the same time I wish you to make your burden as light as may be, & you will know much better how to adjust these two matters than I can at this distance advise you.

So you have had your visions of late, well, I hope you will communicate them when you have time & paper. I have a *waking notion* haunts me very much of late which is the begining a regular drawing & modeling school to train up artists for ourselves. I wo^d. pick up some likely Boys of about 12 years old & take them apprentice 'till they are twenty or twenty one & set them to drawing & when they had made some tolerable proficiency they sho^d. practice with outlines of figures upon Vases which I wo^d. send you to be fill'd up. We could make out lines which wo^d. bear carriage & these might tend to facilitate your doing a quantity of the Patent Vases, & when you wanted any hands we could draft them out of this school. "The Paintings upon these Vases from W & B school"—so it may be s^d. 1000 years hence. Adieu.

I condole with you for the return of your Elephant, & will send you no more such cumbrous Animals 'till you have sold what you have, for as the Lady s^d. I fear we made a *Bull* when we first made an *Elephant*.

ETRURIA, *31 May, 1770.*

I rec^d. your favour of 26th & sho^d. have wrote to you yesterday but it was Saint Amputation day, & my friends came upon me before I could sit down for that purpose, & now I have scarcely three minutes to spare.

I do not know your objections to the Painters working over hours. As you want painting I sho^d. think the more hours they work the better, but I do not know your reasons to the Contrary, so cannot tell that I am right. I only judge from what I do in the like case with my Potters.

I am glad you like the dark Pebbles as I have made a good many of them. Sally said they wo^d. do, & that made me venture to do more of them than I otherwise sho^d. have done. Farewell for a week—I believe you will say *amen*. Oh! that you wo^d. but mark out a place for your seal *as I do*.

ETRURIA, *19th June, 1770.*

With respect to our business answering I have not the least doubt of it, nor do I think you will, now your good sister is recovering; I could *feel* the impression her illness made upon your spirits very sensibly by sundry expressions in your last letters, however there is nothing like demonstration, & if you will let us have the accounts up to the end of Augt. next we will then see what we have done with certainty.

I have form'd a little plan to treat myself with a sort of pleasure journey to London to have a peep at the Russian service, & your enamel work at Chelsea & sho^d. be glad to know when you think I sho^d. set out for that purpose, but before I leave Mr. Cox sho^d. be here, & that about a week before I set out, for I have nobody that I can rely much upon for their steadiness in the Vase work for Danl. will absent himself sometimes when he sho^d. not.

Did I tell you that we had inoculated Joss, he is now at the height of the disorder, the eruption is of a good sort but thick & teizes the poor fellow sadly, but hope he will now be soon well over with it. Jackey Willett is under the same circumstances, only much better.

PS. I am over head & ears in planing, altering, & setting out my works. Mr. Pickford & I shall not agree, I believe, but we must begin to build at all events.

ETRURIA, *2nd July, 1770.*

I have your favour of the 27th acquainting me of your having open'd another Avenue into the Russian Empire for which I return you my best thanks, & have no objection to allowing the five ℔ C^t.

My Father is here today to settle the day of our departure, & I think of going by Soho to order the branches, as I can then see what patterns they have & shall take a Triton, & Vase or two along with me.

I think with you that the answer to my Lady Mayoress may have its consequences, & that no *written answer* will have a proper effect; if you wo^d. be so good to wait upon her Ladyship that is the best possible way of negotiateing this business. You know everything about the white ware *as how that* I have given over the thoughts of making any other color but Queens ware. The white ware wo^d. be a great deal dearer, & I apprehend not much better liked, & the Queens ware whilst it continues to sell is quite as much business as I can manage.

After thanking my Dear Friend for his last
good letter with the drawings &c, & assuring
him that a moment shall not be lost in executing the fair Ladys commands, in the most
pretty, odd, new, quere, whimsical, Vase-like
manner possible, I cannot help telling him
how much I admire his Gallantry—Ovid himself, after a visit to his most favourite Mistress,
could not have infus'd more spirit & vivacity,
into so plain a subject, as the order^g. a few
Potts, than my Good friend has done on the
present occasion.—The Lovely Countess can
elevate him many degrees above the stupid,
common, & vulgar forms of business : quicken
the circulation of his animal spirits, & make
his pen flow like a feather dipp'd in Oyl, or
rather, like his own river Dove, after an April
shower.

After such delicious treats as these, what
can we furnish you with in the Country that
will not be insipid or disgusting. It is true
we had a Mrs. Boverie here the last week.
Do you know the celebrated Mrs. Boverie, she
is truly Elegant, beautifull, & affable, in short
she is a Gem of the true Antique character.
But she is gone ! & may not return again this
summer.—Your Ladys are as kind as beauti-

full, & if they cannot visit y^r. apartments, send a kind summons for you to their own where I find they impart their warmest wishes to you with the utmost freedom.—Happy mortal! how do I envy you, but hush, my Wife is coming, & may look over my shoulder, so that it may be the safest way for me to descend to plain downright business with you.

In the first place then I am advis'd by Mr. Hyde of his having sent me some samples of Clay to London by Land directed as we order'd them, to be left at the Castle & Falcon Aldersgate St., & must beg the favour of you to forw^d. them hither by the first Waggon. His men dug 16 Grafts deeper (8 inches to the Graft) than usual when the sides of the Pitt tumbled in, but no *sand*, or *blue water* appear'd.

Etruria, *30th July 1770.*

We arrived here last night after a pleasant journey, & without any cross accident in our way, my good Father very happy & thoroughly well pleas'd with his journey.—He joins with me in the warmest thanks to you, & your good

sister, for the cordial reception & entertainment, & all the good things we enjoy'd at your
hospitable mansion. We still drink our friends
in the four Counties, with Middlesex at the
head of them, which is likely to become a
fashionable toast at Etruria, & we flatter
ourselves with being remember'd sometimes
over an evening pipe at Chelsea.

We have a good deal of comp^y. come here
constantly & I think we sho^d. have a few more
sorts of painted Etruscans to make a shew
with, though I do not suppose we shall sell
many, yet we sho^d. nevertheless endeavour to
gratify all in our power such of our friends as
bring their company hither to see the works
from Trentham, Keel, &c, &c.—We have had
Mr. Sneyd here this morning with a Mr.
Vernon, Lady Grosvenors Brother, & have
some company or other allmost every day.

We had a S*r*. Charles Bingham from Ireland here on Tuesday last with his Lady & Daughter. They came from Namptwich hither on purpose to see the works *they had heard so much talk about in Ireland*, & immediately set off for London where you will see them in a little time. They told me the Duke of Richmond had made a present of a pair of Vases to the Duke of Leinster who was in Raptures with them, & that the D. is a Gent*n*. of the first Virtu in Ireland.— That some others had seen our Vases & there seem'd to be a violent *Vase madness* breaking out amongst them, & they were sure if we had a room in Dublin, a large quantity might be sold.—This disorder sho*d*. be cherish'd in some way or other, or our rivals may step in before us. We have many Irish friends who are both able & willing to recommend us, but they must be applyd to for that purpose. I am putting down in writing, as it occurs, everything I think likely to be of use to us, & our Agent in this expedition, & I hope you will do the same. L*d*. Bessborough you know can do a great deal for us with his friends on the other side the water by a letter of recommendation or otherwise as he

may think proper—you are to visit him soon—
the rest will occur to you. The Duke of
Richmond has many & virtu—ous friends in
Ireland. We are looking over the English
Peerage to find out *lines channels & connections*
—will you look over the Irish Peerage with
the same view—I need not tell you how
much will depend upon a *proper* & *noble*
introduction. This, with a fine assortment
of Vases & a Trusty & *adequate* Agent will
insure us success in the Conquest of our
sister Kingdom.

With respect to the sale of Vases, it is first,
& above all things *absolutely necessary* that they
sho^d. sell, & that *in quantitys*, therefore if we
cannot sell enough in London we must try
elsewhere & I cannot think of any other places
so proper as Dublin & Bath, unless we can
make an inroad into China which I think we
sho^d. endeavour to effect, but this last must be
a work of time & I think we sho^d. try the
other places in the interim. Lady Bingham
fell violently in love with one of the new Tripods, a waster, I told her we did not sell imperfect ornaments, but she said she sho^d. die
if she had not one of them & begged I wo^d. fix
a price upon it, & as she had promis'd to be a
good friend to us in Dublin I indulged her
with a waster at half price, which half price

she told S^r. Charles was *three Guineas* &
looked so at me at the same time that I could
not forbear saying as she did. This Tripod is
sent to you, where she is to recieve & pay for
it & a small bill they owe besides.

We are making 2 or 3 Rocking. Vases. They
are enormous things—a yard high, & will be
30 inches when fired. Pray for our success, for
they are perilous goods & have many chances
against them. But they are a sacrifice to
Fame, & we must not look back.

We had a Mr. Willbram of Namptwich here
yesterday who has been digging amongst the
Ruins in Italy, & was one of the Party who
spent several months in opening the Mauso-
leums & Caves the figures from which are
nearly ready for publication. I subscrib'd for
them with Doddesley some time since. Upon
seeing the painted Etruscans Mr. Willbram
asked me if they were done by the man in Vine
Street, which question surpriz'd me not a
little, but before I could answer him, he said
—no—they are not so well done. How do
you think he comes to know the man in Vine
St.? Mr. W. asked if we had got the Herculaneum, & mention'd some other books to me,
all which I told him we had, at which he
seem'd both pleas'd & rather surpris'd but as I
am often ask'd these questions & do not know

the titles of all our books I sho^d. be glad to have a Catalogue when you have so much liesure.

ETRURIA, *11th Aug^t., 1770.*

I do not know what to say about the Irish expedition, your hints are very good, but your objections to the whole plan are so powerfull that unless we find an absolute necessity to adopt it I think with you that we sho^d. let it rest at present. As to an Agent, we sho^d. be at a loss, for I durst not venture Mr. C. ; he goes on in the same way here as in London, was out all last night, for which, & his behaviour in London I have been talking to him very seriously. I told him we had a plan in which he might have been employd very advantageously to himself, but he had depriv'd himself of the oppertunity, & without a thoro' alteration in his conduct, I could never do anything for him. He own'd he had done wrong, & promis'd to mend which I shall be glad to see.

It is impossible to make the surface of the black Vases allways alike, the difference being made in the fire, a little more or a little less, a little quicker, or a little slower makes the difference. The last as you observe are the roughest we have had of a long time, oweing merely to their having a little too much & too quick a fire. But I am trying another method to render the surface smoother in general when no accidents happen in the fireing, which is to burnish them when they are pretty hard, with steel burnishers, 'till they have the polish of a mirror; but as this is done by hand, it is very tedious work, but they take an admirable polish if the fire does not destroy it, which I can acquaint you of soon, having sent one of them to Burslem to be bisketed there.

Spen Green, *20ᵗʰ Augᵗ., 1770.*

I shall take particular care of this letter as it contains some excellent instructions for our Dublin plan if we shoᵈ. ever be reduced to put it into execution, but I think we have settled to try awhile as we are, as we certainly have many good advertisers there already.

—New means of exciteing attention to our Vases."—

Wo[d]. you advertise the next season as the Silk mercers in Pell Mell do—Or deliver cards at the houses of the Nobility & Gentry, & in the City—Get leave to make a shew of his Majestys service for a month, & ornament the Desert with ornamental Ewers, flower baskets & Vases—Or have an Auction at Cobbs room of Statues, Bassreliefs, Pictures, Tripods, Candalabras, Lamps, Potpouri's, superb Ewers, Cisterns, Tablets Etruscan, Porphirys & other Articles not yet exposed to sale.—Make a great route of advertising this Auction, & at the same time mention our rooms in Newport St., & have another Auction in the full season at Bath of such things as we have now on hand, just sprinkled over with a few new articles to give them an air of novelty to any of our customers who may see them there.—Or will you trust to a new disposition of the Rooms with the new articles we shall have to put into them & a few modest puffs in the Papers from some of our friends such as I am told there has been one lately in Lloyds chronicle—or something, but I have not seen it, & do not know the particulars.—But I shall never get thro' your letters at this rate.

—Will not the people of Ireland like these things better that come from London &c "—A certain degree of difficulty in coming at fine things may excite, increase & keep up the attention to, & appetite for them; but when this difficulty extends beyond a certain point, the bulk of those who wo^d. otherwise become purchasers will content themselves without such things, & it will only be a few, who have the disorder very strong upon them who will be at the trouble of procuring them from such a distance. For if you consider how many difficultys, risques and disagreeable circumstances a Gentleman in Dublin must submit to in procuring a sett of our Vases, you'l say a very strong stimulus is necessary to carry him thro' them. He must trouble some friend in London to buy them and does not know at what expence, whether at £5 or £20 which circumstance alone, as he wo^d. not limit his friend in the price, may prevent his ordering any. Then he must unavoidably trust to the taste & choice of another Person, which I am certain you will think a very disagreeable circumstance where so much depends upon it, & after all this is submitted to, there is the risque of carriage, & of their being forfeited at the Custom House by a wrong entry as they will scarcely know how to specify them. So that upon the whole I do not think we shall sell many Vases to Ireland under these discouraging circumstances, notwithstanding all our Noble & honourable friends do for us there.

I am sorry his Excellency the R^n. Ambassador chooses rather to have plain ware for the Polish services, than Printed; we could certainly have got them ready in less time than he can have an answer from Warsaw. Could not you prevail upon his Excellency to mix some of our Pebble Vases in the Deserts. If this could be made fashionable it wo^d. open a fine market & is worth trying for every way, at home & abroad. Do you think his Majesty wo^d. set the example? This wo^d. be a finer conquest to us than all Poland, or perhaps even than China.

I am sorry Miss Cox has behaved so ungratefully, but some people I have observed recieve all favours from their friends, as if they were so many debts due to them. I wonder Mr. Cox has not wrote, but do not know how to interfere without making bad into worse. . .

The Pyramid flowerpots dress with flowers so excellently that my Wife says *they must sell* in time, when their good propertys come to be known, however we shall make no more of them 'till farther orders.

I have led a strange rambling life since

Wednesday last. I came here that Even^g.
returned to Etruria on Thursday morn^g.—
Came here again on Friday, returned to
Etruria to dinner on Saturday, yesterday I
came here again, & now we are journeying
alltogether to be, I hope, a little more settled,
when you shall hear again from your most
affect^e. friend J. W.

————————

ETRURIA, *24 Aug^t., 1770.*

"When Roman luxury increas'd, Etruscan
ware gave place to Plate: but when English
luxury seems at the height, your elegant taste
has put to flight Gold & Silver vessels, &
banished them from our Tables &c &c."
The Gent^n. to whom I am indebted for this
very polite compliment recommends the following books to our inspection.

Museum Odescalcum, sive Thesaurus Antiq.
gemmarum a Bartolo.—Rome 1750.

Maffie's, & Agostini's gemms. . . . .

This Gent^n. has presented us with Perriers
Statues, Fecoronis gemms, & Middletons
Antiquities.

We have made a Boy (Autumn) from the mould Hoskins sent us but cannot find any pedestal, or ground for it to lye upon & that sent for the infant Hercules we cannot make it fit. We are under the same difficulty with Neptune, though we have the large shell model'd for him. It sho^d. have been contriv'd like the Triton rock, to support his legs, for they will not bear him without some such support. The making of these figures out of *such moulds* as these sent us is an endless work, for they are all to be model'd over again, & our Statuaries are not qualified for such a task, but if we have the remainder of the moulds I wrote for in my last we shall make one of each sort, but I fear they will be a sacrifice to *shew* & not to proffitt. In truth I fear they will be *Bulls*.

Vases—Vases are the articles for us to get money by, if we can but sell them, & surely the world is wide enough to take 5 or £6000 per ann^m. in these articles off our hands, if they could be sufficiently made known & dispos'd in convenient situations for the purchasers.

We have begun to make the dishes for his Majestys service but we have not a cover for them. I hope you will send us either a cover, or drawing soon, but I had much rather you

could have them all planish'd for us, as we
shall have en°. to do with the other articles to
have them completed in any reasonable time.
We have finish'd one Terrine model & begun
upon another, but they are long—very long in
hand. The Terrines & Sa: bowles will take
us 6 weeks to model—the Compotiers, cover'd
dishes, salts &c as much longer; & the covers
if we model them will not be finish'd scarcely
on this side Feb^y. ! This will be a monstrous
loss of time, & everything else, & there will be
no avoiding it unless you can procure us some
help in Town; besides whilst these things are
in hand at Burslem, I am oblig'd to be so much
there that I cannot spend so much time at the
works at Etruria as I wish, & as is necessary
for me to do.

25th, Saturday morning.

We are drawing a good Kiln of Gloss this
morning, & have nearly finish'd turning 4 large
Rockingham Vases wch. will be about 31 inches
high when fired. They are fine Vases & must

fetch a very good price, or we shall add to the number of our *Bulls* in making them.

I am now going to Leek for some of his Majestys money & must bid you adieu.

Aug. 28, 1770.

What Treasure! & how many good letters, & matters, & things have I to thank my dear friend for, & but three minutes to do it in, being determin'd to catch this mornings post & not wait 'till tomorrow. And first—you acted like a Man, & a Prince with Mr. Baxter & I thank you most cordealy for it. We feel so much alike on these occasions, that you need not wait to consult me upon them. Nothing less than such *spirited*, & at the same time *polite* treatment will do with such Bashaw like Gent[n]. We rec[d]. the packet safe & p[d]. 5s 6d postage. It wo[d]. have come by the Coach & in the same time for 1s. 6d.

As I dare not write by Candlelight or rather cannot, for my Eyes will not bear it, & every moment of daylight is too little to oversee the Vasiers, Statuaries, Potters, Brickmakers, Bricklayers, Carpenters, Farmers, &c, &c; I am oblig'd to pinch a little time out of my breakfast & dinner allowance, to write a few lines to you, but I am really asham'd to see so many of your good letters before me, when I reflect how deficient I have been in making any returns for them; & yet my Conscience will not permit me to stay in the house, whilst so many things are calling for me abroad, & going absolutely wrong if I am not constantly with them. This was the reason I could only send you three lines yesterday when I had an hundred things to say to you, but I hope you will *prevent me in all my sayings* by giving me the pleasure of *saying* them face to face, so that I intend this as my last to you whilst you stay in Town, & shall just give your letters another review to see if there is anything which requires an answer before I have the pleasure of seeing you here.

With respect to making some usefull Etruscan ware at Etruria, I shall *myself* have no

sort of objection to it, but you know I have
another partnership, in which it is stipulated
that he (T. W.) shall have 1-8th share of the
proffits upon *all usefull ware*, & he has bestow'd
a great deal of attention for some time past
upon China bodys for T:pots in brown, black,
grey, &c. &c. so that though I believe he wo^d.
not deny me if I ask him to give up the black
T:pots &c to us, yet I have some fear of its
being a tender point with him. I have not
yet mention'd it to him but propose doing so
in a day or two, & shall be very happy if I can
settle this matter so as to be agreeable both to
him & you.

Stellas book is an admirable one indeed! &
the Roman Antiq^s. is a very valuable addition
to our books of Vases, many good things may
be made out of both.

Have you p^d. your visit yet to L^d. Bessboro'?
I long to be molding from his Porphiry Vase.

I am extremely glad you have got another
so good a neighbour as I am confident Mrs.
Russel, if she is at all like the Miss Sinclair I
knew, will make. I believe you may recollect
my mentioning that Lady as having had the
address to convert a *plain Person* into a most
agreeable Woman. I shall be very glad to
see Mrs. Russel when I come to Chelsea & if
you sho^d. see her before you leave that place

pray make my respectfull compliments to her, & tell her I am sorry I did not know I had a friend so near when I was at Chelsea.

We hope to remove to our other house* very soon, but we want two floor, Oyl cloaths, I think Chocolate colour, to save the floors. Will you be so good to buy them for us & have them sent down as soon as you can.

ETRURIA, *3rd Sept*r., *1770.*

My dear friend

I like your mode of painting companions to great men exceedingly, & I hope it will have a proper effect, & I need not tell you that I shall be glad to travel with my good & worthy friend & the agreeable company he mentions to the utmost regions of *Posterity.* But an Earth Potter shod. not soar too high— however *lead the way*, & I shall have too much confidence in my guide to be very inquisitive whither I am going.

With respect to the difference between *Usefull ware* & *Ornamental* I do not find any inclination in myself to be over nice in drawing

* Etruria Hall.

Etruria Hall

the line. You know I never had any idea that *Ornamental ware* sho^{d}. not be of "*some use*." You knew this from all that we have done hitherto, from the many conversations we have had upon this subject, & from the list we wrote in your commonplace book of the uses to which ornamental Vases might be put; I co^{d}. have wish'd therefore that you had not repeated this idea so often, & ask'd me if my Partnership with T: W. wo^{d}. exclude our making Stellas Ewers." Tell me my dear friend did you ask me this question for information, or were you realy as angry with me, as the question accompanied with any other idea wo^{d}. seem to import. I hope you were not, for I sho^{d}. be very unhappy to think you wo^{d}. be angry with me lightly, or that I had given you any just occasion for the warmth some parts of your letter *seem* to express. I say *seem* for I hope I am mistaken & shall rest in that hope 'till I have the pleasure of hearing from you again. But as this question has put me upon thinking a little more upon the subject, & the situation I am, or may be in, betwixt two Partnerships, it may not be amiss to enter a little deeper into it, & attempt somthing like a line in *Theorie*, though I hope we shall none of us be too rigid in our adherence to it in *practice*. And first Negatively, I do not think that *fineness*, or *richness*, or *price*, or *colour*, or *enameling*, or *bronzeing*, or *gilding* can be a criterion, for our purpose, for though we make a Table, or desert service, ever so fine, rich, or expencive, though they are every piece rich enough to adorn a Cabinet, they are, in my opinion, *usefull ware* still, & I think the same may be said of a Teapot, & on the other hand, though we make a flowerpot, Vase Candlestick &c. ever so plain, it is still in the Class of *ornamental ware* & clearly within the partnership of W. & B. only, & I sho[d]. think I did wrong in making them at Burslem on any occasion without first asking your consent. If degrees of richness, or elegance of form, were to constitute the difference in question, & consequently the making of it be transfered from Burslem to Etruria upon its improvment beyond such a pitch, this wo[d]. not only lay a foundation for frequent disputes, but must have the same effect upon my usefull works, as the King of Frances Edict has upon the Potteries in France to prevent their rival[g]. his works at Seve, for T : W. might with reason in that case say, I have such, or such an improvment to introduce into the desert, or Tea-ware, but I shall then lose the Article, or if I improve such a single article any farther it is gone ! May not usefull ware be comprehended

under this simple definition, of such vessels
as are *made use of at meals*. This appears to
me the most simple & natural line, & though
it does not take in Wash-hand basons &
bottles or Ewers, & a few such articles, they
are of little consequence, & speak plain enough
for themselves; nor woᵈ. this exclude any
superb vessels for sideboards, or vases for
deserts if they could be introduc'd, as these
articles woᵈ. be rather for *shew* than *use*.

This appears to me the plainest line, & the
least liable to objections of all others, but if
you think otherwise, & have a different one to
propose, I am perfectly open to conviction &
am so far from wishing to *limit* our undertaking, or to render it too trifleing for your attention, that I wish to extend it by every means,
& that, I can very truly assure you, as much
on account of my friend as myself. A friend
whom I esteem & love (next to the nearer ties
of nature) before all mankind, & cannot bear
the thoughts of haggling with him about
trifles. I may not continue long in business,
& my life itself is a very precarious one, &
whom have I then to leave my business to,
capable of conducting it in the manner you
know I shoᵈ. wish to have it continued, but
you two, let us therefore, my friend & Brother,
live, & act like Brothers, & friends indeed, &

not suffer any small matters to put our peace
& harmony in jeapordie. All I mean by the
above distinctions, is, to chalk out a path
that I may walk in securely, by defineing
the limits of two interests, at present seperate,
& of which my situation renders me the
connecting link, without giving offence to
either; for if my friend on one side sho^d. tell
me, in any way, that I am too partial to my
Burslem work, & my Relation, & Partner on
the other hand be discontented & think I lean
too much to the ornamental works, & am
throwing every advantageous article into
that scale—Think, my friend, you who can
feel for me, the situation I must be in. Do
you think I could bear it—no, & I am sure
you would not wish me to lead a miserable
life, continually jarring with those I wish
most to be at peace with. Next to my *Wife
& Family*, my *Partners* are those with whom I
must be at peace.

You have for some time past, or at least it
has seem'd so to me, from very many passages
in your letters, been doubtfull of our undertaking being worth the time & attention
you have bestowed upon it; & in your last
you intimate its certainly coming to nothing
upon the present plan. I should be sorry to
think so too, but own I have no apprehensions

of that sort.—Ornament is a field which not-withstanding you have bestowed one years close attention upon it, & I many, yet it appears to me that we are but just stepped or steping into it, & I am fully perswaded that the farther we proceed in it the richer crop we shall reap, both of *Fame* & *Proffit*, & I do upon the maturest deliberation give it as my firm opinion that mixing *usefull* with *ornamental wares* wo^d. *in the end, limit us both,* (in Fame & Proffit I mean) & make no doubt of your being of the same opinion too, if you have patience, & perseverance to proceed on in the same tract a little longer. But how, or in what aspect does this first years essay give either you or me any ground for repineing, or such gloomy forebodeings? If the first year of a business pays all expences, & furnishes any proffit at all, I sho^d. not call it a bad one, but if beyond this, it likewise gives a proffit of £500, or £1000 in Cash for goods *really sold* & an increase of stock in manufactur'd goods *ready for sale* of one to two thousand pounds more, surely we ought to be more than barely content, I think we have reason to rejoice, & are robbing ourselves of what is more valuable than money if we do not take the satisfaction of a prosperous, & very promising business along with us, as a cordial to support us in every hour of toil & fatigue wch. our avocations necessarily require at our hands.

I must now quit this subject 'till I have the pleasure of seeing you here which I hope will be soon suppose you made Etruria in your way to Liverpool came this way back again & then by Derby to London you wo^d. by that route see your works here twice & travel very few miles round for it. Adieu my dear friend, believe me most affect^{ly}., yours at all times

J. WEDGWOOD.

NOTE BY MR. BENTLEY.

Mr. B. rec^d. this letter a few Days before he set out for Etruria. The Difficulty was easily setled, & the Etruscan Tea Pots made by y^e. Company at Etruria. The Company very much wanted some such constant selling Article.

ETRURIA, 13th Oct^r., 1770.

I was very glad to learn by my dear friends kind letter that he was arriv'd safe amongst his friends in London, notwithstanding the perils, & dangers with which he was beset upon the road. I hope you have recover'd your fright, but indeed these Gentry will be so familiar to you soon at this rate that they will scarcely be able to put you into one.

Your stay here, short as it was, was a most agreeable treat to us, & all your friends in this part of the world, as well as myself regret the loss of your good company & often wish— but wishing is the constant hectic of you know what, so no more of it, but in its stead a quiet submission to the will of our good Lords & Ladies who will not permit you any long residence in the Country.

I expected no less than what you have wrote me respecting the invasion of our Patent & I apprehend they will persist in it to the utmost so that a tryal seems inevitable, & if so, the sooner, the better. I shall therefore now just mention what occurs to me upon the subject, & what Mr. Sparrow advises, as I have mention'd it to him.

I think we shall stand a much better chance to have it tryed in London than in the Country, & shall more easily prove the invasion of the Patent ag^t. Neale than Palmer, the first thing therefore we sho^d. do in my opinion sho^d. be to purchase a T:pot from Neale, & afterwards to leave an attested copy of the Pat^t. with him by some person who can evidenc

for us. This sho[d]. be done immediately as I
must have the Patent sent me here that I may
deliver another to Palmer. May not this affair
furnish us with a good excuse for advertiseing
away at a great rate? pray consider of this
& favour me with your thoughts upon it. And
in this advertisement could not you weave in
Count Caylus's lamentation that no Artists
had then been able to imitate the Antient
Etruscan Vases. I think you told me he had
said some such thing, & at this time such a
publication might answer more purposes than
one to us.

We have often talked of introducing these
Vases to the notice of L[d]. M[ansfiel]d which is
now more necessary than ever; & I do not see
why you might not wait upon his L[d].ship with
patterns. He could not be displeas'd with
the compliment, you know we were allways
rec[d]. very politely upon the same occasion by
other Noblemen & had their thanks for our
trouble, why therefore sho[d]. we omit doing this
where it seems the most necessary.

There is a most famous puff for Boulton &
Fothergill in the St. James's Chronicle of the
9th & for Mr. Cox likewise. How the Auther
could have the assurance to leave us out I
cannot concieve. Pray get another article in
the next paper to complete the Triumvirate.

Oct. 17, 1770.

So you will not be content with anything less than the conquest of the Hero of the Age ! Well I wish you success equal to your Ambition, which by the bye is wishing you a great deal. I like your connection with the Universal Merch^t., & long live the King of Prussia !—He sends some desert sets "—Any of the *Royal Purple ? Flora Marine—Royal Marine*—or what have you X^nd. it ?—it must have a name so do not let it go to Vienna without one.

Octr. 29, 1770.

Mr. John Holland of Mobberley was with me last night about a nephew of his, son to the late Mr. Peter Holland of Knutsford, whom he wants us to take apprentice. He says the Boy has a taste for drawing & he sho^d. like him to be a painter with us. I told Mr. Holland I wo^d. write to consult you & know if you had room. They wo^d. ingage to find him with Cloaths in his apprenticeship & we must find him the rest. If we could

order it for Mr. Stringer to instruct him in
the rudiments of drawing whilst he is at home
with his Mother for a year or so he might do
very well for us, it will doubtless be our best
method to bring up a few likely hands to
painting as we shall thereby be more independent &c &c &c.

Sukey & Jack who are at my elbow insist on
my now sending their love & thanking Mr.
Bentley for his most acceptable present & little
Jos says ta ta.

I have glazed some black Vases but do not
like them at all. You must paint & border &
honeysuckle them all over to hide the glaze or
you will never sell them.

I can say nothing to the price of the figures,
only that they will never be sold for so much
as they have cost us. You'l compare them
with other things, remembering that we made
a *Bull* when we *prised* as well as when we *made*
the Elephants. They were certainly too dear,
though I do not think they would be selling
articles at any price.

ETRURIA, *21ˢᵗ Decʳ., 1770.*

You will wonder, I dare say, notwithstanding my fascinating companion, & the many things we had to see, & perform upon the Road, that I did not reach home before yesterday, but there was no avoiding this delay, part of which indeed was oweing to the floods, the rest was fate, which you know there is no resisting. However, I have now the pleasure of thanking you by my own fireside for all the good things you bestow'd upon me at your hospitable Mansion, & I beg Miss Oates & Miss Stamford will accept my best thanks for the very friendly & polite entertainment I recᵈ. at their hands during my widowship at Chelsea.

———————

To MR. BENTLEY.

ETRURIA, *22ⁿᵈ Decʳ., 1770.*

. . . . . When Lᵈ. Shelbourne was here he told me he had recommended it strongly to our Envoy at Lisbon to endeavour to introduce

such of our manufactures at that Court as
were not there already, & to inquire what
alterations wo^d. be acceptable in such as are
now bought of us & to acquaint his Lordship
with the particulars, & he was so kind to offer
us his interest with the Envoy in favour of
our Manufacture & advis'd me to send a set of
patterns & request his advice upon them to
know if they might be alter'd any way to suit
their taste more completely. . . . The usefull
Queens-ware has long been sent thither & is
going continually upon very low terms, some
of the Houses there having a Packer here so
that I have no expectations but from *Desert
ware*, or ornaments, & in these I do not know
that it will be prudent to attempt anything
'till we know if we are to have war or peace.

———————

Sunday morning.

It is *hard*, but then it is *glorious* to conquer
so great an Empire with raw, undisciplin'd
recruits. What merit must the General have
who atchieves such wonders under such dis-
advantageous circumstances. The Glory, &

honour my friend is yours & as the desert is
to be decorated with Vases I hope it will lay
the foundation for your emolument too. To
add still to your Bays I send you two more
Recruits on Monday, Barrat, & Glover. I
believe they will learn in time, but you must
have patience with them. They walk it to
London, & I allow them 12s each besides their
wages. Barrat has 12s. say twelve shillings
per week, 4 of which is to be p^d. to his wife by
Mr. Boardman in Liverpool & the other 8 he
is to rec^{ve}. with you, the other is hired for 3
years, at — I forget what, but will let you
know in time. Please to try them at borders,
husks, & flowers, & dispose of them as you
think best. They have been practiceing here
at the latter, but they make little progress in
their improvment as we have nobody to instruct them or shew them how to manage
the colours in this new way of working.

I am glad to hear you have waited upon
her Royal Highness the Princess Dowager,
though her commands are not great at present,
'tis good to have an opening, & to be known,
the former may increace, & the latter cannot
hurt us. . . . . . .

I need not tell you that I had a most agreeable journey home. We breakfasted at Oxford
on Friday (to gain which we rode 20 miles in
the Dark on Thursday evening) & had an high
feast in looking over the Collection of Paintings & Drawings at Christ Church, I mean a
few of them for there are an immence number
of drawings! enough to take up a summers
week to *run* them over. This we had leave to
do & to offtrace any of them. I saw but few
Vases, *that I had not seen before*, but suppose
there are many more, & some I saw were new,
& very good.—The next morning we breakfasted at Woodstock looked over the fine
paintings at Blenheim with which, accompanied with my companions learned remarks
I was equally delighted & edifyed. We lay
at Warwick that evening tho' it was late before
we got there, & on Sunday we dined at Soho
where we stay'd 'till Tuesday morning & in
the evening after leaving my fellow traveler at

Wolseley bridge I was stopped all night at
Stone by the flood.—But I must now take you
back a moment to Blenheim to tell you how
exceedingly civil Mr. Turner was to us (you
know the inference we have so often drawn
upon these Phenomena) & at our coming away
he told me that his Grace on mentioning the
Cranberrys I had sent to the Duchess said
that perhaps I did not choose to make any
charge of them & order'd him (Mr. Turner) to
send me some Venison. I beg'd leave to
return my best thanks to his Grace & accepted
his favour & promis'd to let Mr. Turner know
when & where to send it. So Mr. Stewart &
I have promis'd ourselves a merry meeting
with you & some of our friends in Town over
a Hanch, but in the meantime pray see if
there is any acc^t. of these Cranberrys in the
books ag^t. his Grace & Cr. the Acc^t. by
V———n.

Mr. Boulton has promis'd to make us some
branches such as I have fixed upon, &
amongst other things shew'd me some bodys
& necks made of Porcelaine colour'd green to
be mounted in Or moleau for Tea Kitchens, but
he wished we wo^d. make him some of them in
Etruscan painted ware which I promis'd to do,
one of which Mr. Stewart has bespoke for Mrs.
Montague instead of a plated one he was to

order for her. They have 35 Chacers at work
& will have a superb shew of Vases for the
spring but believe he has not yet determin'd
upon the mode of sale. He has spoke to Mr.
Adams for Rooms at Adelphi & professes a
good deal of pleasure that we were likely to
be such near neighbours, but Mr. Stewart has
put us both off 'till he shews us a ground plan
of the houses he mention'd which is to be in a
few days, they are in the front of Adelphi,
betwixt & the Strand the very houses Mr.
Adams's want to purchace to complete their
plan. I was sorry to hear this as it may
have disagreeable consequencies betwixt Mr.
Stewart or Mr. Adams & us—But this must
be left to time & circumstances.

Mr. Stewart & I debated the matter at full
length whether it wo^d. or wo^d. not be best for
both partys that Boulton & Fothergill, &
Wedgwood & Bentley sho^d. have their shew
rooms near to each other, or if this alliance
wo^d. throw an advantage into either scale
which wo^d. have it.

We agreed that those customers who were
more fond of shew & glitter, than fine forms,
& the appearance of antiquity wo^d. buy Soho
Vases, & that all who could feel the effects of
a fine outline & had any veneration for Antiquity wo^d. be with us.—But these we were
afraid wo^d. be a minority; a third class were

therefore call'd in to our aid, compos'd of such as wo^d. *of themselves* choose shewy, rich & gaudy things, but who wo^d. be *overruled by their betters* in the choice of their ornaments as well as other matters; who wo^d. do as their *Architects*, or whoever they depended upon in matters of taste directed them; & with this reinforcement we thought Etruria stood a pretty good chance with any competitor; but when it was recollected that to all this we could add *richness & splendour* equal perhaps, if not superior to water gilding, the odds were clearly in our favour, & we decided accordingly, but left the question open to be more thoroughly discuss'd by the learned & very able Triumvirate at Chelsea whose decision we shall be glad to know in due time.

I hope the Ladys increase in their learning & will furnish you with many quotations out of their beloved Count Caylus to embelish the History of the Art of Pottery. . . . .

I am inform'd that Mr. Palmer will stand tryal with us & says that his Vases are not made in imitation of ours but from a book publish'd abroad which they have bought & this I suppose will be one of their strongest pleas against us.

I forgot to tell you that Mr. Boulton was making an immense large Tripod for Mr. Anson to finish the top of Demosthenes Lanthorn building there from Mr. Stewarts design. The Legs were cast & weigh'd about 5 C^{wt}. but they (the workmen) stagger'd at the bowl, & did not know which way to set about it. A Council of the workmen was call'd & every method of performing this wonderfull work canvass'd over. They concluded by shaking their heads, & ended where they begun. I then could hold no longer but told them very gravely they were all wrong—they had totally mistaken their Talents & their metals. Such great works should not be attempted in Copper or in Brass. They must call in some able Potter to their assistance, & the work might be completed.—Would you think it? they took me at my word & I have got a fine jobb upon my hands in consequence of a little harmless boasting.—Mr. Stewart said he knew Mr. Anson wo^d. glory in having the Arts of Soho, & Etruria united in his Trypod & that it wo^d. be a feather in our Caps which that Good Gentleman would delight in taking every opportunity to shew to our advantage. So the matter stands at present, but Mr. Boulton, Mr. Darwin & I are to dine with Mr. Anson on New-years day & shall then talk the matter over again. . . .

Adieu—y^{rs}. affectionately
J. WEDGWOOD.

(Jan. 1771.)

I have neither heard from nor wrote to my dear Friend this year, which methinks is a long silence on both sides.—Permit me to begin this letter by wishing you, & the good Ladies under your Roof many happy years, replete with every good thing your hearts can wish.—We have hitherto had a very dirty Christmass, rain, wind, frost, snow & every sort of weather in the twenty four hours : but these are matters you know little of in the Town, comparatively with us at Etruria.— Unshelter'd & Bleak as we are, not a blast, or drop of rain escapes us. But we now comfort ourselves that summer will return, & with it every rural beauty & pleasure to us poor Villagers. In the meantime you will be so good to let us know what is going forw^d. in the Great World.—How many Lords and Dukes Visit your rooms, praise your beauties, thin your shelves, & fill your purses ; & if you will take the trouble to acquaint us with the daily ravages made in your stores, we will endeavour to replenish them.

We are every day suffering more disgrace at Mr. Boltons from some of my first Vases which I made him a present of & they now stand as a specimen of our Vases compar d, as they must be by all his company, with those of Soho! I could not bear this situation, & the odious comparisons they must give rise to, & the only plausible way of removing them was to offer to replace them, which I did, with Etruscan painted ones. They have a Clock for a middle piece so they will want 2 side & 2 end ones. The room is small & the Chimney piece not large. The present Vases are the two middle size Chetwynd Vases & 2 Orfords Cream-colour, Engine lathed and gilt, such as you have now stow'd in the Garrat out of the way, & such a situation Mrs. Boulton has promis'd me for hers when we send her better.

Please direct for me near *Newcastle* & not near *Stone*.

The Cranberrys sho[d]. be distributed in time for old Xmass—to Mrs. Wright—Mrs. Noades —Mrs. Blake. I dont know who else.

———

ETRURIA, *13th Jan[y]. 1771.*

I have several good letters to thank my dear fr[d]. for, which I sho[d]. have done before now, but I have been extremely busy for a week

past in making a general review of all my
experiment pitchers, & writing to such as were
not wrote to, & have not yet completed this
tedious jobb.   As I am making new experim^ts.
with several diff^t. objects in view, I thought it
wo^d. be best to take this general review, to see
what *I had done* & I do not repent the trouble,
though it has been no little to look over 1,000
experiments, & compare them with their re-
spective registers,—with each other &c &c—
Some of my present views are—first To make
a white body, succeptible of being colour'd &
which shall polish itself in burning Bisket
To make a black body, that shall shrink little
or none in burning.   To make a black & a red
body as light as can be consistent with other
necessery qualitys.   I have made some progress
in these matters & hope to conquer the re-
main^g. difficultys—in due time   The first will
enable us to make wonderfull pebbles & other
fine things—The next to make Tablets &
figures &c without cracking, & the third to
make *real Antiques* you know.   We have fram'd
one of the Herculaneum pictures & I think it
looks very well.

ETRURIA, *21ˢᵗ Janʸ. 1771.*

We are much obliged to our good friend Mr. Shonen I beg my respectfull Compˡˢ. to him & thank you for the gratification of my curiosity in sending me the Daily Advertiser. The article is not much amiss, but I hope the good People of England will not imagine we are the Authors of these puffs, though it has (with me) so much the appearance of it, that in any other instance (besides this of ourselves) I shoᵈ. allmost venture to swear that the Manufacturer & Puffer were one & the same.

I am told this mornᵍ. that Palmer set out for London again yesterday, & has taken his head Enameler (Baker, late of Liverpool) along with him. He says the tryal comes on the 26ᵗʰ insᵗ. & is very confident of succeeding against us. Another of his intended pleas is, that our Patent is not founded upon a *new invention*, but upon an *improvment* only, & they do not fear, if this shoᵈ. fail them, of proving that our Patent will be a *detriment to trade*.

These you will percieve, are points which Mr. Neale & I have discuss'd in an *amicable manner* before, how they may stand in Court I know not. If you must have me to London to attend this tryal I hope you will give me timely notice to prepare my business here before I set out.

We are making some Sphynx Tripods with
the Pestals, & some more Greek & Roman
heads, & Lamps of various sorts, but new Articles of any kind which must be ornamental as
well as usefull move very slowly in their first
processes.—John Wood writes for drawings
of the Vases, but who must make them? we
have nobody that can draw a line. If you
woᵈ. make some for yourselves we woᵈ. thank
you, though Mr. Cox has put some such things
in our book as he can know them by, but such
articles will not pass in London; so provide
for yourselves at least, if you do not assist us.

The frost is leaving us, & will leave us a
miserably dirty Country; for our roads were
in a shocking condition before the frost, &
will now be much worse. Your Gravel defies
every change, & every thing & keeps you upon
Terra Firma let the weather be what it will,
whilst our mire & Clay—but happily my paper
is at an end & will not allow me to complain.

ETRURIA, *23ʳᵈ J.anʸ. 1771.*

Your good letter of the 21ˢᵗ requires a word or two respecting the Application from the India Compʸ. which as the subject strikes me, upon the *first thoughts* shoᵈ. not be complyd with for several reasons.

In the first place I shoᵈ. by selling single patterns give away without any adiquate compensation the result of several years study & application, & many hundred pounds expence, & in the next place it woᵈ. not only be merely giving so much away, but it woᵈ. be giving it to the greatest possible disadvantage, both National, & Personal, for which reason I woᵈ. much rather sink the Articles in the Thames, than send them to China. These are my ideas at present; but if upon knowing more of the business you think otherwise, you will oblige me by acting just in what manner you think best.

I am much oblig'd to my good friend for the honor he does me, in dubbing me Generalissimo, & though I am sensible how much his kind partiallity over rates my powers in War, yet if he thinks my assistance necessary I am allways ready to fight by his side, & he has only to command his affectᵉ. frᵈ. & hᵇˡᵉ. servᵗ.

ETRURIA, *11ᵗʰ Feb. 1771.*

I thank my Dear Friend for the good news he so frequently sends me of the visits he recieves from the great, that most People are pleas'd with what they see, & many buy. May the latter increase daily, that our stock may diminish a little, for I fear it is much too large, & nothing but a *foreign market* as you observe will ever keep it within any tolerable bound.

Do not the East India ships begin to sail, or at least take in their Loading soon. Pray try to ship some of our Vases with them & send Mr. Shonens orders away before the people are all displac'd or dead which they are going to.

––––––––––

ETRURIA, *11ᵗʰ Feb. 1771.*

I have had Mr. Pickford with me yesterday, & all day today, till this moment, & have not time now to answer your last kind favour including Mr. Antipuffado ; but could not let the post go without thanking you for sending me the paper & interesting yourself so cordially

in my behalf. I think Antipuffado a clever
sort of a fellow, & would not say any thing in
reply that should anger or prevent his writing
again, for I think he will do us more good
than any *real puffs* we could have contrived. I
am well pleased too that I am not cut up &
mangled by the hands of a dull rogue. He
shews himself too plainly (for his own credit I
mean) by being so waspish & angry in the
middle of his paper, but that is so much the
better for me. The beginning & end are in
my opinion by much the best parts but the
whole is clearly above the professors abilitys
see his own Advertisement of Ornamental
Architecture &c as a proof. But he may have
given the materials to a better hand & this
seems I think to have been the case. I should
have no objection to the Public being acquainted in *some way or other* that I have not
directly or indirectly been concerned in the
publication of these or any other paragraphs
upon the subject except the advertisements
with my name affixed. What you have
been so good as to send me would be a
proper reply, but in my present way of
thinking I would not repeat the word *puffing*. It would give me the idea of a person
pelting & fuming in repeating a *pointed* word
so often after another who had been abusing;

besides I would not methinks take such *direct notice* of any *words* or *mode of expression* made use of by Antipuffado but I have not time to consider or say much upon this subject at present, & leave the whole to my dear friend, & beg he will do & say just what he thinks proper. Mr. W. or J. W. being at a great distance from town did not hear till within this day or two that he has had the honor of being extravagantly praised & abused in the Public Papers, & as both the praise & abuse may be considered by some as different modes of pursuing the same end, he thinks it his duty publickly to disavow his having had any concern directly or indirectly in publishing either the one or the other. I dont quite like the above J. W. but put my thought into this form as the clearest way of shewing you my ideas on this point.

I think the answer should be grave, too short to be dull & as little pointed to any of Antipuffado's witticisms on particular expressions as possible.

Farewell my dear fr^d. all things shall work together for good &c

Yours affectionately

My Dear Friends kind letter convinceth me
more & more that Antipuffadoes letter is the
best puff we have had from any of our well-
wishers & I hope he will occasionally favour
us with his lucubrations.   But should not we
seem a little nettled & provoked to induce him
to take up his pen again, for if he thinks his
writing is of service to us he will certainly be
silent.   You mention his letter as a foundation for my advertising.   How wo^d. you introduce the mention of it into an Advertisement ?
& wo^d. not that be giving it too much consequence, & seem something like a bravado or
puffing in the very face of our friend Anti—
Whether the *time & circumstance* wo^d. not seem
affectedly joined together I mean.—Since I
wrote to you yesterday I have thought we
might possibly offend the Gentⁿ. who meant to
do us a friendly office by celebrateing our productions, in joining him in our reply without
any distinction with the Man who meant to
do us an injury.   This you'l please to consider
& act as you think proper.

I am very sorry to hear of the Death of Mr. Percy, & sympathize with you very sincerely on the loss of so worthy & amiable a friend. His poor widow must be in great distress, but I know you will do all in your power to comfort & assist her,—God only knows which of us may next stand in need of the like support from our surviveing friends.—

I wrote to you in my last concerning Busts. I suppose those at the Academy are less hackney'd & better in General than the Plaisters shop can furnish us with; besides it will sound better to say—This is from the Academy, taken from an Original in the Gallery of &c &c than to say, we had it from Flaxman & I suppose you must have these in moulds or not at all; so we must be content to have them as we can, & as Oliver, as a plaister figure maker, in selling the moulds, transfers his business likewise to us he must be p^d. handsomely for them. I sho^d. like to keep one hand constantly at Busts if you could dispose of them The Marquis of R [ockingham] has some divine Busts, one you may remember is actually speaking. If he wo^d. lend you some either to mold in Town or send down here. I think Mr. Olivers method is to take a mold, then prepare that mould & cast a plaister one out of it, from which he makes what *sho*^d. *be* a working mould for us, & this long process makes them come so dear. When he takes any casts from Busts for us, let us have the original mould, & that sho^d. not often be more than from 10/6 to a Guinea, & pay him well too.

How do you think, my dear Friend, it happens that I am so very *poor*, or at least, so very *needy* as I am at this present time, when it appears by the acc^{ts}. that I clear money enough by my business to do allmost anything with. The nett proffits of last year appeard by the acc^{ts}. in which I cannot find any errors to be upwards of £4000 in the Burslem works only & yet I have not money to pay my debts & unless something extra can be done in collecting, must borrow money for that purpose! Indeed I find a vast increase in stock this last year, there is upwards of £4000 in London & 12 or £1500 here & in Liverpool, which is too much by one half & must be diminished some way or other. I do not know how the sales run for this year, but observe that in Nov^r. & Decr. last they were not sufficient to pay wages, abo^t. £500 only in 7 weeks?—This seems to point out advertiseing, & if you think you can by the Purple enam^d. & other things, make an adequate shew, so that those who come in

consequence of the advertisement may not
be disappointed & charge us with *puffing* I
will certainly do it. All trifleing objections
vanish before a real necessity. The Ord.^{rs}
from Russia this spring may do great things,
but we have a very full work, & can spare
much, besides supplying the Warehouse, unless
the sales increase abundantly. I wish you
wo^d. speak to John Wood, or any of them to let
me have by every Saturdays or Mondays
post the amo^t. of the precedeing weeks sales in
two lines. I think so much may easily be
done as I do not want it so correct as to make
any entry from it, & it will give me great
satisfaction.

ETRURIA, *20th Feb. 1771.*

Thank my Dear Friend for his final decision
respecting Antipuffado. I had no objection
to a short answer, something perhaps betwixt
what we had each thought of, but as you are
of opinion, that it will be best to treat it with
silent contempt, I acquiesce, but I cannot
help observeing, that the first part of your letter

describes the situation of my mind so exactly, as well as your own, that I often think we shall spoil each other for ever acting seperately again. I feel the same irresolution steal upon me in other matters, & nothing but the distance betwixt us, & my natural aversion to writing prevents your being troubled with many a thing which only requires a moments thought and resolution to determine; for I can scarcely bring myself to think anything *finally determin'd* without haveing your opinion to guide my resolution upon it. In the case now before us, we must again try our united strength, & if matters are as our Antagonists give out, there is occasion for it all.

I hope we shall not stand in need of a Master Potter for an Evidence, it will be very expensive, & I do not know who to ask that wo^d. *come freely*, & *do us any good*. Do you think our Antagonists, & their Attorney are weak enough to give out their *real*, & *strongest arguments*, or do they mean to *throw out a Tub*. If our cause has any weak part & we do not hear of there touching upon it, we must nevertheless imagine they know all, & guard ourselves everyway, & even try all the arguments we can think of to find out any flaw which may at present be hid from ourselves, or our Attorney. But I do not care for saying too much by letter, as I do not think our Country post Offices in general are the most sacred places in the world.

ETRURIA, *23 Feb. 1771.*

I have your favour of the 21ˢᵗ enclosᵍ. a part of the mornᵍ. Chronicle, but the same paper of Anti— was in the St. James's Chronicle, & I suppose most, or all the other papers. They seem to rant, and rave, just as our Burton, & other Antagonists did in the Navigation cause & as nothing distress'd & puzzled them like our long silence in that case, so I suppose it will have the same effect in this & I hope we shall not want *Facts & Reasons* to sum up the whole at last, agreeable to our wishes, or agreeable to truth & Equity which I think is the same thing.

Our Antagonists are moving *Heaven & Earth*, or rather, if you please, endeavouring to *kick up a dust* with the Pottsellers in London, & the Pottmakers here perswading them to join one & all in their cause against us with exactly the same arguments as Anti— is possessing the minds of the Public with, & that if I succeed in this attempt, I shall next get a Patent for some new kind of usefull ware, to the destruction of the whole Manufactory! With the former class (Pottsellers) I could not expect any quarter, & how the latter may stand affected I do not know.—It is natural to suppose that the non inventors wo^d. wish to have every invention laid open for their emolument when it is once made.

Perhaps I might be able to get a declaration sign'd by some of the most sensible & disinterested Potters that the Pat^t. wo^d. not injure the Trade &c &c   But if this step is not *very necessary* I wo^d. rather be excus'd.   I have been acquainted today only with their intentions respecting the Potters at large joining them, & as they stick at nothing, true or false, there is no knowing what notions they may fill the heads of the ignorant multitude with here, for ignorant People we have some, even amongst us, both Masters & journeymen.

I have given this second paper of Antipuffs a second read^g. which it will scarcely bear. There is a great falling off & a very evident *want of matter*.

The falsehood of their Vases being better than ours might be contradicted by somebody who had seen both, without our answer^g. at all.

I should imagine that Antiquaries, Connisseurs & Artists are the only proper persons to prove that no such painting as ours has been done in Europe since the time of the Etruscans & consequently that our Patent is founded upon a real invention. Mr. Stewart,* Mr. Dalton, Dr. Chauncey, Mr. Chambers, Mr. More, Mr. White in New Gate St. or any such Gent^n. of establish'd Character wo^d. certainly be the best evidences we could have. I will speak to Mr. Stewart, & you may do as opportunity & your own prudence directs.

ETRURIA, *13th March 1771.*

I must now trouble my Dear Friend to procure me some Clay to work upon, or we must give over work *or make bad ware*, which is worse, for Mr. Hyde of Pool does not send me any & we have scarcely any left. It is *Pool Clay* I want. The price I believe is from 10 or 12 to 14/- p^r. Ton at the Wharfe, but let the price be what it will I must have it. My Clay

---

* The Architect known as " Athenian Stuart," author of "*Antiquities of Athens.*"

comes from the Island of **Purbeck**, but is nevertheless call'd *Poole Clay*. I wo^d. rather what you buy came from the same place if possible, but if that cannot be obtained, the best Poole Clay of any other sort must do.

ETRURIA, *1st April 1771.*

I went a stage farther after parting with you at Barnet, & lay at Brickhill, from thence I got to Stone about ten O'Clock the next evening 99 miles, & breakfasted with my wife at Etruria on Sunday morning. I was most thoroughly starv'd in some of their bad, open Chaise, in the morn^g. & Even^g., in consequence of which I have been either agueish, or feverish, I hardly know which since I came home, my head has been very Ill all the last night, but I am much better today & hope a good nights rest will set me to rights again.

I wrote to my Dear Friend on Monday, since then I have had two good nights sleep, am quite rid of my cold & very well in health again.

We drew a Bisket Kiln of very good Vases on Monday, nearly all black ones, with some Teapots &c. We have not fired quite so hard this time, I had order'd them to be a little easier on acc^t. of the first being crooked, & other accidents attending a hot fire, but I find nevertheless many of the feet warped, though they (the men that placed them in the oven) assure me that the Vases were set as straight as they knew how, with all the care they could take, to set them. There is a way in which I believe they may be made with *slender* & yet *straight* feet, & that is to make & fire them seperate, & afterwards fix the Vase, foot, & plinth together by a pin, screw & nut, & I believe in this way they may be made to hold water by putting a piece of leather betwixt the screwhead & the bottom of the inside of the Vase. There are objections to this method, but as we must fire our *Vases* 'till they become allmost glass, & are therefore in a very soft state in the oven, I do not know any other method of preventing our having many crooked footed ones.

ETRURIA, *8th April 1771.*

I observe what you say respecting Hutchins, & if there was no other consequence to be apprehended from raising his wages p^r. week there would not be much in it, but I apprehend that Wilcox & the other hands will follow his example if he succeeds, but of this probability you are a better judge than I am & perhaps it may be better to risque these consequences than to part with Hutchins. Wo^d. his working piece work be a better plan? At all events I think you may tell him that you have observ'd he has not got so much work out of his hands as you know him capable of doing, & that if he has more money he must do more work for it, & I imagine that that will be agreeable to him, for provided he may be suffer'd to earn more money I believe he wo^d. be content to work some over hours for it, & if so that wo^d. take away the objection I first mention'd. — Suppose, however you were to propose somthing of this sort to him as a mode of his geting more money 'till I come to Town, & when he is once got into a way of doing it I dare say he will proceed in the same track.

NEWCASTLE, *17ᵗʰ Aprˡ. 1771.*

What shall I say to this good Lady—Her
Goodness to us beggars all thanks—you will
see Mr. Jackson, & settle matters with him &
then you will have much more matter to write
to our Noble Patroness upon, than I have at
present, and there is no impropriety in you
writing, (say Wedgwood & Bentley) upon this
occasion, so I shall trust to you for this time.

I suppose after Lady Cathcarts very strong
recommendation of Mr. Porter we must send
a quᵗʸ. of goods at all events whether the
Compʸ. choose to take them *here* at their own
risque, or not, but I know we are both perfectly agreed to sell them *here* if possible
though we were to make a larger allowance on
that accᵗ.

———————

ETRURIA, *17ᵗʰ Aprˡ. 1771.*

Yes, I will come to your assistance as soon
as I can, but that time must depend upon an
event which we cannot command, it may be a
week, or it may be three or four weeks, for I
do not hear of any symptoms denoteing the

time to be immediately at hand, but I hope you will not want me much before I shall be ready to attend you.

Our fr^d. Mr. Bent, who is likewise an intimate fr^d. of Mr. Palmers, took occasion to observe to me that he was very sorry on all our acc^ts. that we were in a way of spending so much money in Law, in which sentim^t. I join'd with him, & said we did not wish it even to our Antagonists, if it could have been avoided, but he knew our situation, & I did not know how we could consistently avoid protecting our property in the way we were endeavouring to do it—He said it was very true, he sho^d. have done the same himself, which he had often told Mr. P., & that even Mr. P had said the same thing, & therefore did not owe us any *illwill* for what we were doing—but Mr. Bent said he wish'd it could be compromis'd to both our satisfactions, & observ'd that he thought Mr. Palmer wo^d. not be averse to it. I sho^d. wish to hear your *general idea* of a compromise—whether admissable at all in our situation, & if so upon what terms?

The book you mention must be the School of Arts, a small book abo^t. 100 years old, probably the first book publish'd upon the subject of Enameling in England. I have

seen this book about twenty years since, but
have totaly forgot everything relateing to the
receipts it contains, & therefore cannot say
how near they may approach to our P—t
colours—Suppose you try to get one of these
books.—The Elaboratory, the book you suppose they mean, has not been publish'd a quarter of a Cent^y. I believe—I have it somewhere
& will look at the Cont^s.

LEICESTER, *Monday noon, Apr^l. 18*

We want an anatomical figure, wch. I sho^d.
have bo^t., & I think you sho^d. send us by the
next waggon half the Vol^s. of Count Caylus &
some of y^r. other good books for Mr. Denby &
us to study after. It will encourage, & have a
good effect upon him & I hope will not be lost
upon any of us. At present these matters are
unequally divided, you have all the fine books
we are possess'd of, besides your access to the
cabinets & Librarys of our good friends, and
we who are at a distance from all these good
things of our fr^{ds}. have next to nothing of our
own to refresh & enliven our ideas of the
beautifull antique.

This Russⁿ. trade comes very oppertunely for the usefull ware, & may prevent me lower^g. the prices here, though it may perhaps be expedient to lower the price of the Tableplates to 4/- p^r. doz. in London, as our people are lowering them to 2/3 or 2/- here—Mr. Baddeley who makes the best ware perhaps of any of the Potters here, & an Ovenfull of it ℔ Diem has led the way, & the rest must follow, unless he can be prevail'd upon to raise it again, which is not at all probable, though we are to see him tomorrow, about a dozⁿ. of us, for that purpose. They (these Potters), call'd upon me yesterday to consult with me upon this dilemma, & we are to have a meeting at Newcastle tomorrow — Mr. Baddeley has reduc'd the prices of the dishes to the prices of white stone viz. 17 inches for 16^d. 16 inches @ 14^d. &c. In short the *General trade* seems to be going to ruin on the Gallop—large stocks on hand both in London & the Country, & little demand. The Potters seem sensible of their situation, & are quite in a pannick for their trade, & indeed I think with great reason, for *low prices* must beget *a low quality* in the manufacture, which will beget *contempt*, which will beget *neglect*, & *disuse*, and there is an end of the trade.

But if any one Warehouse, distinguish'd from the rest will continue to keep up the quality of the Manufacture, or improve it, that House may perhaps keep up its prices, & the *general evil* will work a *particular good* to that house, & they may continue to sell *Queens ware at the usual prices* when the rest of the trade can scarcely give it away. This seems to be all the chance we have & we must double our dilligence here to give it effect. The same Idea may be applied to Ornaments, & the crisis in which a foreign vent for our goods will be of the most singular service to us, is, whilst the General Manufacture is *degradeing*, & the particular one *improving* 'till the difference is sufficiently apparent to strike the most common purchacers; & that crisis seems to be now at hand, which I am very sorry for, but it seems to me inevitable; for I am certain the Potters cannot afford to work their goods in a Masterly manner, & sell them at the prices they now do, & they will very probably go lower still—I have been thus tedious, & particular on this subject to you, that you may be insens'd of the particular utility of joining heartily in our good Patroness's proposal at this time even though we shoᵈ. be obliged to run some considerable risque in the adventure.

I think what Mr. Weldon says respecting the

taste of the Russians is natural & may be depended upon, but then we have been told that they *have money* & will be led *in matters of taste.*

The gilt Desert ware will want some repairs before it is fit to send so long a Voyage. When the gold becomes in a loose state, so as to be easily rubb^d. off the ware, we have found bakeing over again to secure it very well, but you have neither oven, or anybody to manage it. I think you sho^d. get an oven built in the Kitchen, you have old Crates to heat & Ja^s. Bakewell could shew Nanny, soon, how to manage it for Gilt ware, or suppose I was to send you a Gilder—I have none but Women, & good natur'd ones too—They wo^d. do very well in your house perhaps, & you may if you find necessary procure a gilder in Town, who may, und^r. the direct^n. of Bakewell repair anything which you find deficient—if an Oven is of a proper heat for bakeing household bread, it is for our gilt ware.

I have many good letters & things to thank
my Dear Friend for, if I *had time*, but what
with Bricklayers, Masons, Carpenters, Joiners,
Road makers, levelers, planters, Farmers,
Potters, & Vasiers, I am like a certain Animal
betwixt some hundred bundles of hay or so.—
To say the truth, I scarcely know which way
to turn my head first, & if I sit down to write
a line, a hundred of folks are wanting me. I
sometimes reach Burslem once a week, but
cannot do that every week, & now, indeed, we
have no clay for them to work upon.

I meet Mr. Palmer at our Society & other
places frequently, & we are, or seem to be very
sociable & friendly nobody would imagine we
are over head & ears in Law together, & the
People star'd abundantly at our walking &
talking together so cordially yesterday at the
opening of a Bowling Green—A Neighbour
joind us & said what a pity it was that two
such Men (I am only repeating anothers words
remember) should be at variance & throw our
money away amongst people who did not
know anything of the cause they were to
decide, & that nobody could do it so well as
our selves if we could find in our hearts to talk
to one another upon the subject.—We look'd

at each other, I believe, very foolishly for some time & I was oblig'd to break silence at last by declareing that our suit at Law had not made any breach in my friendship for Mr. Palmer, & he declar'd to the same purpose with respect to me. I added, that I believ'd our business could not now be decided any otherways than by Law otherwise I did not believe we were either of us so fond of spending money in Law, as to do it for the sake of spending money.—Here we were reliev'd by others coming towards us, so we walked off together talking upon indifferent subjects, & went to dinner, but I rather expect the subject will some time or other be bro^t. upon the tapis at our Society.—What shall I say if it is?

_____

15th May 1771.

This is chiefly to tell stories of my Wife— Wo^d. you think my dear friend, she could have serv'd me so slippery a trick, After my waiting here so long to recieve a certain present, that she should bring it forth in my absence, when I had only turn'd my back of home for a few mom^{ts}. without thinking anything of the matter. I left her at near 8 last night, to go for an hour to our Club, quite well as usual, came home before ten, & just as I came into the house, little Tom, (for so they call him) came into the world, & a very fine lad they tell me he is, a month old at least and all are *well as can be expected.*

Now my Dear fr^d. I wait your commands, but as the injunction is not taken off & our cause cannot be bro^t. on soon do let me stay as long as ever you can for I have a great many & very important affairs in hand. The building of my works, & cannot get hands—The point^g. of my house & cannot get these men of Pickfords to do their business either decently or to stand, & there is a half a doz. of them. A Gang of sunk fence makers & levelers &c &c that nothing scarcely in the world, but this P——t business sho^d. divert me from Etruria this summer.

Dr. Darwins two sons, & Mr. & Mrs. Willets just come in.

Adieu & believe me ever y^{rs}.

I do not know whether I told you the result of our meeting of Potters at Newcastle.—They have all promis'd to be very good, keep up their prices, & we are to have a weekly meeting, & to be very sociable & harmonious together. Our first meeting is today & I have at their request drawn up a sort of preamble & a few articles to bind us together. I wish to send a copy of them for yʳ. correction if we do not sign today, but your letter & what I had wrote correspond as exactly, as if we had been consulting together upon the subject—nay some parts were literally the same. But this is nothing new, though my wife thought it a little strange.

———————

ETRURIA, *13ᵗʰ June 1771.*

Last night Mr. Palmer & I smoked our pipes together at Newcastle & discuss'd the subject of the Patent.

Mr. P said he would have given up makeing the P——t ware at first if he had been applied

to before the act^n. was commenc'd, nay more
he declar'd if I had told him of my P——t for
the Vases, & desir'd him not to make them he
would never have attempted them but he
thought himself Ill used by the commencem^t.
of the action without any previous notice,
& as he had proceeded so far he was determin'd to proceed at all events. He own'd
he had much rather compromise the matter
for several reasons—he did not like to have a
Law suit with one who had done so much
service to the trade &c &c nor did he like to
spend his money in Law at all if it could be
avoided—And if he cast us (which he was very
sure of doing) though he won the cause he
should lose the trade as he well knew that if
the P——t was laid open & the ware made
common it would be good for nothing to any
body.

His chief argument was, in substance, that
the same effect had been produced by different
means. I told him I could say nothing to so
positive an assertion, but that it was incredible
to me, that such a thing sho^d. be done, &
neither myself nor any person we had spoke to
upon the subject sho^d. have seen or heard of it
before but if we had committed such a blunder
as to take out a P——t for an invention which
was then in practice, we must abide by the

consequences. I then made the following proposals,—That the suit betwixt us sho^d. be dropp'd,—That each should pay their own costs,—That Mr. P—— sho^d. be admitted a sharer in the P——t & that it sho^d. be left to reference what he sho^d. pay for his share of the P——t & I observ'd that he might percieve by these proposals the aversion we had to being in a state of litigation with a neighbour—& how highly we valued his friendship, & indeed after this I should not wonder much if he did think our cause a weak one.

————————

ETRURIA, *15 June 1771.*

Mr. Hales is this moment come to me from Mr. Palmer to acquaint me that he wo^d. agree to my Proposal for an accommodation. I am now going to Hanley to take a bond of indemnity, or what is necessary on Mr. Neals acc^t. to insure him to decide to the treaty as agreed by us.

You know what we said upon the subject of Queens ware at the Instalation, but I think a little push farther might be still made with *due decorum,* as it is more than possible that though Mrs. Shevelinberg might not think proper to mention the affair to the K or Q herself, yet she might have no objection to our doing it, if it could be bro^t. in when we were in the Presence on another occasion.— This opportunity you will have with the Tablets, & I wish you would consult Mrs. Sh—g when you see her on Thursday with the Edged pattern about the propriety of its being mention'd to their Majestys, & likewise my desire of having the honour of being Potter to the P—— of W. And as my not being P to His M—— is given as a reason for my not serv^g. the Instalation, & there is no such honorary title at present I think it wo^d. not be amiss just to mention that circumstance to Mrs. Shev—g & hear what she says upon it.

Saturday Evening, 10ᵗʰ Augᵗ. 1771.

I should have thanked my dear friend &
thanked him again for his last good letters,
upon which I have had a most excellent feast
to-day, but just as I was sitting down to write
I saw a carriage at the works which proved
to be my worthy neighbours & friends Sʳ.
Nigel Gresleys. They looked at the works &
ware, were highly delighted with both, ordᵈ.
some vases, drank tea with us, & are just now
departed. The visit has pleased me very much
(though I could ill have spared the time) as I
have not till now seen Sʳ. Nigel & his Lady
since their misfortunes, & they have always
shewn themselves very friendly to me & were
ever ready to do me all the good offices in their
power. I have indeed had many such friends.
If I thought I deserved half of them I should
be too vain & much prouder than I am.

This Marquis is an angel, & writes like a
Cherubim & has made you a most glorious
opening into his Country, which I make no
doubt you will improve. Nothing could have
been better contriv'd than to have *such a letter*
and from *such a personage* to pass *open* through
the Merchᵗˢ. hands to us. Woᵈ. you take less
than another £1400 Commⁿ. for this?

Mr. & Mrs. Wilbraham Bootle were here a

few days since, they seem'd vastly pleased &
were very civil & polite, three or four of his
Daughters accompanied them & fine Lasses
they are. I am to dine with them next week
at Rhode & see what ornaments will be suitable for a bookcase there.

ETRURIA, *27ᵗʰ Augᵗ. 1771.*

I have read the Appendix to the last 6
months Reviews & admire some parts of it
very much particularly the Review of Passerius.
The writer seems to understand the subject
tolerably well & speaks with great precision &
very decisively of the difference betwixt *Etruscan, Encaustic & modern Enamel* painting &
speaks very honourably of W. & B. on that
subject. This woᵈ. have come very appropos
had our Tryal gone forwᵈ. & will do us *no harm*
as it is but perhaps you may have seen the
whole if not I woᵈ. wish you to give it the
reading. If I knew the Author I should like
to smoke a pipe with him though I confess I
do not wish to know who the writer is for
reasons which I do not need to point out to
you.

A late Neighbour of mine has left two
Orphans behind him who are now in London
in hopes of finding employment, but they have
not succeeded & do not know any one creature
there. They are two Boys, one about sixteen
years of age & the other fourteen. Their
Grandfather has been with me this morn[g]. &
begs so earnestly that I wo[d]. try to assist them
in some way that I could not refuse promising
him to write to you upon the subject & have
sent them your direction in London to Mr.
Ephraim Chatterley who will send them to
you that you may see how you like them.
Perhaps Mr. Rhodes may want an assistant or
Colour-grinder, & as one of them can write &
the Grandfather says is *Devilish ingenious* perhaps he might learn to edge plates, in which
case he must come apprentice for 5 or 7 years.
But the whole is left to y[r]. discretion when
you see the Lads & if you cannot employ them
or recommend them to any place I sho[d]. be
willing to bestow a few shillings upon them as
you see occasion.

I sho[d]. be glad if you wo[d]. be so good to send
my laced waistcoats down by the next waggon
desiring Nanny to paper & pack them safe.

Pray how is the weather with you? We have
had but one fair day here a long time & to day
we have rain again. I should be very sorry to

have our good friend Mr. Shonning & you here in dirty weather.—A half finished place in such weather being very uncomfortable.

MR. SPARROWS, NEWCASTLE, *2nd Sept'. 1771.*

I do not know whether you will approve of a step I have just now taken respecting our affair with Mr. Palmer. I am perswaded we shall stand as good a chance to have justice done us in London as in the Country, *by any Persons they wo*^d. *consent to have* as referees & umpire. Mr. Sparrow thinks you sh^d. get the bonds completed or have their refusal if possible before you leave London but if the whole could be done it wo^d. be better for as they now have full liberty to sell we have some reason to believe they mean to delay the conclusion as long as they can or to make a hit upon us in the choice of the third Person.

ETRURIA, *7ᵗʰ Septʳ. 1771.*

I give you joy upon your very gracious
reception with their Majesty's & hope you have
sown the seeds of a plentifull & rich harvest
which we shall reap in due time

His Majesty does us great honour in recommending the Boy he has brought up to our
service & we certainly cannot refuse anything
from His Majesty's hands, otherwise I do not
think it very desirable to have a Boy *with such
connections* in our work-shop to know the
prices of our work &c &c—you will by this
hint know my train of ideas upon the subject
but I suppose you cannot avoid takeing him in
& if so we must make the best we can of him.

Their Majestys are very good indeed! I
hope we shall not lose their favour & may
promise ourselves the greatest advantages
from such Royal Patronage & the very peculiar
attention they are pleased to bestow upon our
productions. It was a good hint you gave
them respecting their Portraits. I hope it
will work & have its proper effect, & am fully
perswaded a good deal may be done in that
way with many of Their Majesty's subjects,
but we shoᵈ. if possible do in this as we have
done in other things—begin at the *Head* first
& then proceed to the inferior members.

426

Though we have made a sort of begining in
that way here for Hackwood has been three
times at Crew by Mrs. Crews particular desire
to model the head of her son and heir. I told
her he was quite a novice in Portrait modeling,
but she wo^d. have him try his hand & I could
not refuse her.—What he will make of it I do
not know. I mentioned Bracelets rings &
seals to her, with which she seemed much
delighted, & to these I think we may add
Gemms to be set in snuff box tops, such as
the Cupid and Psyche &c. or a favourite head
& I finished some of these ready for the oven
yesterday. For snuff boxes and Bracelets, I
mean.

We have company at the works allmost
every day. On Wednesday we had S^r. George
Strickland & his Lady with her Father (a
Mr. Freeman of Schute Lodge in Wilts) &
her two Brothers. Mr. Freeman has travelled
& is a man of Taste as you will be convinced
when I tell you *that he admires our works
exceedingly* but says as our materials are so
fine & we execute so well we should to be
complete spare no expence in having the finest
things abroad model'd for us & mention'd a
Man at Rome who for a small commission
would get them done for us. He is a great
admirer of young Flaxman & has advised his

Father to send him to Rome which he has promised to do. Mr. Freeman says he knows young Flaxman is a Coxcomb, but does not think him a bit the worse for it *or the less likely to be a great Artist.*

On Thursday Lord Mount Stuart* with his Broth^r. & S^r. Alexander Gilmour did us the honour of a visit. S^r. Alexander was very lavish in his praises. L^d. M^t. Stuart on the contrary in his haughty manner said everything was dear & that he had seen enough, & when his Bro^r. & S^r. Alex^r. said our Vases exceeded the Antient ones in beauty & variety —yes says his L^d.ship *but we know that they are not Antiques, & that spoils them.*—What a sentiment! is this the son of the Brittish Mæcenas? For he deliver'd this as his real sentim^{ts}. & not as a too prevailing idea of other peoples which he feared might operate to the prejudice of modern Artists.

Yesterday a Mr. Gifford & his Lady call'd here & took a thorough view of the works & express'd great pleasure in what they saw. Mr. Gifford is a Gent^n. of very large fortune & lives near Wolverhampton. He told me he was going to build & sho^d. be a good customer for Bass reliefs both as furniture & to set in stucco. He said a great deal in praise of Mr.

* Eldest son of the Earl of Bute.

Adams as a man of Genius & invention & an excellent Architect & Mr. Freeman assured me that he knew Mr. Adams kept Modelers at Rome employed in copying Bas reliefs & other things for them & he thought a connection with them would be of great use to us.

Your sentiments respecting the impropriety of troubling Mr. H(amilton)* in our affairs especially pecuniary ones are too just, it was the only doubt I had about it. I wish it was not a money matter as I should rather have had an honourable testimony from such a Person as Mr. H in the conclusion of this business with our Antagonists than anything money can procure us. But it must not be in the way of an Umpire—that is clear as the sun—however you may I think acquaint him with our Pat^t. The Reasons for our obtaining it &c. &c. & he may perhaps be led by some delicate touches thrown out for that purpose to declare his sentiments upon the validity of the P——t & perhaps upon the utility of it too for that is no more than Majesty itself has condescended to do in our favour.

---

* Afterwards Sir Wm Hamilton : he was created Knight of the Bath, Jan. 3, 1772.

I am very happy to know the Fawn colour'd articles are agreeable to your wishes. I believe they will sell, for all who have seen them here have fall'n in love with them. I wish you had sent me an acc^t. of the prices you have fixed them at. I have sold one of the least Teapots at 4/- & the Cream bucket & Ladle @ 2/- to Mrs. Gifford & we have others ord^d. by different Persons & are prepareing more Clay for this kind of ware.

I am glad to hear that you are receiving for Mr. Shoning's adventure, & I wo^d. advise if it may yet be done to send parcels with *all* the letters he was so good to write us & for this plain reason that they cannot do *much harm* & may do *a great deal of good*,—you'l consider of it but in all your deliberations you'l be pleased to bear in mind, that as our proffits are — & we want nothing but *sale for our goods*—we may & should *adventure boldly* & this would naturally lead me to Mr. Brock's proposal, but I must first ask you whilst it is in my head whether you have done anything tow^{ds}. makeing the most of our excellent letter from Portugal? —" What would I do with it"—Why I wo^d. take it in one hand & Kent's Directory in the other & shew it to every Portuguese Merch^t.

in London & tell them that we were intro-
duceing a new manufacture at every Court in
Europe & when we have done this they wo^d.
be wanting to themselves & to the interests of
their Country if they did not *do the rest*.—You
know how to talk them over excellently upon
the subject but I hear you at this distance
crying out—where· the D—l must the time
come from.   Why here now I apprehend is a
finer opening for Mr. Brock than he could have
in being nail'd down to any one place, &
business enough too for any one man to be
continually amongst the Merch^ts. *shewing them
Patterns, bringing them to the Rooms, taking
their orders, & receiving their money.*   This is a
first thought just come into my head as I go
on writeing to you.   If you think it worth the
pains, mature it & give it existence.   I do
veryly believe that Mr. Brock would in this
way sell us five times the goods he could do in
any other, & it might be either upon a fixed
salary or a small comm^n. & upon this plan we
do not increase our Warehouses, Stock, book
keeping, cares & vexations after goods in a
strange land &c &c but the whole is still continued under our own eyes & as snugg as may
be.—A tryal an immediate tryal of this may be
made without either loss or risque.   But at all
events *retain* Mr. Brock.   For if this hasty

thought does not meet your approbation I have no doubt but we can think of something that will be of service to both Partys.

———————

ETRURIA, *11ᵗʰ Septʳ. 1771.*

I have wrote a line to you to day & sent it by a Good honest Presbyterian Parson, a Mr. Farrar of Edinburg, who married one of our Potters sisters & she has a sister who keeps the first China & Earthenware shop there & Mr. Farrar believes could sell a quᵗʸ. of our ornaments which it seems are well known amongst the Nobility & Gentry there but there are no Vases at all sold in that City at present.

After telling Mr. Farrar the necessity of keeping the ornaments in a seperate Room &c &c if we shoᵈ. supply them I have referr'd him to you & to our Rooms to see the whole manufacture & our method of disposing of them. I believe the house will be safe to deal with at least it is a shop of long standing & may be as proper for us to put them into as any can be of that Class & seems to coincide with our ideas of extending our sale to other places for the rest we must each of us consider of the proposal till you come into Staffordshire which I now hope will be soon & shall not think of another letter finding you in London unless I am advis'd of the Contrary.

ETRURIA, *Sunday, 13th Oct*. *1771.*

I hope this will find my Dear Friend & his fellow Travelers safe in Town to all & every of whom I beg you will present my best compliments with thanks to those who have done us the favour of a visit to Etruria in which Mrs. Wedgwood desires to join with me.—Mr. De Shoning I hope has found his Paroquets & all his family well. I congratulate him on the sight of his *Dear Oxford Street* once more & hope he will enjoy many happy walks from thence to the corner of Newport St. & the Change without the interruption of a single mountain or any part of the Alps to incommode his motions. I shall be glad to know you have found all well at Chelsea & Newport

Street & that you do not find anything to make you repent this short visit amongst your friends in the Country.

We slept at Ashbourn the evening we parted from you at Matlock & got home the next day to dinner & found all well there—Except that Mr. Ferguson had given two of his Lectures at Newcastle upon Mechanicks which was not so well for I should have been glad to have seen them, but to make me some amends he is to dine with me to morrow when I am to give him some lectures upon Pottmaking & hope to recieve some of his good things in return.

———————

ETRURIA, 26 *Oct*. *1771*.

Our Good Friend Mr. De Shoning's proposal is so very magnificent that it requires some time to take a very cursory view of it on every side so as to form any probable idea of the consequences of complying with it.

In the first place if they have any Earthenware manufactures of their own in Italy or

Genoa our sending such a qu^{ty}. at once & to all the Noble Familys at the same time such a Deluge of Earthenware coming upon them all at once may alarm the state & cause them to return the whole at least they must think it an odd kind of a push in Trade—but their speculations upon the Phenomenon are of no great consequence to us if we can sell the adventures & open a future trade into those Countrys.

This object is great indeed & my general idea upon it is to close heartily with it to the utmost verge of prudence or rather beyond. The rest you will be so good to manage as circumstances occur—But I think we sho^d. not sell all to Italy & neglect the other Princes in Germany & elsewhere who are waiting with so much impatience for their turns to be served with our fine things unless you think it better to send all to one place at a time that one Agent may first do the business in Italy then in Germany & so on to Spain Mexico Indostan China Nova Zemble & the L^d. knows where.

So—more great news from Russia. Very well—we will make & paint & do all we can for the spring.

I wish Lady Cathcart would put some proper and orthodox notions into the heads of

these good Russians respecting the colour of
the *real Original & Genuine Queens Porcelain*
for they are very heterodox in that respect at
present.

ETRURIA, *2ⁿᵈ Novʳ. 1771.*

Mrs. Wedgwood thanks you & Mr. De Shoning very kindly for your purchase of Green tea
which will be very acceptable   The Ladys it
seems have no objection to stretching their
Consciences a little upon such tempting occasions nay my Dame says if you had offer'd
twice as much to her she should not have
cryd out so much is she harden'd in these
matters.

Upon considering & reconsidering Mr. Shoning's Plan I think we shoᵈ. close with it to
as great an extent as we can get up the Goods
for it seems almost the only mode in which
our Goods can get into such Familys as he
will direct them to & by this means they have
them at prime cost & they will not be dear to
the Purchaser as the Merchants & shop keepers

proffits are saved to them & the qu^{ty}. sold will be so great that we may have more time to seek after other markets.

Mr. Shoning will want to shew these things to the Ambassadors but I beg you will first review & trim them *secundum artem* or this whole species of ware will be ruin'd & undone. —So you'l consider what has been said as our good Parsons say & the L^d. give you understanding in all things. Are you ready for young Holland from Knutsford? Pray let me know that I may send him to you, for I suppose he is doing nothing where he is.

ETRURIA, *6th Novr. 1771.*

The Fawn colour body must be made upon another principle to made it stand for which purpose I am now making some tryals. The present has lead in its composition (though that must not be mentioned) I must make it without. Thickness or Thinness has nothing to do with its flying. I have tryed several pieces at home & they all fly so you had better sell no more of them.

FF

I wrote to you yesterday, since which I have been favour'd with a letter from Mr. Burdett signifying that he had very much improved in his new manner of Engraving, both in *Execution & strength* & that Mr. Sadler as well as himself, believ'd it would suit my purpose to the utmost of my hopes, & that he should think himself happy if the advantages he proposed to himself by the possession of this Art would coincide with my proffit.

It will be a very capital stroke for our manufacture if L^d. Rochford can procure the liberty of Entry for our goods into France, & I am very glad you mention'd it to him, & without something of this sort can be done, I do not see how we can send any parc^{ls}. of goods thither.

I hope you may send many of your finest things away to these Princes & Nobles abroad, they will be exoticks there. If they were so here, I expect we should not keep them long.

LIVERPOOL, *Thursday Morning,*
21ˢᵗ November 1771.

Mr. Burdett & all who have seen the painted
patterns you sent me are very much struck
with their elegance & beauty. The taste in
the disposition of the flowers & the excelence
of the painting. Mr. Burdett says the sight
of these things has quite made a revolution in
his ideas of Earthen ware for he did not think
it possible that anything of the kind could
have been made to look so rich & elegant; at
the same time he is fully perswaded that he
can by his new method of ingraving produce
upon our ware, *Vases,* & *Tablets* the *full* &
complete effect of painting *in one colour* & from
what he has shown me I am convinced that he
may approach very near if not equal to it &
you will have some idea of its *capability* when
I only tell you that his ingraving is done with
a *Camel hair pencil !* by which he can produce
every tone of color from the most tender and
delicate wash to the deepest shade without a
stroke of the graver.

Here is a field opening my Friend in which
there certainly may be found some flowers
worth the trouble of gathering. A revolution
in these little matters of decoration seems to
be at hand.

We have not yet spoke to Mr. Burdet upon

the main point. In what way or how much he means to be paid for his invention. I have spoke to Mr. Sadler* upon the subject & to Mr. Green* & do not find they are either of them dispos'd to pay any premium. Mr. Sadler says that Mr. Burdet & he set out jointly in quest of this new art both equally strangers to it. The fact seems to be that Mr. Burdet has made the discovery the first of the two but how far Mr. Sadler's communicateing his experiments to Mr. Burdet may establish his claim upon Mr. Burdett for the like partici-pation in his discovery, I have not heard what he has to say upon the subject sufficiently to discover.

Friday Morning.

I find Mr. Burdett does not mean to discover his Art to us nor therefore to be paid by way of premium but as he does not like surveying & is fond of designing drawing etching &c. he means to make the most of his discovery by working at it himself. He has now 4 or 5

* Sadler & Green of Liverpool printed the designs on the cream-colour ware.

months leisure before him, however, has very little to do in that time, the greatest part of which he would employ in ingraving for us & repairing any of the plates that might want it in that time on being paid a reasonable price for his work. He then intends going to Rome to copy subject for his ingraving & so pursue this branch of business.

Mr. Sadler observ'd that unless they could depend upon having somebody always at hand ready to repair the plates it wo^d. not answer. I proposed to Mr. Burdett that he should take an Apprentice for 7 years, a Boy who could draw a little, that he should teach him to repair the plates & leave him in Liverpool to attend the press, which wo^d. leave him more at liberty & at the same time multiply the means of doing what we all mean by following any business viz. *getting money*. Mr. B was pleased with this idea & I believe will close with it.

Mr. Burdett has taught me how to edge our dishes & plates by a little machine by which they may do 6 or 8 for one & ten times as well which I think is no small discovery for us & may help us wonderfully in completing the setts for our friends the Princes & Nobles abroad, if you will please to sett one of the people who fit up tweezer cases &c. about it.

MEMORAND^M.

Mr. Burdett has done a small Landscape with the utmost delicacy & they reverse with the greatest precision & exactness therefore may be very valuable for our Encaustic pictures. For Table Ware we have two subjects under consideration. 1st Dead Game. All Country Gentlemen are Sportsmen there is scarcely anything gives them so much pleasure to look upon as dead Game, a good representation of it is the next thing, you know, you will easily conceive the rest.

Our next proposed subject is Shells & Sea weed in groups &c. These may be placed on the ware just as our flowers are at present. They will be very pretty but uninteresting— Game is not quite so. Shells & weeds have been somewhat hackney'd in prints (Ladys amusement) & printed Linnens. Dead Game but little so at least upon Cloaths or Furniture you'l see which way I lean but I sho^d. be glad of your & *your Cabinet Councils* opinion.

I wish to have one plate or dish here exactly the same as the Kings Service even though it was a broken one being often asked after it.

These Dublin & Edinburgh adventures with Mr. De Shoning—The Enameling & the Bass Reliefs about which something should be done to make them go. These are matters I own about which our personal Consultations seem next to absolutely necessary, & I will endeavour to put things in a train here for leaving them in a little while & perhaps may not trouble you with any more of my long letters 'till I have the pleasure of seeing you at Newport St.

Oneal works quick—Spilsbury slow. The consequence is that the latter has much more of the fat oyl in his colour than the former & his works sho^d. be thoroughly stoved & be made allmost red before they are put into the Kiln to be burnt. Another consequence of fat Oyl is Phlogiston*—you'l consider how that may affect the colours.

I have bought a Chemical Dictionary translated by Mr (late Captn.) Keir with which I am vastly pleased but I shall send mine to Mr. Green & beg you will buy me one half bound & Lrd. & send it as soon as possible for I wo^d. not be without it at my elbow on any account. It is a Chemical Library. I think you sho^d. buy yourself another & charge them to Company.

* The combustible element in air, according to the theory then prevalent. When Priestley discovered oxygen, he called it " dephlogisticated air."

I allways mean my Love & duty to the Ladys whether I tell you so or not in which my wife joins with her Goodman.

ETRURIA, *5th Dec'. 1771.*

I have spoke to John Wood & he is willing to go to Dublin for a few months say from the latter end of this month to the latter end of Apr'. He has only to ask his father who he believes will have no objection.

I do not know when I can come to Town but I shall want a world of money from thence soon.

NEWCASTLE, *2nd Feb'. 1772.*

I need not tell you how shockingly bad the weather has been for traveling since we parted. —Severely cold, & since the snow fell again

not a track to be seen of any road so that the
frequent meeting of those monsters, the broad-
wheel'd Waggons to turn us out of the way we
were in was really terrible, & in the uninclos'd
Roads it was more like sailing, than traveling
upon Terra Firma.

However I had set my face homewards, &
was determin'd not to be stopped by trifles.
I slept at Dunchurch the first night, & arriv'd
safe & well at this place about seven O'Clock
yesterday evening, but could not prevail upon
my Landlord to trust his Chaise to Etruria, so
here have I been locked up all night within a
mile of home, after traveling 150 miles with
the flattering idea of seeing my Wife & Children by my own fireside, to cure my fatigue &
repay me for a troublesome & hazardous
journey after a six weeks absence.

ETRURIA, *17ᵗʰ Feb. 1772.*

I wrote a line to you advising you of Mr.
Burdetts coming to Town & inclosed a specimen of his new ingraving, which I wish you
may be able to apply ; but great caution should
be taken that the idea of *printing* does not get

abroad, as that may do us more harm than the printing itself can ever benefit us. For if our customers once concieve that we can print the figures upon our Vases, they will not know where to draw the line betwixt *printing* & *painting* & may take it into their heads that we apply the former to everything. I endeavoured to make Mr. Burdett sensible of this danger & he has promis'd to say nothing.

Mr. Christy told me the Barrel Organ was to be sold the 10th Ins^t. but as you suspect that all is not right with that machine I am in no such haste as to wish you should risque the buying an imperfect one, & I would not give you any farther trouble about this trifle, knowing how precious a thing *time* is with you, but that I think you will have a better opportunity whilst Mr. Burdett is in Town, than may offer of some time again. He is an excellent judge of musick, of the *Tone* & other qualitys of an instrument, & if you will be so good to tell him what is expected from the machine—that it is to put, or keep us in *good humour*, & to make us laugh, sing, & dance—& tell him too that Joss sends him a nod, Jack a scrape, & Sue a Curtsey, he will perhaps be so good to take the commission off your hands, or at least assist you in it; but after all, if nothing clever offers to your wishes in that way, I am in no violent haste, & can wait patiently another opportunity.

Those brown T.pots had *lead* in their composition which material must be omitted, & we must endeav^r. to find out somthing else to make the body close.

ETRURIA, *March 1772.*

I am glad you have changed the name of our large Bacchante to Cassandra, I like it much better & hope it will sell, now it is regenerated.

Mr. Mather tells me in a L^r. I have rec^d. this morn^g. that the Turkey Captn. sails in a week or 10 days, & will in that time come with Mr. Foley to look at some things to take with him. I am now makeing models &c from these drawings & Mr. F—s instructions for that Trade, but it will be some months before a proper assortm^t. can be made, enameld &c & I wish you wo^d. say so much to Mr. Foley, & to the Captn. if you think it will not prevent his takeing specimens of what we have now by us. —Or perhaps he had better not to take anything 'till we can send a *proper* & *strikeing* assortment to produce a due sense of their beauty & importance upon the minds of the Infidels.

I am endeavouring to make some Lamps more usefull & less intricate than those we have hitherto made. For this & other purposes I have found it necessary to spend a great part of my time in these Work-shops, & particularly in the Lathe Room where I am now writeing at such intervals as James can spare me.

If Mr. Burdett is still in Town I beg you will pay my respects to him, & if you think it proper to tell him that I am far from wishing him to be a sufferer on my account & am very willing to pay him for the sketches of Dead Game.

When I talked with him upon the subject he seem'd pleas'd at the idea of exerciseing his talents with his new art upon subjects so much superior to the Dead Game & Cream colour, as Gemms & pictures wo^d. be, & did not seem at all uneasy exchanging one for the other but by what you now mention, he seems to think & speak of it as a branch of business dropped by us, & lost by him without his having anything else in its stead which I suppose will not be the case, & is therefore a wrong point of view for him to see it in.

With respect to our purchasing the secret,

I think that wo^d. not be a good plan for us—
We rather stand in need of the *execution* than
the *secret*. Indeed I do not think there is
so much mystery in it but that numbers will
soon be in possession of it without paying any
purchace money. Different modes & degrees
of Corrosion are the whole—the lights are
scraped in, as in Metzotinto's, which I apprehend to be $\frac{3}{4}$ of the work, & in this
scrapeing which perhaps others have not attempted, thinking to finish all by corrosion,
the superior excellence of Mr. B——s execution
seems to me to consist; in proof of this idea
I now inclose you a copy from his plate before
he had scraped in the lights, which he left
with me, & told me it was in that state, & that
the lights & softening were produced by
scrapeing.

There may be no harm in knowing what
value he sets upon the secret & then we can
consider what is best to be done but I apprehend it wo^d. be the same thing to our selling
the secret of Throwing, Turning, or handling,
which after all the instructions we could give
the purchacer it wo^d. require several years
actual practice before he could do anything to
the purpose.

The Organ arrived safe & a most joyful
opening of it we have had. About twenty

young sprigs were made as happy as mortals could be, & danced, & lilted away, It would have done your heart good to have seen them. I wish we had your little Sprightly Neece with us, but give my love to her & tell her that when the Organ is sent to Town again which It will be soon it shall be sent to Chelsea for her amusement a week or two.

ETRURIA, *7ᵗʰ March 1772.*

Success to your visions—Dream on my Dear Friend & fear nothing. If you wake too soon, the phantoms may vanish, dissolve in air, & be no more; but with a little more brooding over, a little more fostering in the brain, they may in time be hatched into *real substantial forms*, & as substantial fame. Your idea of gilding the Etruscan borders in *water Gilding* is a very good one, if it can be executed, of which I have some doubt, as I think it is scarcely possible to gild the ornaments in that way, & leave the *ground* ungilt, but upon this subject it may be necessary to consult a workman. In the mean time I shall indeavour to prepare you some Cups. I have five different shapes in the Loom, & some of them nearly finish'd.

We have had two good letters here from Dublin, & I suppose Mr. Brock has wrote you duplicates, or nearly so, mine are from Jn°. Woods pen, who writes very well, & seems much pleas'd with the prospect before them. They seem to have settled the entry of the Vases & ornaments at the Custom House by the assistance of Mr. Berrisford upon a very good plan at last as the parc^{ls}. from London, amo^t. £185, are ch^d. only £25 upon which they pay 15 ℗ C^t.—This will do, if they can establish it as a president for the entry of future parcels. I hope you will write your friend, & acquaintance Mr. Berrisford a *very fine letter* of thanks upon the occasion.—He certainly deserves our warmest acknowledgments.

The same noble contempt for Gold reigns, I find by J. Woods letter, at Dublin as in London—They cannot bear anything Gilt beyond a picture frame, & their stomachs are a little squeamish even about the frames!—What will this world come to! Gold, the most precious of all metals is absolutely kicked out of doors, & our poor Gilders I believe must follow it.

I hope you have sent some purple edge, & deserts to Dublin, J. Wood says their visitors have nothing but purple edge in their mouths, & we must endeavour to satisfy their longings.

Mr. Swift tells me we have over drawn A & H near £600 !!! I shall be undone—I am in a fine condition to buy Estates indeed.

———

ETRURIA, *22ⁿᵈ of March 1772.*

The sun shines, & the birds sing so finely, & we have had so little tolerable weather lately, that it goes against the grain to be confin'd in a room, when every living creature ought to be in the open Air swelling the chorus of universal praise for the chearing influence of the Sun, & the prospect of a returning spring. We have had a vast deal of *hard weather* as we call it here, & I suppose you have not had much fine weather hitherto, but we have now two summers before us for one winter, & must endeavour to make the most of them.

I am glad you have taken Rooms to your likeing at Bath & hope they will answer to all the Partys concern'd. I should know what time they are intended to be open'd as it will require six weeks or two months to prepare a sortment of usefull ware here, services &c, & to get them to Bath by water.

With respect to Glazed flowerpots, I believe they are worse for plants growing in than soft bisket, or porous ones, but then the latter will not stand the frost, & the mischief of the Glaz'd ones does not I believe proceed from any pernicious quality in the Glaze, but from the roots matting to the outside of the soil, & the inside of the pot, where it is worse for them to meet with a *polish'd surface* of any sort, than with one approaching nearer to the nature of earth, say a porous, bisket body. When the plants are in this state therefore they sho^d. be shifted into larger pots, & the vacancy between the matted root & the inside of the larger pot sho^d. be filled with fresh soil, which if it was dry they wo^d. fill it up better than with moist soil, & the plant will then grow & thrive in either a glazed or unglazed pot, however we will make you some of the latter for those who will not take the necessary pains with the others.

We will likewise try to make some middle Teapots, both for Bath, Dublin, Liverpool & London, but as to *cheap Vases*, I am afraid of danger there. Would it not be better to sell our 2^{nds}, I suppose you have some in London & we can furnish you with some from the works but if you think they sho^d. be of a new

GG

colour & make, I can make plenty of new sorts whenever you please to say the word. The greatest difficulty I have ever found is to check & keep my invention under proper subordination, if I was to give it the reins, I should soon become an errant schemer in the common acceptation of that term. *Ise make you new Vases like lightning* when you think we may do it with safety.

23ᵈ of March they tell me it is.

ETRURIA, *30ᵗʰ March 1772.*

When do I bring Mrs. Wedgwood?—God knows. We had Dʳ. Derwin with her yesterday, He says he is afraid her disorder will be stubborn, they have bled her twice & are now going to blister her. She is very ill, not the least help for herself. Her wrists, Shoulders, neck, Hips, knees, Ancles, & feet are all violently affected, & she is as complete a Cripple as you can easily imagine. Dʳ. Derwin has order'd her to Buxton, to bathe there as soon as she is able, & I am nail'd down here as fast as a Rock, so that it will be impossible

for me to come & attend the W—— house
whilst you go to Bath, which I sho^d. be glad to
have done.

———

ETRURIA, *11th Apr^l. 1772.*

Mrs. Wedgwood joins with me in thanking
you very sincerely for your good wishes to
her, & I have the pleasure to tell you she is
got so much better as to take an airing on
Horsback yesterday, but we have now a rainy
morning, & she is not quite so well today,
which may be owing to the weather. The
return of the Sun, with the approaching
spring, & the aid of some one or other of our
Watering places, will, I hope, restore her to
her wonted state of health again.

We are much oblig'd to our good, & very
polite friend S^r. W^m. H [amilton] for his repeated favours. I hope we shall be able to
make a good use of his hints respecting the
Pebble Vases, by greatly reduceing, if not
totally banishing this *offensive Gilding*. For
this purpose I have for some time past been
mustering up my different colour'd bodys, &

been contriving the shapes of the Vases, &
their handles for Pebbleing ; but I do not find
it an easy matter to make a Vase with the
colouring so natural, vairied, pleasing & *un-
pot-like*, & the shape so delicate, as to make it
seem worth a great deal of money, without
the additional trappings of handles, ornaments, & Gilding.

Any kind of Teapots with the *inside Glazed*,
& the *outside unglazed* will, I fear, be apt to
fly now & then with hot water. The common
red China ones do the same. We can send
you some unglazed ones & your customers may
then have their choice.

I make no doubt of our friend Mr. Boultons
things being very excellent, both in contrivance
& execution, & wish him every encouragement
his ingenuity, spirit & industry deserve, but
Mr. Cox has so far *outshone* him that I am
afraid he will be under some little bit of an
eclipse in that respect, this season ; & I am
not without some little pain for our Nobility
& Gentry themselves, for what with the fine
things in Gold, Silver & Steel from Soho, the
almost miraculous magnificence of Mr. Coxes
Exhibition, & the Glare of the Derby & other
China shews—What heads or Eyes could stand
all this dazzleing profusion of riches & ornament if something was not provided for their

relief, to give them at proper intervals a little relaxation, & repose. Under this humble idea then, I have some hopes for our black, Etruscan, & Grecian Vases still, & as I expect the golden surfeit will rage with you higher than ever this spring, I shall almost tremble even for a gilt listel* amongst your Vases, & would advise you by all means to provide a curtain immediately for your Pebble ware shelves, which you may open or shut, inlarge or diminish the shew of gilding as you find your customers affected.—In earnest I believe a Curtain before the shelves of pebble Vases would be very proper on several accounts. It wo^d. *moderate the shew* at the first enterance— hide the Gilding from those who think it a defect, & prevent the Gold from tarnishing.

I have been thinking over the subject of *cheap Vases*, & am perswaded you may have a range of shelves for that purpose, without any injury to the sale of your—must I say *dear*, as that answers to *cheap* Vases. The furniture of these shelves may be composed of your small odd vases, of the bronze & other sorts. Of *2nd & pieced Vases* of which you have some, & we can furnish you with more, & of *ugly ones* in color or form of which we can always furnish you with a sufficient quantity. If you

* A fillet, a slightly projecting ledge.

had an assortment of these, a number of your
customers, who have more taste than money,
or want to place them at a great distance
from the Eye, or collect odd things, of *fine
forms* for their Cabinets, or those of your
Customers who are fond *in the extreme* of his
Majestys picture *in gold* & yet wo^d. wish to
have some of the fine things in vogue, in
their houses or Cabinets—These Gentry altogether make up a numerous class, & may
buy up a large qu^{ty}. of our odd, & second rate
things, which at present are a dead stock, &
not at all in the way of being sold, & are
daily accumulateing, at about half the price
of good ones, & would never buy any of our
first rates at all, but go to St. P[aul]s or other
shops for *something like them at a lower price.*

ETRURIA, *20th of Apr^l. 1772.*

We hear from Liverpool that T: Byerley is
coming over from America & expected every
fair wind at that Port.—We likewise hear
from Liverpool that our Good Friend Mr.
Bentley is just upon the verge of the Holy

Estate of Matrimony, & we rejoyce in the intelligence, knowing how happy two good People may make themselves, even in this state of things; & firmly believing that will be the lot of Mr. Bentley & the Lady of his choice, whenever they shall consent to let the union of their hands follow that of their hearts. —Under this perswasion, & remembering with gratitude the good offices I have in times of yore, & under somwhat similar circumstances recieved at the hands of my worthy friend, I cannot forbear my sincerest wishes that the Good Lady would consent to make him happy, & that they would mutually agree not to waste any more of that precious time which never can be recall'd.

ETRURIA, *9th May 1772.*

My Dear Friend will think I Joke when I tell him that I had the pleasure of drinking Tea with his friends Mr. & Mrs. Rasbottom on Wednesday last at their own house. But so it was in reality, & they send their best respects in the most friendly manner to you. To unriddle this matter you must know we

had three little Lasses to be put under the
care of Mrs. Holland in Manchester, & nobody
to take them.   Mrs. Willet is too forward in
the world to venture upon such a journey for
fear of consequences.   My Wife was not able
to take such a journey, & the Bratts wo^d. not
go contentedly without one of us three, so I
was pressed on all sides into the service, &
when I was at Manchester I thought it would
lose the least time then to go to Bolton &
look at the school intended for Jack when
there is a vacancy for him.   Indeed it did not
lose me any time as I must stay one day at
Manchester to see them a little settled, so I
took Mrs. Holland & her little son with me to
Bolton, call'd upon Mr. Rasbottom as we went
past in the morn^g. drank tea with them as
we return'd in the afternoon & brought Mr. &
Mrs. Holland with us from Bolton & made a
very agreeable day of it altogether.   Jenny &
Kitt Willet & my Daughter Suke are the
Lasses who ran away with me.   I have left
them with a very good Woman, & hope they
will be happy, & improved.

I saw Peter Hollands Bro^r. at Knutsford &
find that he & they too are dissatisfied.   He
tells them he cannot get more than 20s per
w^k. when he comes out of his time, & they
think that is not enough.   I said a good deal

to him, & told him ultimately that Peter was at liberty if they chose it.

A house in St. Martins Lane or the Acre, or about Convent Garden, with plenty of room backwards to build cheap & large skylight rooms with store rooms under them, would do better for us even than Adelphi.

I had an opportunity of thanking S^r. W^m. Bagot at Mr. Sneyds last week for voting for S^r. W^m. H^s. Antiquitys being left with us in England* which he told me he had done.

ETRURIA, *12th May 1772.*

Mrs. W. is not yet able to dress herself & in so precarious a state for traveling that she begs a few days—to the latter end of the week, & you know I am *a most indulgent Husband.* Indeed, betwixt friends, it seems to me to be the most extravagant, out of the way thing, to leave home at this time, that ever I did in my life. If you saw what confusion we are in half remov'd, the men all unsettled, both in body & mind, nothing in a finish'd, settled

* Sir William Hamilton's collection was acquired for the British Museum in 1772.

state, you would say it was the next thing to
a man leaving his house on fire. And yet I
must leave them so farewell my dear fr^d. The
good things you write me are a Cordial to
my heart, but I have not time to thank you
for them scarcely.

BATH, *6th June 1772.*

I am glad to find my Dear Friend will have
no more plague with Mr. Burdett—I suppose
it was necessary he sho^d. recieve some such
sum before he left Town, & perhaps his leaving
at all might depend upon the event.*

You are tired of living by yourself, & wish
to know when we think of returning "—Poor
Man! he counts the minutes for hours, &
thinks Old Time drawls along like a Broad
wheel'd Waggon. How many years now do
you think it is since some good Ladys departed
into Derbyshire, or can you count over the
months since we left you at Chelsea.—Be
comforted my Good Friend, the time will come,

---

* Wedgwood paid Burdett a portion of his demands, but kept
the sketches of dead game which he had painted for him : these
were afterwards returned to the artist.

however tardy he may seem; but every body tells us Mrs. W. must stay about three weeks longer. In the mean time we drink your health every night, wish you could be convey'd here some how or other to spend your even^{gs}. with us at Bath, but as that cannot be we pity your solitary condition, & hope you will take care of yourself in the best manner you can 'till we arrive at Chelsea to set you at liberty for a week that you may be made a——— Happy Man for life.

The Stone Vases here are most of them in good stile & very well executed, several are taken from Kent, & others from the large bronze ones. They make immensely large ones, ornamented in a good taste with Vines &c all over, & quite free, larger, & of better forms than our largest black ones & ask only 50s a piece for them! We could scarcely make them in Clay for so many pounds.

We met with a large assortment of Mr. Boultons Vases in a very rich shop in the Market place. The Gent^{n}. told me a long tale of Mr. Boltons having ingaged at several £1000 expence the only mine in the World of the Radix Amethyst, & that nobody else could have any of that material. I heard him patiently, but afterwards took an opportunity of advising him when we were alone in a corner of his shop, not to tell that story too often as many Gent[n]. who came to Bath had been in Derbyshire, seen the mine, & knew it to be free & open to all the world, on paying a certain known mine rent to the Land owner.

The Gent[n]. star'd, & assur'd me upon his honor that he had not said a word more than Mr. Boulton had assur'd him was true. Well done Bolton says I *inwardly*. I told the Gent[n]. Mr. Bolton might possibly have ingaged them lately as I had not been in that country since last summer—Nay says he 'tis three years since he told me this story. I was glad to change the subject, & inquir'd how they sold —but so so says he, I am afraid they will never answer Mr. Boultons end as a manufacture." He then told me he had a new shop building for him & would have shewn me the Plan, but more company coming in we parted.

We are now loseing time & *opportunity* sadly in Westgate Buildings for want of somthing to open, you had better take the men from Chelsea to pack a day or two than let us want a few crates to complete our assortment. I hope you will send us some enam[a]. Tea ware, & in short everything to make a complete shew of it, or we had better do nothing for I think the Toy, & China shops are richer &

more extravagant in their shew here than in London.

I understand that I have a Wig come from Etruria. I wish you would send that, Borlaces History of Cornwal, & the Adelphi plans by the next Coach. However pray send my Wig or I must buy a new one for this old one I have is quite shabby.

I do not quite like this situation. The street is full of Coal Carts, Coal horses & Asses—& great way from the Town & Parades & not very near principal Pump Room. It might do perhaps for the seasons, but it will have little Town business the rest of the year.

———————

BATH, *13th June 1772.*

We have now nearly completed the shew & store rooms here all to the paper & Cloth. The season seems completely over here, & the Town is scarcely habitable for heat. We take a mouthfull of fresh air on the Downs in the morning, drink three or four glasses of scalding hot water from the Pump, & sweat it out in the *least hot* places we can find out the remainder of the day.

The opening our Rooms now at the conclusion of the season will have one bad effect. It will shew the China men & Pott-shops what they want for the next season, & teach them how to shew their goods & rival us in every respect much more effectually than they could have done had we begun our shew with the season.

Mrs. Wedgwood begins to Bath on Monday, she joins with me in wishing you a pleasant journey into Derbyshire. We wish you everything that is good, & have no doubt of your returning to Chelsea a real Benedict—may you remain so thro' every stage of this sublunary Pilgrimage prays your most affec^te. friend.

BATH, *14th June 1772.*

Mrs. Wedgwoods lameness continues so long in her knees & feet without any amendment that I cannot help being much concern'd least it should fix in those parts, especially her knees, as they seem the most affected, & make a crackling noise like dryd parchment whenever she bends them. I have some hopes from bathing, & if it agrees with her in other respects I suppose we must try 'its effect a fortnight or longer in which time I know she will have such a longing after home & her Bratts that I have some doubt of our coming by London that being about 140 miles extra which will be equal to 1000 at another time.

I sho^d. be glad if Simpcock (for I wo^d. not take up your time now, nor indeed engage your attention too much at present as I would wish you to go upon your expedition as thoughtless & gay as a Boy of fifteen) would give me some account of the new mode of printing you mention & try to put somthing in practice that we may have painting done cheaper in both our branches, for unless somthing of that sort can be done I am really & truly perswaded we must diminish that branch of buseness very much.

But no more of business—leave it all behind you.

BATH, *24th June 1772.*

By this time I hope my Dear Friend & his
Good Lady, after the pleasantest journey they
ever made, will be safely arriv'd at their
habitation in Chelsea, & I need not tell you
that I most sincerely wish you every comfort,
& every joy that your own good sense, & good
nature can bestow upon each other, or that a
kind providence can bless you with, & I never
made a prayer with a stronger perswasion of
its being heard, & answer'd, than that which
I now put up for your mutual happiness &
felicity thro every period of your lives.

We have often amused ourselves over our
evening glasses with wishing to be of your
party for an hour or so, but the vain wish hath
as soon been checked as made, & after a little
harmless play at guessing how our friends
were employd, who & who was together &c &c
we have been oblig'd to content ourselves with
drinking their healths, & wishing them every
felicity the enjoyments of friendship & the
convivial hours could bestow.

I must not omit to tell you that though we
have not open'd the Rooms we have nevertheless taken hansell.* S͏ʳ. Harbord Harbord
desir'd he might bring Lady Harbord (his
Mother) to our Rooms before he left Bath,
which he did yesterday morning. She boᵗ. a
pʳ. of Green fluted Flowerpots, & a painted
Etruscan Teapot &. S͏ʳ. Harbord boᵗ. a plain
purple Edged Desert service but he wants to
complete it 4 Twiggen baskets of the smallest
size oval—less than any we have, & Lady
Harbord desires to see a Glaucier in three
parts, I believe either purple or plain will do.

Mrs. Wedgwood has left off bathing, it did
not agree with her, she is now trying the pump,
but thinks of leaving the Pump, & Bath, &
Water, & the City too behind her, on Monday
or Tuesday next.

S͏ʳ. Harbord has been particularly civil to us
here & I hope will be a good friend to the
Rooms in Westgate as he certainly has it in
his power to be. He mention'd a very white
Clay he had found in his Estate, & full of
shining Mice—by his description it is like the
Cherokee Clay.

* Handsel, earnest, first act of sale: "The apostles term it
. . . the *handsel* or earnest of that which is to come." Hooker:
Ecclesiastical Polity.

HH

I have now the pleasure of dateing from Etruria once more, & thanking you & your good Lady in which Mrs. Wedgwood joins me most cordially, for your goodness to us at Chelsea. We have often you know wish'd, but wish'd in vain, to annihilate, or at least to lessen the distance between Chelsea & Etruria, but I am afraid we must submit to these things as they are at present, — love one another wherever we are, & meet together as often as we can. Under this idea I am not without some small hopes that we shall have the pleasure of seeing Mrs. Bentley & you here towards the latter end of the summer, but I dare not say too much upon this subject whilst you are so busy. A month or so hence you will perhaps hear me better, & when our orders are completed, our Hay & our Corn got into the barn, I shall then be more at liberty to quaff the social bowl, & smoak the Calamut (is that right spelt) of peace with my friend, & our good Governesses will ramble thro' the fields & Garden &—*wherever they please,* as good Wives should you know.—Well then 'till these Halcyan days arrive I must beg leave as usual to talk to you in my *dull* way about a little *dull* business now & then.

We call'd upon Mr. Boulton on Friday Even^g. & saw his superb Gallery in which there is a great many good things of his manufacture besides the Vases. A silver Coffeepot from St. Non, some silver cups—*moderate* & silver plated ware of the best forms I have seen, a small spicemen of which—4 Candlesticks you will recieve by the Bir^m. Carr^r. & hope you will do me the favour to accept them.

I wish you would be so good to tell Thos. Mier that I am sorry to find he does not know when he is well, & that he is geting into a way of trifleing with a good place 'till he loseth it. As to the allowance he wants me to make him for washing & lodging, I shall not consent to any such thing, for we shall not keep a bed less if he leaves the House. He has thirteen pounds a year, meat, drink, washing & lodging, which he knows is considerably more than he could get here, & if that does not content him, nothing that we could afford to give him would do so long, & he had better let me know at once that I may provide another for Martinmass. I do not like to part with old servants, but I have often found that some servants may be kept too long, 'till nothing will content them.

This morning I have had an opportunity of consulting with Lady Gower & Lady Teignham & their two Lords (who have been at the works here & bo^t. some flowerpots) upon the subject of Boughpots, & find that they prefer those things with the spouts, such as the old Delph ones, they say that sort keep the flowers distinct & clever.

Bough Pots instead of Cheap Vases.

Vases are furniture for a Chimney piece— Bough pots for a hearth, under a Slab or Marble Table; I think they never can be used one instead of the other, & I apprehend one reason why we have not made our *dressing* flowerpots to please has been by adapting them for Chimneypieces where I think they do not place any pots dress'd with flowers. If I am wrong in this idea I should be glad to be set right as it is of consequence in forming these articles to know where they place them.

ETRURIA, *5th Augt. 1772.*

I rejoyce with my Dear Friend in the continuation of such agreeable dispatches from the Princes in Germany. May they hold out to the end 'till we have a good account from all our remaining adventures. I shall be glad to hear from you every time you hear from your Princes & Great Men of the Earth.

We have had a visit from Mr. & Mrs. Southwell at Etruria. They like our new flower & bow pots very much. They are both adepts in these matters & I did not miss the opportunity of proffiting from their knowledge in this pleasing Art—The Art of disposing the most beautifull productions of Nature, in the most agreeable, picturesque, & strikeing manner to the eyes of the beholders. We fixed some general principles, & then examin'd every flowerpot we had by those principles, & we found all those we have hitherto made & *which have not sold*, to be very deficient in some of these *first principles.* I now have much clearer ideas of bow pots &c than before & believe I can make them to *please your customers.* Mrs. Southwell is a Charming Woman I am more & more in love with her every time I see her & having such a Mistress in the Science of flower dressing, I hope our future productions will shew that I have proffited accordingly.

Every *Gentle & Decent* push should be made to have our things *seen & sold* at Foreign Markets. If we drop, or do not *hitt off* such opportunities ourselves we cannot expect other People to be so attentive to them, & our trade will decline & wither, or flourish & expand itself, in proportion as these little turns & opportunitys are neglected, or made the most of. I see you smile, & say nobody can blame us for any neglect of this sort in *Germany*— We have not been over shy there. Very true we were both agreed that there we made somthing beyond a *Gentle push* —however I hope all things will work together for our good even there, & that we shall have no cause to treat the Majority of the German Princes in the end, as Hereticks, Goths, or Vandals.

ETRURIA, *19th of Augt. 1772.*

Last night I had a visit from Minshals Father who came in a violent bustle to let me know that he had recd. a letter from his son at Chelsea by which he found that his Lad was very uneasy,—that it was a sad thing for a Child to be in such a situation so far from his

Parents & friends, & that his Mother was just
out of the World abo^t. him.—He then shew'd
me the letter which set forth that he had not
for some time past liked their goings on at
Chelsea & had determin'd not to stay their
long but Mr. Simpcock having quarrel'd with
him lately & told him that he was idle & they
could do better without him than with him he
was determin'd to leave immediately, but he
said that I had agreed, if he did not like, to
pay his expences back & desir'd his Father
would ask me for so much, but whether I
wo^d. allow it or not he would come into the
Country again.

I told his Father that I suppos'd his son
wrote in a heat after some trifleing quarrel
which might be over by this time, & desir'd
him as a man of sense & understanding to
quiet his wifes mind & assure her from me that
her son sho^d. take no harm, that I wo^d. write
to you today, & did not doubt but you wo^d. be
able to set matters right, & make her son easy
in his place, but if that could not be done he
should come down to her as soon as we could
provide ourselves with one in his place.

I Did promise that when he came up if he
did not like his place I wo^d· pay his expences
down again, but he did like his place & I
did not mean that I would Frank him down

into the Country again at any distance of time whenever he should capriciously take it into his head to leave his place. When he had been a reasonable time to *try* his place, *liked* & was *settled in it*, I looked upon myself as discharg'd from this ingagement. But if he stays quietly 'till you can get another in his room, does his duty & saves some of his Wages for his Voyage I will lend him what is necessary to bring him down taking his acknowledgment for the money.

I do not think it answers any good purpose to send our Country People up to Town. The Change is so great that not one in ten can stand it without being ruin'd or spoild or being siezed with the Swiss disorder which I suppose to be the case with Minshal.

I observe, & lament your want of plates, & ware to enamel, but could not possibly do more than we have done, our men will go to the Wakes's one day if they were sure to be carried to the D——l the next. I have not spared them in threats & I would have thrash'd them right heartily if I could.

I am now ingaged in a very serious subject & a more difficult one than I at first apprehended it to have been. Some of my difficultys I have laid before you, but what perplexeth me the most is, that although I am very positive what I have allow'd for the expences of makeing & selling our goods is quite enough; yet it appears from comparing the expence of Manufacture for a year, with the amoᵗ. of the goods made, to be little more than half the *real* expence attending the making & selling so many goods.

You have an excelent talent at Analising. I wish you would *turn this subject in your thoughts* & see if you can enable me to make somthing of it.

I have had several serious Talks with our Men at the Ornamental works lately about the price of our workmanship, & the necessity of lowering it, especially in Flower pots, Bowpots & Teapots, & as I find that their chief reason against lowerᵍ. their prices is the small quantitys made of each, which creates them as much trouble in *tuning their fiddle*, as *playing the tune* I have promis'd them that they shall make dozⁿˢ. & Groces of Flower & Tea pots, & of the Vases & Bowpots too, as often as we

dare venture at such quantitys, & the consequence of *lowering the price of workmanship*
will be a proportional *increase of quantity* got
up; & if you turn to the Columns of calculation & see how large a share, *Modeling & moulds*
& the three next columns bear in the expence
of manufacturing our goods, & consider that
these expences move on like clockwork, & are
much the same wether the quantity of goods
made be large or small, you will see the vast
consequences in most manufactures of *making
the greatest quantity possible in a given time.*
Rent goes on whether we do much or little in
the time. Wages to the Boys & Odd Men,
Warehousemen & Book-keeper who are a kind
of satelites to the Makers (Throwers, Turners
&c) is nearly the same whether we make 20
doz of Vases or 10 doz per week, & will therefore be a double expence upon the latter
number. The same may be said in regard to
most of the incidental expences, Coals for the
workshop fires (no small expence) which must
be rather increas'd than diminish'd when the
Men are idle, in order to keep them warm.

We have now upwards of 100 Good forms of
Vases for all of which we have the moulds,
handles & ornaments, & we could make them
almost as currently as usefull ware, & at one
half the expence we have hitherto done, pro-

vided I durst set the Men to make from abo^t.
6 to 12 doz of a sort.

The Great People have had their Vases in
their Palaces long enough for them to be seen
& admir'd, by the *Middling Class* of People,
which Class we know are vastly, I had almost
said infinitely, superior in number, to the
Great, & though a *great price* was I believe, at
first necessary to make the Vases esteemed
Ornaments for Palaces that reason no longer
exists. Their character is established, & the
middling People would probably buy quantitys
of them at a reduced price.

Etruria, *31st Augt. 1772.*

Joseph Unwin wants to see his son R in
the Country for a few weeks if we could make
it convenient. Suppose he was to come &
stay the winter here & take drawings of all
our Vases, or at least stay 'till he has finish'd
a book of them for each of us, finish'd drawings, to leave behind us for the advantage of
our Children & Posterity.

By the inclos'd acc^t. it appears that the

expence of our Manufactory at Etruria for one year was _____ 1802: 4: 8

The Produce exclusive of the increased value by painting is _____ 5755: 12: 10

This Acc^t. is very exact as to the *whole* but we cannot make it agree with its parts Viz the seperate pieces—It agrees with the small Vases very well but those we sell at 2 or 3 G—s do not appear to cost us $\frac{1}{10}$ of that money. We are now taking stock & shall then try another method.

ETRURIA, 7th *Septr. 1772.*

Mrs. Wedgwood has had an extreme bad night, & miscarried this morning. Her situation is attended with much danger. Mr. Bent says her case is the most singular one he has ever known & nothing but the greatest attention in nursing & keeping everything quiet about her can save her life.

Wednesday 8th (I think) Sept'. 1772.

I know my dear Friend will rejoyce with me
in hearing that my poor Girl is somthing
better today. She has rested pretty well, &
her vomiting is stay'd, the two great points
upon which her safety depended, & I have now
some flattering hopes that she may still be
continued to her family & friends, who had
almost given her up for lost.

My head is a good deal better, but not
quite well. A little Air & exercise on Horseback, when I can leave the House, with the
continued recovery of my Wife will in a little
time, I hope, set me to rights again.

I should have been very glad to come &
take my share of the trouble you are likely to
have, but there is no probability of my being
able to leave this place at present even if Mrs.
Wedgwoods illness would permit me to think
of leaving her for I have at this time so many
other things demand my constant care &
managem'. that it would be highly imprudent
to leave them to themselves. For instance,
yesterday I stopp'd the Men at the Ornamental
works from working over hours, 'till I could
find out some other work for them, for the
fact you know is that we have not work
enough for them the common hours. Upon
this they told Dan¹. they would all leave us, &

they know Mrs. P[almer] wo^d. take them in which makes them almost unmanagable upon any terms. Now though our business may be a little over done in qu^{ty}., I do not think it is in such a desperate way that we should set our best hands adrift to the establishment of our Antagonists. I know they wo^d. promise our hands anything—mountains of Gold, to gain them, but if things go well with us in the house I must spend as much time as I can this week at the works.

———————

ETRURIA, 10th *Septr. 1772.*

My Dear Sally continues to recover, & has been up today & bore it very well. But well as we think her compared with her situation a few days since, you never saw such a changling, nothing but skin & bone, pale as her cap, & does not seem to have a drop of blood in her body. Her lips today begin to incline towards a blush of red, & as she relishes what she eats I hope to give you a better account of her soon.

Doct^r. Derwin has left me to act as Physicion in his absense but I believe I shall not gain much credit in my office amongst the female Nurses here, as I have prescribed what they durst not think of for my Patient.

When nothing would stay upon her stomach I gave her fruit, ripe plumbs &c as often as she would eat them, & she has never vomited since.—For the wind, I have given her Cyder that blows the Cork up to the Cieling. She relishes it vastly, & it does her good.

Mr. Swift will shew you a letter from a Mr. Clark a young Gent[n]. from Boston with whom I sho[d]. be glad to have you spend an hour when you have time to chatt a few politics with him on American affairs. He is sensible & clever, & I think you will like him. I have sold him some goods here, & he will look at our things in Town with a view perhaps of buying some of them if they are not *too dear*. He says they are not ripe for expensive things at present in New England.

I would not say anything to you about Mr. Swifts return before he is well got to Town, but may just hint that he left poor Mrs. Swift in tears, she was very loth to part with him at this time having only a few weeks to count, she therefore hopes that *whatever he has to do he will do it with all his might*, that he may return in time for the merry meal, & to nurse

& comfort the poor Woman in the straw. I hope he had a safe journey to Town, Minshall & Holland were thrown off the Coach, & were very near breaking both their necks, they both pitched upon their heads & were some time before they recover'd the stunn it gave them.

———————————

18th Sept. 1772.*

We cannot be insensible to the loss of some friends, & the afflictions of others especially of those who are most near & dear to us, & these have oppress'd my spirits much more than any other of the disagreeable circumstances we have lately experienc'd, but having now a fair prospect of my Dear Sallys perfect recovery, as every day brings an addition to her strength & spirits, & your Good Lady being in the same good way, I have no doubt but our days will brighten upon us again, & the subordinate parts will be brought to run smooth & regular in a little time.

With respect to my health, I scarcely know what account to give you. Too much attention to anything I can feel would hurt me at present, & I must avoid it. I shall therefore endeavour to regulate the People, & things here so as to need as little of me as may be, & endeavour to bestow my chief attention upon *essentials*, & I beg you will do so too, & not overload your mind with care & anxiety about the subordinate parts.

I have been to see Mrs. Brindley this morning by her desire, & she has a particular favour to beg of you—Mr. Parsons you know took Mr. Brindleys Portrait which he was to have had, but they had a little fracas about the terms.— Mr. Parsons demanded 60 Guineas for the piece & frame.—Mr. Brindley meant to make Mr. Parsons a handsome present for the picture, but did not like the mode of demanding so much from him, & in short told him he would not have it. Mrs. Brindley always wish'd to have the picture, & she begs you would be so good to see Mr. Parsons & tell him so, & that now she is at liberty, she readily complys with his terms, & hopes he will not refuse her the picture, if it is not already disposed of. She has set her heart much upon having it, so if Mr. Parsons has any new terms to propose, you'l please to send them, & stop him from disposing of it 'till you hear from her again.

I have just been reading Lady M—— W——
Montagues letters (a few of them) with a view
of learning somthing relative to their eating
& drinking, & the inside of their Houses,
where I find this comfortable passage in the
32ⁿᵈ letter, that between the Windows in the
Ladies Harams are little Arches to set *pots of
Perfume,* or *baskets of flowers*" Alias Beaupots
—Pray are they *Beau* pots or *Bough* pots ?—
now as there are double rows of windows in
these rooms, & Arches between every window,
what is a single chimney piece in our solitary
rooms to twenty or thirty of these charming
little Arches, if they were but comatable for
us—Let who will take the Sultanas if I could
but get at these delightfull little nitches, &
furnish them, is all I covet in Turkey at present.
If you read a little farther you will find in Lʳ.
34ᵗʰ that the Walls of their Mosques are in-
laid with painted Japan China!—And in
another place—Thier Baths are all set round
with the richest Vases. These People have
right notions of things, if we had a clever
Ambassador there somthing might be done,
especially now they have given over fighting
with the Russians.

I have now recᵈ. all the accᵗˢ. up to the 12ᵗʰ
insᵗ. & promise my self much satisfaction in

recieving them weekly. Nay, bad as their aspect is at present, I really feel more comfortable upon that subject now, than when I was 4 or 5 months without seeing them at all, & when they did come they compos'd too formidable a volume for me to attempt, besides it was somthing like reading an old newspaper. But now as I shall have all your good company pass before me weekly I shall interest my self more with them, & with every transaction in Newport Street, & I am perswaded we shall neither of us upon this plan ever permit a Cashier to be so long behind hand with his accounts, or keep such a balance of our Cash *aparently* in his hands.—If these weekly accounts had been made out, which it appears Ben had time enough for, it would have thrown too much light upon his affairs, & his riotings & feastings must sooner have been at an end ; but had it been done, the evil we now suffer would have been prevented, & what is more, a human being, & usefull member of society might have been saved from that ruin which now apparently hangs over his head.—You must estimate the integrity of your servants *in general* by the opportunity you give them of doing wrong, says a friend of yours & mine the other day (D^r. Derwin) one is sorry to entertain such ideas of ones fellow creatures, but I believe it is a safe maxim, & I am afraid its truth will be a sufficient excuse to ones self for bearing such a disgusting idea pretty often in ones mind, & to apply it to our affairs in Newport S^t. I think whatever plan is fixed upon, whether commission or otherwise this sho^d. be a Law, unalterable as the Medes & Persions that the Cash & sales acc^t. should be settled, & the Cash deliver'd to you every week, & for my own part I am determin'd that if the acc^{ts}. are not sent to me by the head Clerk weekly,—if they miss one week I will come for them myself the next.

ETRURIA, *26th Septr. 1772.*

I have been at Turnhurst almost every day this week, & can give you but a melancholly acc^t. from thence. Poor Mr. Brindley has nearly finish'd his course in this world. He says he must leave us, & indeed I do not expect to find him alive in the morning. His disorder I think I told you before is a Diabetes & this malady he has had upon him for seven years past most probably, which occasion'd his constant fever & thirst, though I believe no one of his Docters found it out 'till D^r. Derwin discover'd it in the present illness, which I fear will deprive us of a valuable friend, & the world of one of those great Genius's who seldom live to see justice done to their singular abilities, but must trust to future ages for that tribute of praise & fair fame they so greatly merit from their fellow mortals.

Poor Mrs. Brindley is inconsolable, & will scarcely be prevail'd upon to take either rest or food sufficient to support nature, but she has promis'd me to exert herself in bearing this afflicting stroke all in her power for the sake of her Aged Parents & her helpless Children.

ETRURIA, *28th Septr. 1772.*

I told you in my last that Mr. Brindley was extremely ill, & I have the grief to tell you he is now no more. He died the 27th Ins^t. about 12 at Noon, in a sound sleep, for about 3 O'Clock in the morning, after giving him somthing to wet his mouth, he said '*its enough—I shall need no more*, & shut his Eyes, never more to open, he continued to the time of his death, (about 9 hours) seemingly in a fine sleep, & yielded up his breath at last without a single groan.

He has left two young Children behind him, & poor Mrs. Brindley inconsolable for the loss of a sensible friend, & affectionate Husband.— What the Public has lost can only be conciev'd by those who best knew his Character & Talents—Talents for which this Age & Country are indebted for works that will be the most lasting monument to his Fame, & shew to future Ages how much good may be done by one single Genius, when happily employd upon works beneficial to Mankind.*

Mr. Brindley had an excellent constitution, but his mind, too ardently intent upon the execution of the works it had plann'd, wore down a body at the age of 55 which originally promis'd to have lasted a Century & might give him the pleasing expectation of living to see those great works completed for which Millions yet unborn will revere & bless his memory.

Do I need to tell you that he bore his last

* The canals laid out by Brindley, though not all executed by him, were the following:— Bridgwater Canal, Grand Trunk, Worsley to Manchester, Wolverhampton, Coventry, Birmingham, Droitwich, Oxford, and Chesterfield.

illness with that fortitude & strength of mind which charecterised all his actions.

If you have so much leisure perhaps you will send an account of this event to some of the papers, with such accompaniments as your esteem & friendship for the deceac'd shall dictate, & if a prem^m. is requir'd from the printers I will gladly pay it. The Duke of Bridgewater might & indeed ought to have a handsome compliment paid him on this occasion, to encourage others to *bring Genius to light* & support its first efforts as he has nobly done.

Do be so good to thank Mr. & Mrs. Cooper for me & tell them I love them both & will write to tell them so myself the very first opportunity but if they see how I am hurried to & fro—call'd here, & sent for there, & toss'd about continually they wo^d. pity & excuse me awhile I am sure.

ETRURIA, *4th of Octr. 1772.*

I am glad to hear of D^r. Priestleys noble appointment,* taking it for granted that he is

* Priestley had been appointed "Literary Companion" and Librarian to Lord Shelburne.

to go on writing & publishing *with the same freedom* he now does, otherwise I had much rather he still remain'd in Yorkshire. I rejoice too on your account, as you will have one more of your friends within your reach, to injoy & converse with occasionally.

With respect to your discharging Ben, [Mather] I still think some caution necessary, both on his account & our own.

That we cannot continue him in our service, I suppose we are both clearly agreed; but charity may incline us to hope that after a little cool reflection, & seeing the folly & danger of his past conduct, there is still some chance of his being reclaim'd, & in these hopes I shall gladly acquiese in any measures you, who know his friends & connections much better than I do, can propose as the most likely for that purpose.

If he is immediately turn'd adrift, with the total loss of his character, he may probably be driven to a degree of desperation beyond any effort of amendment. He should have *some hope left him* that upon a change of conduct he may still be restor'd to the favor & confidence of his friends, which if he has one ingenuous feeling left, will be a stronger motive for his reformation than any other he could possibly have, *when bereaved of that hope.*

I have not wrote to you of a week past. Indeed I have not wrote a single letter in that time that I recollect & believe I must *write* & *think* & *act* rather less than I have done. Writeing, sometimes even a single letter only, has for some time past brought on an uneasy sensation of straightness across my breast. I let writeing alone all last week to try what effect it wo^d. have, & it had a very good one, for my breast was quite easy, but being oblig'd to write a few letters this morning I feel it will return again.

Another symptom has alarm'd me a little. I have been growing thinner for some years past, but this summer I have lost a great deal of flesh. When I came from London last I could not wear any of my Cloaths 'till they were taken in several inches, & showing D^r. Darwin by one of my Wastcoats how much I was sunk in 9 or 10 months, he said it was wrong, & I must be very carefull of my health.

After examining me very particularly, he said he wo^d. not order me any Physick at present, as I was in rather a delicate situation in respect to my health, but he ord^d. me to live pretty well, to take moderate exercise & to keep free from care & anxiety, & let him know if I still sunk in my flesh. I am writeing to him this morning to tell him that I do not percieve any loss since I saw him (near 3 weeks) & hope I may continue my present bulk by proper care—or rather by casting care behind me as much as may be.

ETRURIA, *27ᵗʰ Octʳ. 1772.*

I thank my dear Friend most sincerely for his many affectionate letters, & the good advice they contain, which I know would be most salutary to me, if I could put it in practice as I ought, but that I find, at present, most difficult to do, for no sooner is one disagreeable event subsided a little but others succeed to keep my mind, & body too upon the fret, though I employ all the Philosophy I am master of to prevent it.

We have lately discover'd a scene of vilany amongst our servants in the House, who have a long time been robbing us of everything they could carry off, or dispose of amongst a score of my out-of-door servants. I mean every eatable & drinkable, for I do not know that they have gone any farther, but in these

matters they have form'd such a correspondence, & proceeded to such a degree, as it is
not easy to imagine, & this will render it
necessary to sweep the House of every serv^t.
we have in it, Male & Female, some from the
field Men & others from the works. My head
Farmer is in this list, whom I have turned
adrift, & given several of my Tennants notice
to quit their houses. Add to this a combination amongst our servants at the works, the
usefull works I mean though it may for aught
I know extend to the other, to have their own
prices, which are most exorbitant ones, or to
leave us. The ring leader who was to try the
experiment with us yesterday, after several consultations amongst themselves, insisted on
having *his own price* or *his discharge*. Our T: W.
as we had agreed gave him his discharge, at
which the man was visibly chagrin'd, for he
had an excellent place & got near £50 a year
with so much ease that I verily believe he
could have got near double the money in the
time if reasons of policy had not prevented
him. However he took his discharge & is gone,
& I expect more will follow him.

In this situation, it is true, I can convey
my *body* from the works, & from my domestic
concerns in the house but 'till these matters
are in a little better order my *mind* will be

with them, & the more I absent myself, or my attention from them, the more difficult they will be to conquer. I have therefore resolv'd to set myself in earnest to redress these matters, that I may the sooner come at a little peace & comfort.

The most distressfull part respecting my houshold affairs is Mrs. W——s being so ill prepar'd to bear any uneasiness in her family, on which account I had kept the knowledge of these things to myself near two months, & now have taken all upon myself, & charged the servants not to say a word to her upon the subject, for I found them inclin'd to attack their Mistress in my absense.—We have hired a Housekeeper, & two other servants, who can come at a days notice, & I intend to complete the revolution whilst Mrs. W. is on a visit to her Bro^r. in Cheshire that she may see & feel as little of it as possible. She knows & consults with me about these matters, but then we do it *quietly*, which could not be the case betwixt the servants & her, if they were to transact these affairs in *propria Persone*.

P S Mr. Whieldon has lost his wife & we have lost an excellent neighbour—she died suddenly at Church on Sunday se'nn^t.

My poor Girl is in a very dangerous situation, much more so than she is apprehensive
of, & I am almost distracted with my fears for
her, & for myself, for I should in loseing her
go near to lose myself also, & I fear, though I
shudder at writeing it, that she has but a poor
chance for recovering her present illness. An
Ugly fever hangs upon her, with a sort of Ague
fitts at uncertain periods which Mr. Bent says
are very bad symptoms & he thinks the only
thing that can save her wo^d. be going to Italy
or the south of France. Pray does the D. of
Gloucester, or D^r. Jebb[*] go there this winter?
I have sent for D^r. Derwin when he has been
here I will write again.

When you write to me only say you are
sorry she does not recover faster or so—I wo^d.
not alarm her.

[*] Afterwards Sir Richard Jebb, the well-known physician
(1729-1787).

Nov. 5ᵗʰ 1772.

We have appointed Mr. Henshall Engineer to our Canal with the same salary we gave to Mr. Brindley & the Gentⁿ. of the Chesterfield Canal have solicited him to be their Engineer. He intends to succeed his late Brother in law, who always desir'd he should & long before his death consulted with him upon all his great undertakings & all the difficultys that occur'd in the execution of them.

My poor Lass is much the same as when I wrote last, Dʳ. Darwin has been here & invited her to come & stay with him a few weeks, & we are to go on Sunday—Adieu.

LICHFIELD, *9ᵗʰ Novʳ. 1772.*

I thank my Dear Friend for his last kind letter, & the agreeable intelligence that the K: of Denmark, or somebody for him, has paid for his crockery ware, & that our Rooms begin to fill with good Company again. I have some good news too to tell you, in which I know you will rejoyce with me—My wife has not had any of her shivering fits since Wednesday last, & as she gets strength very fast in their absence, I am very willing to flatter myself that she will have no more.

I brought her to this place yesterday & we were lucky enough to find the good Doct^r. at home. He has order'd her to continue taking the bark & hopes it may prevent her fever fitts from returning.

I shall return home tomorrow & leave Mrs. W. with her Doct^r. for a week or ten days, & hope the change of place, Air, & company will have a good effect—In her absence I am to make the revolution in our houshold, & if I can make so much time, take a trip into Lancashire to see our Children there.

Mrs. W. laughed heartily at your droll account of the Italian Merchant, & I thank you as heartily for making the most of the adventure, & for the hopes you give me of its turning to so good an account.

I left my Wife with her Doct^r. in Lichfield on Tuesday last. She had then been six days without any of her shivering fits, & I have hopes they will not return again.

We are to have a House-keeper come on Wednesday next when we shall part with most or all of our present servants. Our Nurse since she has thought of being turned off has doubled her efforts to make the Children fond of her. Poor Joss told me the other morning with all the concern imaginable, that Sally Hand had never a home to go to—that he loved her, & has somthing of this kind to tell me every day—The Artfull Jade has succeeded wonderfully in interesting so young an advocate to plead her cause, & I assure you the young rogue touches my heart, though my judgment speaks another language.

I can scarcely tell you the state of my health. I am not bad, but I am not so *stout at heart* if you know what that means as I used to feel myself, nor quite so well as I sho^d. be. I find the most advantage in an hour or two of real labour in the fields every day that time or the weather will permit.